Classroom Success for the Learning Disabled

Classroom Success for the Learning Disabled

by SUZANNE H. STEVENS

With an introduction by
ALBERT M. GALABURDA, M.D.

JOHN F. BLAIR, Publisher
Winston-Salem, North Carolina

Fourth Printing, 1991

Library of Congress Cataloging in Publication Data

Stevens, Suzanne H., 1938–
  Classroom success for the learning disabled.

  Includes bibliographical references and index.
  1. Learning disabilities—United States—Case studies.
2. Slow learning children—United States—Case studies.
I. Title.
LC4705.S74 1983   371.92'6   82-25726
ISBN 0-89587-035-5 (pbk.)
ISBN 0-89587-036-3

To John,
Mitch,
Jerry,
and all the other LD children
who've suffered so needlessly

Contents

Introduction

THIS BOOK deals with learning disabilities in general and tells a story of a young man with developmental dyslexia in particular. More importantly, though, this book deals with the world around the affected individual. Ever since the interest in the study of learning disabilities began to grow about twenty years ago, there has been a large number of works devoted to the behavioral, educational, psychological, and cognitive performance of people with learning disorders. It has become progressively clear, however, that attention must be turned to the world around the learning-disabled child. There is a growing realization that the difficulties of learning-disabled children are apt to affect the workings of the society as a whole. Unfortunately society, by its collective ignorance, has notoriously worsened the manifestations of learning disabilities in affected individuals. The social problem is not trivial. Learning disabilities may affect a very large proportion of the school population. In fact, we may be dealing in numbers as high as ten to twelve percent of school-age children. Inadequate handling of such large numbers of individuals can bring on disastrous consequences to a society that requires skilled education and productivity in virtually every member in order to help deal with the growing requirements of an overpopulated world.

The high number of learning-disabled persons brings up another issue. If one assumes that learning-disabled children are simply disabled and nothing more, one must also address the question of why evolution has allowed the high prevalence of learning disabilities to persist. After all, it was not long ago even in the developed nations that food was at a premium and employment difficult to obtain and hard to hold on to, situations which probably go back to the beginning of civilized time. How could countless generations of learning-disabled individuals survive in such a competitive world—unless there were also special abilities present in the same individuals? Consider for a moment what a reading disability would mean in an illiterate society. Most of the world is still illiterate, and until recently even the so-called developed nations had huge numbers of illiterate people. In such a society, dyslexic individuals would not have been recognized and, instead, their special abilities may have been more important than their disabilities.

The learning disability known as dyslexia, of which Al (the young man in the story) appears to be a standard case, was first described during the end of the nineteenth century by a school physician. The doctor wrote to a specialist on learning difficulties and cognitive disorders in children, stating that he had found a boy who appeared intelligent, emotionally stable, and otherwise motivated, who had tremendous difficulty with reading, writing, and spelling. The specialist then set out to collect similar cases and eventually published a monograph describing the clinical symptomatology of "congenital word blindness." This occurred during the golden period of neurology. Fifty years earlier a French surgeon had described, in a patient who could no longer speak, the presence of a small injury in the left hemisphere of the brain. This landmark discovery set in motion a research movement which was to inspire the interest of neurologists around the world in language and other behaviors and their relationship to the brain.

Soon, multiple conditions impairing language in one way or another were being described in large numbers of patients with autopsy-proven brain lesions. German and French neurologists described reading disturbances acquired from lesions in adults who previously had been able to read and write. These lesions affected specific portions of the left side of the brain. It was not surprising, therefore, that the first researchers of developmental reading disabilities suspected the involvement of parts of the brain. Perhaps, they argued, the same areas which when lesioned in adults resulted in acquired reading disturbances might be developed abnormally in the reading-disabled children, preventing normal reading performance from developing. However, time ran out for the neurological period and no demonstrations of abnormal development of the brain were at hand.

During the period between the two wars, interest in behavioral disturbances turned from brain-based, neurological explanations to psychological and behavioral explanations. Investigators were no longer interested in the machinery responsible for normal and abnormal language and cognitive performance, but rather in the performance itself. Expectedly the study of learning disabilities was handled in the same fashion. In the fifty years that followed, many books and articles appeared which dealt with the behavior and performance of learning-disabled individuals. However, just as the neurological period came to an end because it could not by itself explain all the phenomena observed in normal and abnormal language functions, so did the psychological period begin to show weakness in explaining everything simply from behavioral analyses.

The 1970s represent a turn toward a greater cooperation between the neurological and psychological approaches. Brain structure, brain physiology, psychological performance, and other non-behavioral medical associations are being examined for the purpose of developing models that take into consideration the whole biology of learning disabilities. Thus, it is being shown that the anatomy of the brain in certain dyslexic individuals may be altered, and that the alteration can be dated to the period of brain development in the fetal stage. Likewise, neurological approaches are disclosing differences in brain electrical activity, as well as differences in the brain x rays obtained by computerized methods. At the same time psychological, educational, and linguistic testing is discovering subtypes of learning disabilities that are useful not only for research considerations of causality but also for practical remedial use.

The findings in the anatomical studies of the dyslexic brain cannot be interpreted in isolation from discoveries related to brain development made during the past ten years. Most of these studies have come from animal experimentation. In experimental animals, manipulated during critical periods of brain development, one discovers interesting phenomena. For instance, the effect of lesions in immature brains can be dramatically different from the effect of the same lesions in the adult animal. This has to do with the remarkable ability that a developing brain possesses to reorganize after an injury.

It has been shown that monkeys sustaining lesions during fetal life involving one side of the brain show a remarkable growth and reorganization of the parts of the brain that were not lesioned. This illustrates the enormous capacity that the young brain has to compensate for an injury. One can, at least on theoretical grounds, consider that the same mechanisms are available for the developing human brain. If the alterations found in the left side of the brain of dyslexic individuals occurred at a very early stage of development, it is reasonable to suspect that the parts of the brain not affected would have significantly reorganized. Specifically, if the injury was to language areas of the brain during fetal life, other non-language-related portions of the brain might have had the opportunity to restructure, reorganize, and grow in different ways. Thus, again on theoretical grounds, it is possible to say that in developmental dyslexics one might expect superior abilities in non-language portions of the brain.

It should be clear from the above statements that the compensatory abilities often seen in individuals with learning disabilities probably are not psychological in nature, but rather biological and explained by the mechanisms cited above. It is often said that dyslexic children are good in art and athletics because they could not excel in language-related tasks. One could also argue that they are superior in those other tasks because their brains have reorganized after early injury or maldevelopment of language areas so that they are better suited to carry out non-linguistic tasks. Although psychological compensation also may play a role, the presence of superior special skills in family members who are not learning disabled argues for biological explanations for these superior skills.

Those interested in keeping up with the field of learning disabilities are having a growing difficulty in doing so. Why then another book on learning disabilities? The major difference between this book and others on the market is that it deals with the society in as strong a fashion as it deals with the affected individual. Despite the fact that dyslexia and other learning disabilities may be increasingly associated with medical conditions, the handling of the problem is still in the hands of educators, parents, and psychologists. A direct corollary of the statement that learning disabilities are accompanied by learning superiorities in other fields is that the medical suppression of a learning disability may result in the suppression of a special welcome gift. Medicine is still far from being able to change the disability without also altering the other, special abilities. On the other hand, early detection and early application of special teaching methods continually prove to be highly effective in helping the learning-disabled individual. These educational programs aim at teaching individuals how to handle tasks that are difficult for them.

Unfortunately, almost nothing is done to develop the special abilities that many of these children have even by the time they first arrive at school. A learning-disabled child is reminded on a daily basis of how difficult life is, of how arduous it is to achieve satisfactory results (while all the other children seem to be having an easy time), and of how impossible it is to excel. During those early formative years the learning-disabled child is reminded only of his inferiority with respect to the rest of the children. It seems reasonable at this time to weigh the benefits of teaching a dyslexic child how to read and write at an early age against the indignities suffered by the child during the course of this learning. Instead, the child first could be taught to develop those skills for which he is likely to be better than the rest of his classmates. In this manner self-esteem could be built early to help the child cope with the difficulties to come.

The story about Al is a story about a child for whom society failed. It is also a story about a sensitive educator who understands the value of developing self-esteem in disabled children who nevertheless have special abilities. The world needs these special abilities. Society must find a way to bring them out lest they be lost in a sea of shame and failure. It is with approaches such as the ones outlined in this book, carried out individually with each learning-disabled child, that we can hope to minimize the disabilities and maximize the superiorities. Those parents and educators who are able to carry out these suggestions may succeed in producing individuals like Leonardo da Vinci, Rodin, and Albert Einstein.

Albert M. Galaburda, M.D.
Harvard University Medical School
Director of the Dyslexia Neuroanatomical
Laboratory at Beth Israel Hospital

Section One

APPROXIMATELY ONE-TENTH of all children are learning disabled. Although they are *not* mentally retarded, emotionally disturbed, or physically handicapped, these children fail to learn to read and write and spell when taught in a regular classroom by standard classroom methods.

As a result of the failure of these students in school, parents, teachers, classmates, and friends accuse them of being stupid and lazy.

The learning failure is bad enough, but constant criticism and ridicule cause really serious damage. They kill the child's feeling of self-worth, so that he grows up angry, guilt-ridden, and lacking in self-confidence.

Understanding learning disabilities can help classroom teachers stop the vicious circle of failure and frustration that damages ten percent of our children needlessly.

The learning-disabled child's worst enemy is the ignorant adult.

Chapter I

An Afternoon with Al

WHILE ON A LECTURE TOUR, I found myself in a strange town with a whole afternoon free. It was a very hot, sultry day. I decided to find a shady spot down by the river and laze away the hours.

Before I'd even had a chance to pick my spot, a cruising policeman stopped to warn me, "This is no place for a lady."

Scanning the expanse of the gravel parking lot and weed-choked field adjoining it, I saw no sign of human activity. The place was somewhat cut off from the rest of the downtown area but certainly didn't look dangerous.

"A lot of bums and winos hang out down there," the cop explained, gesturing over his shoulder toward a clump of large poplars at the river's edge.

A glance in that direction revealed nothing. A small knoll blocked the base of the trees from view. With a confident smile, I assured the patrolman that I was perfectly safe. "I've got my dog with me," I said, pointing to my Weimaraner, Max.

The officer didn't seem impressed with my seventy-pound protector and traveling companion. "You be careful," he cautioned, and drove off.

Never having been one to take someone else's word for something, I gathered lawn chair, lunch, books, and dog and headed for the shade of the poplars. I'd gotten about halfway to the trees when I noticed the sound of voices coming from that direction. Moving more slowly, I proceeded forward until the weeds thinned enough to allow a glimpse of the area. Sure enough, a group of men were lounging on the rocks at the river's edge. It irked me that they had the best shady spot right down by the water.

I beat a hasty retreat to the only other shady area available. Max and I set ourselves up in a patch of grass in the shadow of a cement wall about a hundred yards back from the river. It was too hot for him to be interested in exploring or for me to pursue thoughts of irritation about the bums. With a pleasant breeze and a magnificent view, he and I pondered and dozed contentedly.

After about an hour, one of the winos came staggering up from the water's edge. He was thin and gaunt beneath a shock of unkempt gray hair. Our eyes never met as he passed. He returned shortly, the neck of a bottle sticking out of the brown bag he was carrying. Following his lurching gait as he returned to the shade of the poplars, I was relieved that he hadn't stopped to bother me or ask for a handout.

Max and I drifted through another peaceful hour. Then, again, one of the winos approached from the river. This time it was a young man. With blond hair sticking out around a cloth cap, T-shirt and blue jeans covering his husky torso, he looked straight at me. Max barked furiously. I drew him in on his chain so that he stood close by my side, and hoped the youth would just pass on by.

Max acted as though he'd rip the boy's arms and legs right off if given half a chance.

"Will he bite?" the youth asked casually.

"Only if you do something to make him feel threatened," I replied curtly. The policeman's warning echoed in my mind and made me very suspicious of the young man's easy manner and unknown intentions. From the way he walked, it was apparent he'd been drinking. From his eyes, I could tell he'd been smoking marijuana. Whatever the reason for his friendliness, I tried to discourage him with a cool, aloof attitude.

He asked a lot of questions about Max. I stuck to one-word answers in the hope that he'd see my lack of enthusiasm and go away.

Instead, he moved into the shadow of my wall, hunkered down in the grass, and told me about his own dog.

It took a long time, but gradually I realized that the boy meant no harm. He was just lonely and wanted to talk. Max and I became comfortable with the stranger as he told us about his home on the other side of the river, places he'd been, things he'd seen. More and more, he revealed himself to be a perceptive, intelligent, sensitive, resourceful person.

As my interest grew, I began asking questions and taking a more active part in the conversation. He talked freely about dropping out of school when he was in the eighth grade. Except for winning a third-grade poetry contest and having one good history teacher in junior high, school had been nothing but a hassle and a source of pain. He said he was a poor reader, a dismal speller, and never could learn math at all. He said he often got "mixed up" and couldn't keep letters and numbers in the right order. At fourteen he joined a rock band. For the next two years he spent his nights playing in nightclubs and his days skipping school and "doing" drugs. As soon as he turned sixteen he dropped out of school and hit the road. He'd been hitchhiking all over the country, living by his wits, ever since.

By this time our conversation was flowing along as smoothly and easily as the river before us.

"What are you doing here in town?" he asked me. "I can tell from your accent you ain't from around here."

My crusade to help the learning disabled interested him tremendously. He knew firsthand about the pain of failure.

When I explained that LD children are badly hurt by adults who accuse them of being stupid and lazy, my companion nodded his head sadly. "Oh, yeah. Tell me about it. . . . That was the story of my life—until I dropped out of school. Really, I guess that was the *reason* I dropped out . . . the kids always thinking I was stupid and the grownups telling me I was lazy." He paused, staring at me earnestly. "But, you know, they were wrong. I ain't lazy. If I'm broke and I need money, I'll work to earn it. I don't mind working. I built a redwood deck for a lady this summer. She paid me over four hundred dollars. And it didn't take but a few days. If I need money, I can earn money."

"How could you build a deck if you can't use numbers?" I asked. "How'd you do the measuring?"

"Shoot . . . don't need to use 'rithmetic for that. You just give me a piece of string, a T-square, and a level, and I can build you anything you want. And not just carpentry work, either. Ain't nothing I can't build."

The topic of how he made money when he needed it was all but inexhaustible. He'd done every imaginable kind of construction job and had even worked with an animal trainer for a while. It became increasingly apparent, and reassuringly so, that panhandling and larceny were not part of his approach to living by his wits. Except for drugs and vagrancy, he lived within the law.

When the subject worked its way back to success and failure, his philosophy amazed me. He spoke with a profound wisdom seldom found in someone twice his age. That boy understood real achievement that motivates by offering more than the hollow rewards of money and approval. He knew why life was worth living. And his answers coincided with the ideas of great mystics and sages recorded in books he'd never read.

"What's the biggest success you've ever had in your life?" he asked.

For that one, I didn't even have to think. "The publication of my first book."

"Oh, wow, what a high!" His eyes widened with understanding. We shared the thrill of my success for a while, then he asked, "Do you want to know my biggest success— the thing that makes me *know* I'm not stupid or lazy?"

I nodded.

"I was a junkie—and I kicked the habit all by myself."

"A heroin addict?!"

"Yeah—smack. It was going to kill me and I knew it."

"And you got off it without any help?"

Nodding slowly, he smiled with deep pride. "All by myself."

"I thought that couldn't be done."

"It can—I did it." He shared the delight of that success, then added, "I was a speed freak for a while, too. . . ."

By this time my companion seemed clear-headed and sober, and the afternoon sun was rapidly eating into our small area of shade. We'd been talking for well over an hour but had no desire to quit. He had no commitments. I still had nearly four hours until my 7:00 P.M. speaking engagement.

"Hey, there's a little pond over on the other side of the river . . . my most favorite place in the whole world. Let me take you there. . . ." He paused to see what my reaction would be, then continued enthusiastically, "It is so beautiful. I'd really like you to see it. We could even go swimming."

In the face of the afternoon heat, the idea of an old school marm and an eighteen-year-old bum traipsing off to the old swimming hole together didn't seem at all ridiculous. We quickly gathered up my belongings and started toward the car.

As the youth entered my car, he said, "By the way, my name is Alvin," and stuck out his hand.

I gave him my name, we shook warmly, and he took his place in the front seat beside me. "My friends call me Al," he added.

"Okay, Al it is," I said as I started the car. "Don't forget you're going to have to navigate. I don't know a thing about this town," I reminded him as we pulled out of the parking lot.

"No problem," he replied. "I know this place like the back of my hand." Pointing ahead, he instructed, "Go down to that first light and take a left. We want to go up over the bridge."

The huge steel girders of the bridge rose in plain sight on our right. When we reached the traffic signal, it was red. As we waited, I gestured in the direction of the bridge. "That way?" I asked, to get verification of the right turn I was about to make.

He nodded. "Yup."

Up over the bridge, down into a small area of heavy traffic, past a few stores and a row of houses—in less than five minutes we were on a winding country road. Al pointed out the interesting sights. He seemed to know who lived in every house we passed and had a story to tell about each. In an easy, free-flowing style he told of living by himself in the woods for months, of fishing, camping, and living off the land.

The pond that was our destination was even lovelier than I'd imagined. Its clear green water was rimmed by cattails, lush tall grass, and woods. The scene had the perfection of a picture postcard. Al helped me out onto the rickety old dock. Removing our shoes, we sat on the weathered gray boards and dangled our feet in the cool water.

Al broke our comfortable silence by asking, "If I get my

jeans wet, you got something I could sit on so I wouldn't ruin your seats?"

"Yes, I've got an old towel in the trunk."

"Good, then I'm going in for a swim." With that he stripped off his shirt, removed his leather belt, and slid from the dock into the water.

For a while, time and the world and appointments just didn't exist. Al floated lazily on his back, tried to touch bottom, gathered a handful of moss from a leg of the dock and studied it carefully. I splashed my feet in the water, relaxing and talking and enjoying.

A powerful thirst, an uncomfortable awareness of a no trespassing sign, and five o'clock all hit me at about the same time. Al picked a couple of the cattails I wanted, helped me off the alarmingly wobbly dock, and we headed back to town.

We wanted to stop by his house on the way so he could change into some dry jeans. But first we stopped at a tiny gas station–grocery store to pick up cold drinks.

Al and I stood side by side surveying the contents of the store's drink cooler. Noticing what I wanted way down at the end near him, I requested, "Fish me out a Coke, will you?"

He reached in with his left hand, snapped the top off in the opener attached to the cooler, and handed me the bottle.

"I didn't know you were left-handed," I commented casually.

"I'm not," he replied, removing a drink for himself with his right hand by way of demonstration. "Most of the things I can do with my right hand, I can do just about as good with my left hand." With a grin he added, "Comes in handy when you're working in tight places trying to hammer up molding and stuff."

The little old lady behind the counter exchanged greetings with Al but obviously didn't approve of him. She asked me a lot of questions in an effort to find out just what I was doing with such riffraff. Al was oddly silent. We finished our drinks and left.

Al's house was on a small side road just a mile or two from the country store. As we pulled up the steep gravel driveway, I gasped, "Your house is an authentic log cabin?!"

"Yup." Al grinned. "The real thing."

We stopped by the side door and parked. While Al went in to change, Max and I prowled around the back yard. A couple of junked cars and a varied assortment of old, rusty parts rimmed one side of the area. A small house trailer, the cinderblock foundation of a building, and two old wooden sheds circled the other side.

Al returned, bringing his young Doberman with him. After proudly telling me how he'd trained his loving, obedient pet, he asked, "You want to see the pigs before we go?"

I nodded with interest and followed the youth over to the cinderblock foundation walls. There, penned inside, three mammoth hogs snuffled and snorted at us in greeting.

"Did you know pigs are smart?" Al asked. Without waiting for my reply, he picked up a long, stout stick. "And they love to have their backs scratched." As soon as they saw the stick, the huge beasts pushed and shoved to get closer, grunting with anticipation. Al leaned contentedly against the wall, rubbing the stick up and down the broad, bristly backs and explaining to me about raising pigs.

The subject was fascinating. But the stench and the heat were overwhelming. As gracefully as possible, I proposed that we leave. "I want to be at the university by six, and it's a quarter of now. I think it's time we headed back toward town." After the pigpen, the country air on the ride back to town seemed especially cool and sweet.

As we crossed the bridge, I asked Al where he wanted me to drop him off.

"There's one more thing I'd like to show you," he replied.

I checked my watch. "It's five to six."

"From the top of this one building downtown, you can see the whole city," he said.

"Would it take long?"

He pointed off to the left. "It's just right there."

"If we run too short of time, I'll have to leave you downtown," I half apologized in explanation.

"That'd be okay. Ain't nowhere I need to get to that I can't get there by thumbing."

We agreed to take in this one last sight before parting.

Al directed me to the entrance of a large parking deck. We took a ticket and drove to the top. Happy to be released from the car, Max loped joyfully around the vast expanse of concrete. Al moved slowly from one vantage point to another, pointing out special features in the tremendous panoramic view of city, river, and hills beyond. As we looked away from the river and back toward the downtown area, even the rooftops across the back alley were interesting. We were particularly captivated by a tiny vegetable garden planted in tin cans and clay pots on a roof below. Languidly leaning against the railing, Al speculated about the size and quality of the small crop about to be harvested by some inner-city farmer.

Increasingly anxious about my tight schedule, I tried to hurry my companion along. He didn't seem to notice my concern. He was digging through the pocket of his jeans, looking for something. As I was about to protest about my schedule once more, Al produced a nickel, held it up for me to see, and grinned. Without a word of explanation, he reached far out over the edge, dropped the coin, then watched it closely as it fell the five floors to the pavement below.

A quick glance at my watch startled me into realizing that time was becoming a serious problem. It was ten after six. Mentally, I computed how long it would take to drop Al off, get to the university, change clothes, eat dinner, and get to the meeting. Quickly deciding I could forego dinner if necessary, I announced, "Al, we have *got* to go. It's nearly a quarter after six."

In our fascination with the view, we'd forgotten all about Max. Now, he was nowhere in sight. I called him. Al whistled.

Some rather frustrated barking came from one of the corner stairwells. I hurried over and looked down. My poor dog, confused by one level that looked the same as the next, was moving farther down the stairs in his attempt to get back up to where we were.

"Come on, Max," I shouted. "Up. We're up here."

Al sauntered over, sized up the situation, and said, "I'll go get him." Talking to the dog in calm, soothing tones, the youth padded casually down the stairs. "You just stay there, Max. I'll come get you. See, I'm up here. No, don't go down—you need to go the other way. Atta boy, now you got it. . . ."

From above, I could hear slowly moving sneakers and clicking canine toenails on concrete. Max bounded out at the top; Al followed shortly with a wide grin. "Ole Max doesn't know up from down," he chuckled and gave the dog a fond pat.

I was so far behind schedule that Al and I had to part without much fanfare. Clasping hands warmly, we said our good-byes.

Several times during the afternoon, the youth had said he often wondered if dropping out of school was a mistake. As I pulled away, I wanted to shout out one piece of advice to him in farewell: "It was no mistake. You're learning disabled. They had ten years to recognize you. What makes you think it might be different now? The first ten years, they damaged you—the next four might have destroyed you." But I didn't say anything. With tears in my eyes, silently, I waved good-bye.

Chapter II

Recognizing the LD Child

How DID I *know* that Al was learning disabled? What could I observe in such a brief, informal encounter?

To those who know what they're looking for, Al had revealed a tremendous amount of significant information strongly suggesting a severe learning disability. From his own words and the circumstances of his life, there is ample evidence that the youth failed to learn successfully in school. Anyone who's only in the eighth grade when he drops out of school at age sixteen can be safely categorized as an academic failure.

But Al's poor scholastic performance is merely one of many pieces of evidence suggesting that the youth had a learning disability. His strengths and successes point just as surely to the same conclusion. Al's entire pattern of significant differences is typical of the learning disabled. A definitive diagnosis would include careful probing for physical, intellectual, and psychological assets and deficiencies. Yet, without benefit of such formal procedures, clues are readily available to any observant person.

Causes of Failure

By definition, the LD child's failure to succeed in school is not caused by a physical handicap. If it is to be suggested that Al is learning disabled, then it must be shown that his learning failure was not the result of some physical condition.

In vision, hearing, and general state of health, Al showed no signs of any physical problem. It takes good visual acuity plus tracking ability to follow a nickel as it drops from a parking deck to the pavement five floors below. No hearing problem was observed or mentioned. Al showed that he was well coordinated. Playing a musical instrument in a rock band, doing carpentry, and engaging in heavy construction work all demand at least adequate agility. Long-distance hitchhiking and living off the land are not for the weak, puny, sickly, or faint-hearted. All of the evidence strongly supports the assumption that Al was alert, quick, responsive, and strong and had a great deal of stamina. From the things Al *could* do, it would not be logical to assume that his learning problems were caused by a physical condition.

Also by definition, the LD child's academic failure is *not* caused by lack of mental ability. The problem is not mental retardation. The learning-disabled youngster has average or better intelligence.

There is much evidence to indicate that Al had adequate mental ability. At fourteen he could play a musical instrument well enough to make money in a rock group. From sixteen to eighteen he managed to support himself as a carpenter and construction worker. By the age of eighteen, he himself had come to realize that his parents, friends, teachers, and classmates were wrong in believing that he was stupid. He knew about raising pigs, training dogs, and fishing. Al hitchhiked all over the country without getting lost or arrested. Despite his poor grammar and slang expressions, he had a good vocabulary and communicated effectively. He asked intelligent questions, was curious and highly observant of his surroundings. Al was definitely not retarded or "slow."

In addition to the type of mental ability that is measured by an IQ test, Al seemed to have a great deal of common sense. Anyone who could figure out a way to build a redwood deck with a piece of string, a T-square, and a level as substitutes for measuring would have to possess considerable ingenuity. "Living off the land" and "living by his wits" would demand alertness and quickness of mind. There *are* LD children who don't have sense enough to come in out of the rain—but they are not in the majority.

The definitions also exclude psychological problems as the cause of the LD child's lack of success in school.

This is a tricky area. Any child who is the dumb-dumb of the class will develop some strange behavior patterns out of frustration, shame, and anger. By the time he gets to junior high, the unrecognized LD student is usually unmotivated and either hostile or withdrawn. In the classroom, he is a behavior problem. Outside the class, he has social problems. Al's truancy and drug use at age fourteen are typical examples. Obviously, he was not a model student.

By the age of eighteen, Al could demonstrate his emotional stability and flexibility clearly. Despite the drugs and alcohol, the youth lived in and talked about reality. He was respectful of a dog that might bite him but neither recklessly bold nor unreasonably afraid. Asking about wet pants damaging my car seats before deciding to go for a swim clearly shows that Al considered the consequences of his behavior *before* acting.

Although school had been a miserable experience for the youth, he expressed no anger or hatred toward former teachers, schools, or society in general. His thoughts on the past were not full of guilt or despair. His thoughts about the future were not full of wild, impossible dreams. By being honest about both his weakness in math and his capability at building, he showed that he had a realistic attitude about himself. Al said he gave up heroin because he didn't want to die. That action demonstrated that he not only valued life but considered the quality of his life to be important as well. The will power needed to overcome heroin addiction could be found only in a person with a very strong desire to have control over his life.

Al's attitude toward me provides further evidence of emotional stability. While being very friendly and unusually assertive, he was always respectful and considerate. He was careful not to hurt my car seats, kindly rescued my dog, and even seemed to watch his language to avoid four-letter words that might have been offensive.

Al never did anything odd or peculiar. He was "oddly silent" in the grocery store but that was an understandable and logical way for him to deal with the situation. We were in a tiny rural community. He was a "local." The old lady at the cash register not only knew him but openly showed her disapproval. She asked me a lot of nosy questions in her attempt to find out what I was doing with a person she considered to be a good-for-nothing bum. In the face of the actual circumstances, Al's polite silence was extremely reasonable behavior.

There are those who would say, "A healthy, intelligent eighteen-year-old who spends his days drinking and smoking dope with the winos—there's got to be something wrong with his head." The young man definitely was a misfit. It would take a psychological examination to evaluate his state of mental health precisely, but from everything that happened during that afternoon, there is no apparent reason to consider him emotionally disturbed.

Mixed Dominance and Directional Confusion

Human beings have a natural tendency to develop a strong preference for using one half of their body rather than the other. In strength, agility, coordination, and acquisition of skills, the body becomes increasingly one-sided. When an activity allows a choice of feet, hands, eyes, or ears, one side will be consistently favored. For most people, the dominant half is on the right.

The learning disabled aren't built that way. More often than not, they have mixed dominance. Their bodies aren't strongly one-sided. Al was partially ambidextrous. Although he did most things with his right hand, he sometimes found it more convenient to use his left. In getting our soft drinks, Al used his left hand for both removing the bottle from the cooler and applying the top to the opener. Very few right-handed people would attempt such a maneuver. For most people, the nonfavored hand is just hanging there for ballast, and occasionally for holding things while the other hand works on them. Al was proud of the fact that this was not the case for him. He commented that the ability to switch back and forth came in handy when doing things like tacking up molding.

There is nothing wrong with having mixed dominance. Sometimes it's an advantage, as with Al's carpentry and those who become switch hitters in baseball. Sometimes it's a disadvantage, as with a youngster who tries to learn to shoot a gun right-handed while sighting with the left eye. When dealing with concrete objects and body movement, right-sided, left-sided, and mixed all work out about the same.

The inability to tell left from right is one of the most common symptoms of a learning disability. Al demonstrated his problem in this area when he gave me the instruction to turn left at the bridge, while he and I could both plainly see the big steel structure looming over us on the right. From any person over the age of seven or eight, such a mistake should *not* be considered a meaningless slip of the tongue. And whether or not the individual notices and corrects his own error does not change the fact that it was made. Those who are learning disabled will *not* have trouble with the labels "left" and "right" every time they use them. But most people never have trouble with them at all.

Poor Concept of Time

Al never once talked about what time it was. Even when my schedule was tight and we were discussing the possibility of seeing the view from the parking deck, he responded without ever referring to time. I announced the hour; he said there was a great view of the city from the top of the parking area. I asked how long it would take; he pointed, replying that the building was right over there. I explained that my schedule might force me to leave him abruptly; he responded that he could get anywhere he needed to go by hitchhiking. Throughout the entire exchange, Al and I were operating on different wavelengths. I was very conscious of the moments moving past. He was totally oblivious of them.

All through their lives, the learning disabled tend to live in the here and now. As youngsters in school, this shows up in many ways.

LD children have extreme difficulty learning to use a clock. But it is very unusual for a teacher to notice or even suspect that one of her students can't tell time. It just never comes up. Everyone assumes that once a child passes the second or third grade, he's mastered the skills and concepts involved. Teachers often say, "I told you to have that paper finished by one o'clock. It's now a quarter after, and you still haven't handed it in." Teachers never ask, "What time is it?" If, by some fluke, the LD child gets trapped into a showdown, he can be counted on to use his wits to bail himself out. In such an emergency, a wide assortment of nonanswers can allow the student to avoid revealing his problem. The humorous response of immediate innocent cooperation usually works well. "What time it it? OOOOooooops, it's time for me to give you my paper."

And, all smiles, he dashes forward, scribbles in his name at the top of the page, gives the paper a pat, and nods as he leaves it on the top of the teacher's desk. If the inquiry is made by a friend or classmate, a flippant "You got eyes. Look for yourself" will usually suffice. As for the LD child revealing his weakness by asking someone else to tell him the time, it never happens. He doesn't *care* what time it is! Like Al, the learning disabled just flow along in the now.

Once we got up on the top of the building, Al and I clearly demonstrated the difference in our approach to time. I was in a hurry. I bustled and scurried around, trying to get as much as possible out of the few moments available. But not Al. He sauntered casually from one vantage point to another, pointing out the sights. He leaned against the wall in easy comfort while offering his observations on a roof garden below. Fishing the nickel out of his pocket and dropping it over the edge was done at a super-relaxed pace. The unhurried movements with which he savored life would have driven most people crazy! This is the nonvariable pace so commonly found among the learning disabled.

Clocks, time limits, and schedules do not motivate LD children. Those who move, think, and work slowly can seldom be forced or coerced into speeding up. Those who run around in high gear tend to stay on fast no matter how strongly they're urged to slow down. Very few of the learning disabled ever recognize the fact that their inflexible pace is an irritation and inconvenience to others. Instead, they think parents, teachers, and the world in general have made a ridiculous fetish out of punctuality.

Because they live almost exclusively in the present moment, the learning disabled rarely think in terms of the appropriate time for a particular action. If they think of something they want to do, they do it immediately. Al showed some of this behavior in proposing that I join him in a trip to his favorite swimming hole. It was terribly hot. The idea of the cool water was very appealing. But he knew that middle-aged ladies don't usually join young vagrants in such adventures. His urge to act was expressed the minute it crossed his mind. In some children this type of instant implementation of an idea constitutes impulsive behavior. When observed in the learning disabled, the quick decision to action is more likely related to a sense of timing that allows only for now.

In addition to demonstrating a poor concept of time, Al described his inability to keep numbers, letters, and words straight and in the right order. Although there was no opportunity to see it first-hand, it can be safely assumed that Al had all the difficulties with sequencing that are typical of the learning disabled.

Sequencing is a technique that orders objects or events in time. First comes this, then comes that, followed by something else. Since LD youngsters have such a poor concept of time, they have no feel for sequencing, either.

This one problem has a devastating effect on almost all areas of schoolwork. From kindergarten, where they can't learn the order of the alphabet, to high school physics, where they can't keep the steps in an experiment straight, the inability to sequence makes routine tasks impossible for the learning disabled.

Upon close analysis, the majority of the activities in a traditional school program are based on doing things in a specific order. (1) Schedules. Throughout the school day segments of time are allocated for various subjects. As long as the periods stay in a fixed order, the LD student will develop a feel for the rhythm of the day. But he'll never remember that art replaces science every other Tuesday. And he'll frequently forget that there's a vocabulary test every Wednesday. It's pointless to hope that he'll fulfill some obligation that comes up once a month. To keep an LD child moving smoothly on schedule, teachers have to supply a lot of advance warnings and gentle reminders. (2) Instructions. Explanations of assignments almost always include instructions that the steps involved must be done in a particular order. Details such as first you break the words into syllables, then you mark the vowels, are likely to be overlooked by LD youngsters. Unless there's some logical and necessary reason for one step to come before another, the precise progression will often be forgotten. Multiple assignments are especially likely to cause frustration. If the child can remember the directions for a single worksheet of math problems, that's enough for one sitting. Adding some corrections from yesterday's work and a page in the workbook plus two story problems on the board will throw most LD youngsters into hopeless confusion. (3) Alphabetizing. Dictionaries, encyclopedias, card catalogues, library shelves, glossaries, bibliographies, outlines, indexes, etc., are based on alphabetical order. Because of the difficulty LD children have with sequencing, all forms of alphabetizing are troublesome for them. This means they are often unable to use the materials necessary in completing an assignment. Yes, they can find a word in the dictionary. But it takes them three to four times as long—provided they don't get furious and quit, get desperate and cheat, or lose interest and start drawing airplanes. (4) Teaching techniques. The human brain uses gimmicks to aid memory. For most people it would be impossible to name the months of the year without saying them in order. Sequencing is the trick that enables us to recall all twelve easily. In teaching anything to anybody, the method of instruction is likely to use sequencing as the tool that makes learning possible. Little first-graders are told, "To make an *m*, first you make a stick, then you make a hump, then you add another hump." This is how youngsters are taught to write. For most of them, it makes the process as easy as one, two, three. But not so for the learning disabled. No amount of repetition will teach them to put two bumps on an *m* if their memory must rely on sequence.

"What comes next?" "What do I do now?" Learning-disabled students constantly ask these questions. Every time they express such confusion, they're announcing the fact that they're having trouble with sequencing.

Unusual Powers of Observation

From the way Al studied the moss on the dock, told me about raising pigs, dropped the nickel from the building and watched it fall, it is clear that he was observant and perceptive. He was interested in what went on around him. He noticed everything.

The learning disabled seem to look at the world through a wide-angle lens. Nothing escapes their attention. They do not focus narrowly on one task and tune everything else out. In fact, it seems to be impossible for them to ignore anything that's going on around them. In a classroom, they're the ones who comment on the teacher's new hairdo and the fact that her slip is showing. While they are trying to focus on an English test, their attention will be drawn to the sounds of footsteps in the hall, the glint of sunlight off the pencil sharpener, the cool breeze blowing across the room, shuffling feet, turning pages, tapping pencils, the feel of initials carved in the top of a desk, the breathing of other students, the great-looking skier on the calendar behind the teacher's desk, and the growing rumbly emptiness of a hungry stomach. The LD student would make a splendid Sherlock Holmes. But in a traditional classroom, such a fantastic power of observation is a handicap. By not zeroing in on the work at hand, they fail to pay attention in a way acceptable to teachers. When a pupil is seated at a desk in a school, the wide-angle lens approach means he is distractible and has a short attention span.

The LD youngster's talent for being observant does not apply merely to what can be seen, heard, or felt. It also applies to people. Most LD individuals are very sensitive. The set of a shoulder, the tilt of a head, the rise of an eyebrow, voice tones, body language, silences and pauses—the unspoken messages in the realm of feelings are noticed by these very perceptive children. They are usually extremely adept at reading people.

Al gave an exceptionally good demonstration of this type of special sensitivity to people. While I was determined not to get involved with any of the bums and winos, he easily made light conversation until my defensive attitude evaporated. My haughty air of disinterest didn't fool him a bit. Somehow Al sensed that my dog and I were both friendly. All afternoon, Al's consideration for me continually reflected his keen awareness of my feelings.

Unusual Creativeness

Learning-disabled students are often much more creative than their classmates. They approach problems in a different way and express themselves and their ideas differently. The products of their inventive thinking are often so amazingly simple, yet so totally original that adults gape in wonder, saying, "What an ingenious idea."

From an early age, Al showed unusual creativity. In the third grade he won a poetry contest, at fourteen he was in a rock band, at eighteen he could figure out how to build a redwood deck without even measuring. Very few youngsters would be creative enough to succeed in even one of these areas, not to mention three.

Al's greatest strength was in the area of building three-dimensional objects. "And not just carpentry work, either."

The LD child is the one who can build a gocart out of an old lawnmower and a pile of scrap lumber, or design a special holster to keep his cap gun on hand but safely out of sight while in school. He tends to build things in unconventional ways, however. Part of this is due to his unusual creative ability, part to the fact that he's not likely to be using written directions or doing a lot of standard measuring or planning. With hammer and saw, screwdriver and pliers, the LD child can do some amazing things.

Research has shown that most of the learning disabled are "spatially gifted." They tend to have a talent for understanding and creating objects that are three-dimensional. This means they make good sculptors, mechanics, automotive designers, architects, interior designers, plumbers, and engineers.

The mechanical wizardry of the learning disabled is pretty much common knowledge. The other areas of their exceptional creativity are not so often recognized. The walls of my classroom were always covered with outstanding art work done by my LD students. They won many blue ribbons and awards at fairs, exhibits, and other children's art contests. Some of them showed unusual skill in drawing, painting, or design. Almost all of them demonstrated the LD child's wonderful talent for coming up with original ideas. This special skill in producing novel ideas often carries over into creative writing and the interpretation of literature. Despite poor spelling and halting reading, the LD child often uses language with real flair. If appreciated for the imaginative person he is, an LD student can add sparkle, mirth, and new depths of insight to an entire class.

Misfits and Loners

To his classmates, the LD child almost always looks as if he were stupid. Since the youngsters around his neighborhood know about his lack of success in school, they too consider him to be dumb. Teased, picked on, and rejected, the LD child is often forced into the role of outcast.

Generally, LD children do not find acceptance from the adults in their lives either. Teachers believe they're lazy; parents accuse them of being stubborn. Relatives usually think they're spoiled. Neighbors consider them troublemakers. Socially, on all fronts, learning-disabled youngsters are rejected.

Through no choice of his own, the LD child is forced to be a loner. The only companionship and acceptance available to him is from other losers or strangers.

"... skipping school ... doing drugs ... dropped out ... hit the road. ..." Like Al, the LD teen-ager seeks escapes. He's frustrated and miserable in school. And his social life and home life are rarely much better. Life is *not* pleasant.

Escape-type activities hold great appeal. For the younger children, doodling, drawing, and daydreaming are typical. For the teen-agers, it's escape through drugs, alcohol, and travel. Traveling and bumming around become attractive because they offer opportunities for quick, easy acceptance among strangers.

Al's behavior was typical of this pattern. For the most part, he was a loner, escaping through drugs and alcohol. With me, a stranger, he was relaxed, friendly, and comfortably outgoing. With the old woman, who knew all about him, he was quiet and withdrawn. And faraway places held a very special attraction for him. As a stranger, outside a school or neighborhood where he was known, he could be accepted as totally normal and okay.

It's unfortunate that psychiatry probably would not have helped Al. Teaching children to live joyously with failure has been tried many times. It doesn't work. The LD youngster doesn't need counseling. He needs to learn to read. He needs to learn to do his math. He needs acceptance. He needs confidence. He needs success.

Poor Organization

If there's any group who have *no* natural inclination toward organization, it's the learning disabled. They are the world's original absent-minded professors. Can't find their glasses, lost their pencil, don't know what day it is, forgot where they put their jacket, left their book home on the dining room table. Their work is messy, their environment a shambles. They're forgetful, preoccupied, and frequently off in the clouds. Mothers, teachers, wives, roommates, and colleagues are driven crazy by their total lack of order.

Al is a beautiful example of the lack of organization so typical of the LD person. By the age of eighteen, he'd completely abandoned any attempt to live within any kind of structure. No plans, no regular job, no possessions, no commitments, no schedules—he just went along with the flow. Al created a life-style where it didn't matter if he knew what day it was. He turned lack of organization into an asset.

LD individuals are unable to live comfortably within the limits of deadlines. As children, they're chronically tardy. As adults, they're famous for being late for most of their appointments. This is not simply a part of their lack of a concept of time. It is also a result of their lack of organization.

The little square on the LD student's report card for "Uses time wisely" is likely to be checked for "Needs improvement." When faced with a task, he has a standard ineffective pattern: First, he gets ready to get started. This usually includes a trip to the wastebasket or drinking fountain, a joke with a classmate, and some fun with a toy kept stashed in his pocket. Teachers often put an abrupt end to this stage with admonitions like "John, get down to business." Second, he takes a long time to get out his materials. The jumbled mess in his desk makes the search for pencils, paper, and books a very slow process. And, of course, he also tends to dawdle. When the youngster finally picks up his pencil to begin work, his classmates are already way ahead of him. (That is, of course, assuming he can find a pencil at all!) Third, the LD youngster struggles to figure out the directions. He never seems to remember what the teacher said to do. Sometimes he pesters his neighbors for guidance; often he comes running up to the teacher's desk for help. His confusion and uncertainty are usually quite obvious. Fourth, he makes his big attempt. He fills in a few answers. When that proves difficult, he shifts to some part of the assignment that looks easier. As that proves to be of no help, he resorts to pure guessing. Frustrated, he pauses to sharpen a pencil, take a breather, or gaze out the window. And, fifth, his mind drifts off to something else as the rest of the class period slips on by.

This pattern isn't just the result of poor reading skills and distractibility. It's also caused by an inability to get organized.

Failure in the Basic Skills

LD children fail to succeed in learning the basic skills. As a third-grader, Al understood poetry well enough to create a contest-winning poem. As a junior high student he could succeed in learning history. This is typical of LD students. They can think and learn the material involved in subject matter courses, but they can't succeed in learning reading, writing, spelling, and sometimes math. When they fail subject matter courses, it's usually because they couldn't read the book, couldn't write the answers for assignments and tests, didn't pay attention in class, or didn't study. The learning-disabled student's primary problem is with the basic skills.

From the blackboard side of the teacher's desk, it is rarely obvious that the LD student's newest failure is caused by his lack of success in learning the basic skills! It almost always looks as if his problem is laziness, lack of motivation, poor attitude, or absences. The academic failure usually appears to be the *result* rather than the cause of his behavior problems.

When faced with a real LD child in a real classroom, we teachers fail to recognize what we're seeing.

We say, "If there's anybody who can't afford to sleep through math class, it's you. the least you could do is *try!*"

Why should he try to do multiplication? He can't even write the numbers down so they face in the proper direction!

We snarl, "Young man, I'll take that yoyo you've been playing with, and you can get down to business right now. You could get all four of those English worksheets done before lunch if you'd put your mind to it."

Why should he put his mind to writing sentences? He can't read the questions or the story they're based on. If he did know the answers, he could neither spell the words correctly nor copy them out of the book accurately.

We threaten, "You take this note home to your mother. And when you walk in that door Monday morning, I want to see that book you say you're reading for your book report."

Why should he bring that book to school with him? He can read only about half of the words in it. If he skipped over the hard parts, he couldn't follow the action. He can't spell, can't express his ideas in writing. He's never written a decent sentence in his life. Even if he could read the book, he couldn't possibly write an acceptable book report. So why should he bring that book to school on Monday? It would be just another hassle.

To the LD student, effort would be pointless. Failure is inevitable.

To the teacher, the child doesn't look as if he *can't* do the work. He looks as if he *won't* do it.

Even if a teacher is fully aware of an LD child's lack of skill in reading, spelling, and math, there is a strong tendency to find excuses to justify his poor performance. "He doesn't pay attention," or "He's too busy fooling around," or "He just doesn't really care." Adults are almost always convinced that, if the youngster would really try, he could succeed. For Al, his teachers probably blamed socio-economic factors with words such as "What can you expect from a kid who lives in a shack?" Because he came from the wrong side of the tracks, Al wouldn't have been expected to succeed.

When the learning-disabled student has a pencil in his hand, it is glaringly obvious that the real cause of his difficulties is not lack of motivation. We didn't get to see Al do any writing. If we had, he'd probably have made many of the writing errors that are typical of LD students. (1) LD children often have very strange methods of gripping a pencil. They'll hold it at an odd angle, wrap their thumb around to some weird, useless position, use four fingers instead of three. The traditional three-fingered triangle formed by thumb, index finger, and middle finger is rarely the grip they prefer. (And they are very resistant toward changing their personal style of holding a pencil, no matter how much the teacher insists.) (2) Their papers are messy. Although they can control their hands well enough to make great spit wads and paper airplanes, they are seldom able to do a nice, neat job of handwriting, even when they try. (3) When they are motivated to do their very best, their papers show that they've made many errors which were corrected. Learning-disabled children erase a lot. (4) Older LD students usually prefer to print. They continue to use manuscript writing even when pressured to do cursive. By the seventh or eighth grade, they may improve their skill in printing but often refuse to shift to cursive. (5) They tend to use only their first name on papers. LD youngsters have trouble learning to spell and write their first name. Last names are often more difficult, and the young child doesn't get much practice writing his surname. Many teen-age LD youngsters *cannot* write their last name correctly. (6) Most of the errors look as if they're caused by carelessness. (Some of the more common mistakes are undotted *i*'s, uncrossed *t*'s, *m*'s with missing humps; letters facing the wrong way, put in the wrong place, or missing altogether; letters that are the wrong size or shape, or not placed properly on the line; strange mixtures of manuscript and cursive writing.) (7) Much to their teacher's dismay, LD students can't even write well when all they have to do is copy. In their attempt to reproduce what they see written clearly before them, LD children leave out words and letters and make all their usual reversals and handwriting errors.

The same kinds of problems seen in the LD child's writing also appear in his reading. (1) Letters will be read upside down or backwards, so that *bad* becomes *dad* or *mash* becomes *wash*. (2) Letters will be reversed or scrambled out of their proper order, so that *slot* becomes *lots*, or *salt* becomes *slat*. (3) Entire syllables, words, or phrases will be rearranged or omitted altogether. Suffixes frequently get left off, and the little words get changed and altered at random. *For* becomes *from*, *who* becomes *which*, *he* becomes *she*, *mother* becomes *mom*.

Most LD children have adequate or good reading comprehension. It is in the mechanical process of decoding words that they have difficulty. Even after specialized instruction, they tend to rely on guessing rather than systematic word attack.

Spelling is the most sensitive indicator of a learning disability. By combining the demands of reading with the difficulties of writing, it hits the LD children in two of their weakest spots. In trying to spell even the simplest words, they make reversals, omissions, and strange alterations. The relationships between sounds and symbols rarely make sense to the learning diasbled, so without special instruction they seldom even spell phonetically. Even with a very high IQ and the finest therapy, very few LD individuals ever become better than barely adequate spellers. Most never do that well.

Although poor handwriting and spelling mean that LD children cannot express themselves well in writing, they usually have no difficulty expressing themselves orally. Al was typical of the learning disabled in that he loved to talk and was a very good conversationalist.

As much as possible, on what little work they do, LD students tend to confine themselves to writing very brief answers. A worksheet that requires complete sentences will get answers of one or two words. An assignment that asks for paragraphs will get a few sentence fragments. When allowed to respond orally, LD pupils can almost always think of several intelligent sentences in answer to a question. Yet, when the ideas have to be put into writing, they'll condense it all down to one word. As a general rule, the more writing an assignment requires, the less likely it is that an LD student will complete it successfully.

Al's main area of disability was in math. From what could be observed directly, it is easy to surmise the types of difficulties he had. Mixed dominance and directional confusion would have given Al a strong tendency to turn numbers around backwards or scramble them so they were out of order. Twenty-seven would become 72; 465 would become

564 or 645 or 456 or 654 or 546. This means that even copying the problems out of the book could cause errors.

Al said he couldn't learn math at all. As is the case with most LD youngsters, no amount of drill and practice would have helped get the basic math facts firmly planted in his memory. And even if he had mastered the facts needed, it can certainly be assumed that he would have had a lot of trouble manipulating numbers. In the process of working a problem, Al's directional confusion would have made him get lost in the maze of up, down, right, left. Carrying would have caused problems because he would have had trouble remembering which number to write down and which to carry. In subtraction, Al would have been perfectly comfortable taking the top number away from the bottom one. And, of course, borrowing would have been impossible for him. Multiplication, division, fractions, decimals, all advanced arithmetic depends on the student having a strong and sure sense of direction. By his own admission, Al never did learn to work math problems. His total lack of ability in this basic skill no doubt had far-reaching effects on many other areas of schoolwork.

Like most learning-disabled children, Al failed because he couldn't successfully use the tools that—in our educational system—make all learning possible. All of his unsatisfactory grades were really F's in reading, writing, spelling, and math. Because he lacked ability in the basic skills, he was locked out of a chance for success in all academic areas. Effort was totally pointless.

Why didn't somebody recognize Al's real problem? How is it that a system dedicated to helping children damages some of them so badly? How can we prevent this from happening again?

Prior to the late 1960s, learning-disabled youngsters suffered and failed all but totally unrecognized. As with Al, untold damage was done to children who deserved a better fate. It wasn't that teachers didn't care. The problem was ignorance. Only a handful of specialists knew how to diagnose and help these students, and their work was confined to expensive private schools and clinics. In those days, the average classroom teacher might have heard the word "dyslexia"; but that one mysterious term was likely to be the full extent of her knowledge of learning disabilities.

Throughout the 1970s, programs were set up for these long-neglected LD students. Now the special instruction they need is widely available in state-supported school systems. Many counties have merely added learning disabilities to the list of responsibilities of some already overworked member of the special education department. In other systems, entire staffs of experts have been assigned to every single school. Regardless of their size or scope, these new LD programs are almost always based on one assumption: those who have direct contact with the students are expected to single out the ones with special needs and refer them for testing and services. Thus, the burden falls directly on the classroom teachers. They are the ones who must recognize learning-disabled pupils. No matter how desperate a youngster's need, no program can help him until some teacher considers him a logical candidate for evaluation.

The classroom teacher is the key. It's an awesome responsibility.

Learning disabilities cut across all racial, economic, and cultural backgrounds. Many children have unusual family situations that can be mistaken for the real cause of learning failure. The very poor and the very rich, the baby of the family, the spoiled child, the child from a broken home, the youngster who has moved a lot, foster children, adopted children, abused children, runaways, youthful offenders; children whose parents are alcoholic, physically handicapped, chronically sick, mentally ill, hospitalized, institu-tionalized, or in jail—many youngsters live in horrible home situations. Their family problems *can* cause failure in school. But to the unwary teacher a child's home situation can mask a learning disability.

It can be devilishly difficult to recognize the LD young-ster. To be successful, the process of investigation must be a child-centered activity. That's why this book will focus on the child: the child's schoolwork, the child's attitude, the child's behavior, the child's strengths and weaknesses, the child's failures and successes. Always the emphasis will be based on direct observation narrowly focused on a specific child. What is he actually doing in class? What do his papers look like? What are the things he can't do no matter how hard he tries? Always the aim will be to explore beneath the surface—to probe in an open, investigative, problem-solving attitude—to find and understand what's *really* there.

These children can be found and helped. Classroom teachers *are* capable of recognizing symptoms of a learning disability, recommending youngsters for testing, under-standing the special needs of LD students, and making the classroom adjustments that will enable them to succeed.

Beautiful young people like Al do not have to be crushed by the system. The vicious cycle of failure and frustration that damages LD children needlessly can be stopped by caring, well-informed classroom teachers.

Section Two

OUR PRESENT-DAY APPROACH to education emphasizes development of a pattern of strengths and weaknesses that is the direct opposite of that possessed by the learning disabled. Anything that enables these youngsters to succeed in today's schools will be, at best, a compromise.

Teachers want LD students to succeed with the "regular" program. For the vast majority of them, this is not possible. When faced with the regular classwork, LD pupils fail to succeed. They become discouraged, lose their interest, motivation, and self-confidence. When assigned appropriately adjusted schoolwork, these children learn successfully.

The choice of whether or not to adjust a learning-disabled student's schoolwork is basically a question of whether the focal point of education should be the system or the individual child. We often get so caught up in the ethical ramifications of this issue that LD youngsters end up going unhelped.

There is no way to adjust a student's assignments so that it is totally fair to his classmates, future teachers, college admissions officers, and prospective employers. This book is aimed at helping the LD child succeed. As much as possible, the established structure of education and business will be treated fairly. But when there is a conflict, the best interests of the individual student will take precedence over all else. Others will have to solve the ethical questions. Our aim is to solve the problems of the learning-disabled child.

Chapter III

A New Approach to an Old Problem

LEARNING-DISABLED CHILDREN have always been in regular classrooms. They were in the bottom reading group. Their work was messy, incomplete, and full of errors. Bribes, punishments, and special attention didn't help. No matter what was done on their behalf, still these youngsters continued to fail.

We teachers consoled ourselves by saying, "This year I helped thirty-three out of thirty-four children. I didn't do a bit of good for Frank. But, then, you can't win them all. Maybe next year he'll. . . ."

These children passed on through the grades. Their lack of success was merely accepted. Nothing much was expected of them. They were those sweet but rambunctious boys destined to fill the low group. They weren't retarded, hard of hearing, or physically handicapped. There were no special programs into which they fitted. So they became an accepted part of every class—the unmotivated, nonachieving boys in the back row.

We didn't know they were learning disabled. But always they've been there.

Research into the puzzling failure patterns now called learning disabilities began in the early 1920s. Intelligent children who could not learn to read and write were investigated by medical experts in the United States and England. Remedial programs were designed based on their findings. In the 1930s, some private schools began providing special facilities for these "dyslexic" students. However, even among the most exclusive independent schools, such programs were by no means prevalent. Among educators, these programs were extremely controversial. Many believed that dyslexia was an imaginary condition being remediated by quacks and charlatans.

In the 1960s, researchers again began focusing attention on this group of unsuccessful students. Investigations probed to find why perfectly normal children failed to succeed in school. In response to a mass of convincing new evidence, public schools began taking a serious interest in learning disabilities. Throughout the late 1960s and early 1970s, this new area of exceptionality emerged as education's newest craze. States began developing LD programs. In response to the growing demands made by parents and educators, most state legislatures passed bills guaranteeing a free and appropriate education to the learning disabled.

The cat was out of the bag. Those underachievers in the back row *could* be helped!

To cap things off, federal law 94–142 was passed and implemented. It said that LD children *had* to be given appropriate special services—while remaining in a regular classroom as much as possible. Neglecting underachievers was no longer a moral or educational issue. With PL 94–142, the success or failure of the learning disabled became a legal matter! And mainstreaming was the law.

The legislation has not created a new situation. Mainstreaming did not *put* LD children into the classrooms. The statutes have merely made it mandatory that, while remaining in regular classrooms where they've always been, LD youngsters must be given the special services they need in order to learn successfully. Trained professionals must be available to provide evaluation and remediation for the child. These specialists must also provide support and guidance to the child's teacher.

If all the statutes were abolished, it would not put us back to where we were twenty-five years ago. The fact that there is such a thing as a learning disability has become public knowledge. Parents and teachers now *know* that LD children can be helped.

The Teacher's Role

Let's dispel one myth at the outset: mainstreaming does *not* ask the classroom teacher to become a learning disabilities expert. She is not expected to "cure" the child and solve all his problems.

The classroom teacher *can* be a positive factor in helping LD students overcome their learning difficulties. But that is a goal for the future. That *might* be achieved after several years of practice and experience under the guidance of a good LD specialist. The teacher's first objective is to see to it that no damage is done to LD students within the classroom.

Some readers will be insulted by the implication that classroom teachers harm these children. Nevertheless, it is a fact we must accept. For years teachers have done all the wrong things in their attempts to make learning-disabled pupils learn successfully. They have punished, badgered, shamed, and bribed. Their actions were based on frustration and a sincere desire to help. Mainly, however, their actions were based on ignorance.

As a first-grader, Marcie's mild learning disability made it hard for her to learn to write. Her terribly messy papers were always dog-eared and torn from all the erasing. Since her unusually high intelligence made it possible for Marcie to succeed in all the other areas of her school work, the teacher assumed the sloppy papers were caused by laziness. She made many attempts to motivate the child. Most of them were harmful, but one was devastating.

Before an end-of-the-year penmanship test, the teacher tried to inspire the entire class by holding up two examples of student writing. One paper was perfect. Lovely, rounded letters marched precisely across the page. The other paper was ghastly. The children snickered at the ugly, heavy black marks sprawling above the lines and around the splotches and holes. The sample of "what we don't want our papers to look like" was Marcie's work.

The public ridicule hurt Marcie so deeply that she turned off—not just to writing or that teacher or that class. She turned off to school in general. Once she was past the second or third grade, her slight learning disability caused her no further problems. But Marcie never regained an interest in learning. Her high intelligence was channeled into mischief and defiance. The pursuit of boys, drugs, partying, and truancy made a four-year high-school into a five-year project. Then it took her six years to squeeze through a four-year college.

If that one teacher had only understood the real cause of Marcie's poor penmanship. . . .

We teachers smile and say, "Well, yes—but that was twenty years ago. Nobody knew anything about learning disabilities back then." We think things like that don't happen anymore. We believe we know better now. Do we?

The following two incidents happened in the early 1980s.

Freddie, a third-grader, was diagnosed as learning-disabled and provided therapy in a resource room. By late April the youngster was making very good progress but was still far behind the other students in his regular class. The psychologist, LD teacher, classroom teacher, principal, social worker, and parents all agreed that repeating the third grade was definitely in the boy's best interest. The child accepted the plan with calm optimism. He believed another year in the third grade plus continued LD therapy would give him his first real chance for success in school.

Everything was fine until the last day of school. As Freddie's teacher handed out the report cards, she announced where each child would be in school the following year. Her roll call went something like this: "Johnny will be moving upstairs with the fourth-graders. Peter is moving this summer. He'll be in the fourth grade in his new school in Denver. Lucinda will be upstairs in the fourth grade. Freddie will be staying right here in the third grade with me. Paula will be. . . ." When a student asked why Freddie would be staying in the third grade, the teacher casually replied, "You all know Freddie didn't do very well this year." The children snickered and tittered. Embarrassed, the poor little repeater fled from the room in tears.

Retention no longer seemed like a chance for success. Staying in the third grade had been made to look like punishment.

*   *   *

Walter's learning disability was diagnosed after his second un-successful year in the seventh grade. The school system in his small hometown did not yet have any LD teachers. During the summer Walter was given private therapy in a nearby city. In the fall the private lessons continued, and an LD consultant was brought in to work with his school. All the boy's teachers cooperated fully. As they developed an understanding of his special learning prob-lems, they eagerly made the kinds of adjustments that would help him succeed.

Reading was the only class where Walter continued to fail. But with his particular learning disability, that seemed understand-able. The LD consultant and the reading teacher had several con-ferences. Both believed that every reasonable adjustment had been made.

It was mid-December before anyone realized that Walter would be passing his reading course if it weren't for the weekly vocabu-lary tests. One look at the weekly word lists showed the logic behind Walter's failure. The boy was reading on a low sixth-grade level. He had no dictionary skills at all, no study habits, and no self-confidence. The reading teacher had adjusted all his work to fit his level of ability. Yet she had continued to assign him the regular eighth-grade vocabulary list. Every week Walter was ex-pected to look up and memorize thirty hefty five- and six-syllable words that he couldn't even read!

Those vocabulary tests ruined Walter's grade average. He flunked his reading course.

The teacher did not see the part she had played in the boy's failure. In discussing the situation with the LD consultant, she confidently explained, "I think Walter needs the challenge of doing at least some of the regular work—don't you?"

The above stories are not examples of uncaring, incompetent teachers. They are typical of situations occurring in classrooms all over the country. Teachers are just beginning to learn how to deal with learning-disabled students. And as beginners, they make mistakes. It takes time to break away from the old habits and attitudes that have harmed LD children for years.

Teachers are idealists. They want to leap from total ignorance to wonder-working wisdom in one bound. They don't seem to realize that before they can learn to be part of the solution, they must first learn how to stop being part of the problem.

Developing New Ways of Thinking

Before classroom teachers can even begin to help their learning-disabled students, they need to learn to look below the surface to find the real causes of a child's failure.

Traditionally, teachers have believed that success in school depends on only two factors: mental ability and motivation. Thus, it was assumed that any normally intelligent child who wants to learn can learn. The only possible causes for failure were stupidity and laziness. Such an old-fashioned, simplistic view makes it impossible for teachers to deal effectively with LD students.

At the end of the fourth grade, Tommy's teacher told his parents that he hadn't learned a thing that year. The boy had done all the reading and passed all the tests, but he hadn't turned in one single piece of written work. All the B's and C's on his report card merely reflected what his teacher believed he would have gotten if he'd done the work.

The family and the school agreed that the boy was spoiled and did only what he liked to do.

In an attempt to remedy the situation, Tommy's parents enrolled him in a private school, insisting that he repeat the fourth grade. Since the youngster scored well above grade level on all the admissions testing, the headmaster was determined to place him in the fifth grade.

As a compromise Tommy was given a two-week trial period in the private school's fourth grade. Unless there were problems during the probationary period, he would be moved up to the fifth grade, where he belonged.

By the end of the first week of school, Tommy's total lack of motivation was painfully apparent. Several very strong courses of action were considered, including psychiatry. Since everybody was totally convinced that Tommy's problem was a matter of simple laziness, the youngster was not referred to the LD specialist for testing.

On the routine LD screening test given to all fourth-graders during the first month of school, Tommy scored very poorly. When the matter was discussed with his teacher, she talked quite openly about the child's total lack of interest in doing any of his schoolwork. Waving her arms in frustration, she said, "For all I know, the kid could be allergic to pencils. I don't know how he does it, but that boy has wangled his way out of every single writing assignment we've had." She tapped a stack of papers with her red checking pencil and snorted, "Ten days of school—and I haven't gotten him to write anything more than his name!" She shook her head in resignation and concluded, "Never before have I had a student I honestly believed was basically lazy."

A time for testing was set up. As the LD specialist departed, the teacher called to her, "Ask Tommy why he doesn't do his work. You know what he'll say?—'I'm lazy'!"

Testing revealed that Tommy had an IQ high enough to place

him in the "genius" range. That was not surprising. We all knew the youngster was bright.

Much to everybody's amazement, the test results also explained Tommy's lack of motivation. It wasn't that he didn't *want* to write. the boy *couldn't* write. Although he was an excellent reader, he couldn't tell whether letters were written backward or forward. Even though he was a fourth-grader with an IQ over 140, there were letters of the alphabet that he couldn't produce in either manuscript or cursive writing. Tommy had a very severe writing disability.

If a youngster's good mind has not been recognized, limited mental ability can be thought of as the cause for his learning failure. When it is believed that a child is doing the best he can, there is no motivation to search for alternatives that might improve the situation.

In the second week of the fall semester, Jerry was added to my seventh-grade "remedial reading" class. The boy's records showed that he had "barely average" intelligence. Without analysis or additional testing, that verdict was accepted.

Jerry was an industrious young man and wanted very much to please. But the results of his efforts were meager. On classwork, homework, tests, and compositions, his grades were barely passing. Jerry found our program of vocabulary development especially difficult. When the weekly list of words gave him trouble, he'd grumble, "I don't see why I have to learn all these big fancy words."

Throughout the seventh grade, Jerry's complaints and slow rate of progress were pretty much ignored. Convinced that limited mental ability was the cause of the boy's difficulties, we saw no reason to investigate further. It was assumed that, whatever his problems, they couldn't be helped.

Jerry's special instruction in language arts was extended into the eighth grade. In his second year as my student, the youth surprised me with insights not typical of a child of his modest intellectual ability. At first, his flashes of intelligence were attributed to increased maturity.

One particular incident stands out in my mind:

Jerry and I were walking to class together. As we sauntered past the physics lab, a little glass orb shaped like a light bulb with a whirling silver pinwheel inside caught our eye. Jerry had never seen a radiometer before. Fascinated, he stepped up near the window to have a closer look. The minute his shadow blocked out the sunlight, the tiny silver-and-black spinner stopped turning. Amazed, the eighth-grader looked at me and asked, "Why'd it stop?"

I grinned. From my own high school physics class I knew the mechanism's movement was caused by the heat of the sunlight being absorbed and reflected. But I felt it was Jerry's right to figure that out for himself.

As I stood there in silence, Jerry reasoned his way to a solution with amazing speed. He immediately recognized that his shadow acted like an "off" switch. Based on that observation, he jumped in and out of the radiometer's light supply while analyzing aloud. "The light makes it spin. . . . When it's without light it stops. . . . The black sides go away from the sunlight and the silver sides race toward it. . . . It must be some way of proving that black absorbs heat or light and silver reflects or repels it. . . . That's it! That would mean that. . . ." Jerry snapped his fingers and looked up at me with great excitement. "If you reversed the black and silver sides on the arms of that little gismo like a weather vane, it would rotate in the opposite direction!"

Startled, I took another look at the little revolving wheel, then replied, "Yeah, you're right, it would. I never would have thought of that, but. . . ."

Before I could finish agreeing, Jerry used his discovery to launch off on a whole new course of investigation. "Do you think this is related to the greenhouse effect?" he asked.

Since I'd never heard of that scientific phenomenon, I couldn't answer.

As we walked the rest of the way to our class, my eighth-grade student did a masterful job of explaining the greenhouse effect to me.

And sometime that night, the idea dawned on me: Jerry is bright! That eighth-grade boy couldn't possibly have limited mental ability!

The school's psychologist agreed to give Jerry an individual intelligence test. The resulting new set of scores was astounding. The youth wasn't just "barely average." He wasn't even "just average." Jerry's IQ was over 125, well into the superior range! He had gotten all the way to junior high school before anyone even suspected his true mental ability.

Because everybody believed he wasn't very bright, all of Jerry's teachers accepted his lack of academic success without question or investigation. All LD specialists can tell of similar experiences. Even to experts, a child's true intelligence can get hidden behind his learning problems.

When intelligence and motivation are considered the only essential ingredients in success, the LD student cannot be understood. Blame the child for his failure or accept the failure—neither attitude helps the struggling, frustrated learning-disabled student.

Teachers who have LD students in their regular classes will constantly be challenged to deal with failure. They will have to learn to see beyond what appears to be lack of motivation or lack of ability. They will have to learn to recognize lack of success in all its many guises. Whether camouflaged by the child's bad attitude, hidden by the teacher's own desire to ignore the problem, or excused by absences, the covers that usually explain away failure will have to be removed. Teachers will have to develop a whole new arsenal of techniques for solving students' problems.

Defining Success

Problem-solving techniques are useful only to those who know how to find the problems.

In my self-contained LD class, we had one hard-and-fast rule: everybody did his homework every night.

No excuses were accepted, ever! The first thing each morning, along with the attendance and before the lunch count, the completed home assignment had to be shown publicly. After each page was scanned for general appearance, a check went into the grade book. The work was rarely collected.

There was no set punishment for those who failed to produce their homework. Once in a while I would bluster around a bit and make a few outrageous threats, but that was mostly for show. Day after day after day, like clockwork, those forgetful-disorganized-LD students came to class with satisfactorily completed homework. It was wonderful. I was proud of them. They were proud of themselves. And our days started off great.

Then Tony joined the class. Daily, after regaling me with his explanation for why he didn't have his homework, he'd be sent to the back of the room to produce the pages that would allow him entrance to class. It normally took a few weeks for a new student to get into the habit of doing home assignments. Patiently, I waited for Tony to see the light and change his ways.

By the end of the third week, it had become apparent that Tony was not about to change. My students didn't like Tony—and neither did I. We resented the way he disrupted our morning routine. It didn't matter why he didn't have his homework; we were bored with his excuses and tired of his problem. Days no longer started with success and enthusiasm and optimism. The tone of the class's whole day was being ruined by this obnoxious new kid who couldn't get his act together. He was despised.

The idea of spending so much time straightening out one student was appalling. Bidding Tony farewell as he moved to another school district or back to the regular classroom was a vision in which my imagination took delight.

In an effort to restore the serenity to our morning routine, I put a new homework procedure into effect for Tony. He was no longer allowed to launch into any explanations or protests at the time everybody else presented his work for approval. If he had his done, fine. If he didn't, he was allowed one word: "No." The punishment and special arrangements were preset. Anytime Tony came to class unprepared, he had to give up his morning break to make up the work. This improved the situation somewhat. At least Tony no longer missed a big chunk of reading class every day. And it gave me a breather.

Tony quickly fell into the routine of doing his homework during morning break.

I pretended that I had worked out a solution to my student's problem. After all, something *was* being done about it.

It was nearly a month before I saw the truth of the situation with Tony and his homework. Rather than solving the boy's problem, I had merely found a way to avoid dealing with it first thing every day.

Finally, in a conference with Tony's father, a real solution for the youngster's problem was devised.

It turned out that the youth had been faithfully completing his home assignments every night. His difficulty occurred in the mornings, when he was so foggy-headed that he could never remember to take his papers with him to school.

With the father's cooperation, a simple solution was devised and put into action. As soon as the boy completed his assignments, he folded up his papers and put them into his school shoes. Since he never forgot his shoes, he never forgot his homework anymore, either.

Tony got away with doing his homework in class because I lost sight of what the *real* problem was. The basic issue was: Tony was not bringing in his homework daily. The unpleasant, disquieting influence he had on our morning activities was the *result* of his failure to do his home assignments. My solution was about as effective as the actions of a person who furiously swats the flies in the kitchen while leaving the screen door standing wide open. Making Tony do his work during the morning break did *not* get him to fulfill the fundamental requirements of the assignment. By definition, homework is to be done at home. It is independent work. My system had not converted failure to success. Tony was still not doing his homework under his own steam. And he still wasn't getting it in on time, either.

If I had stopped to define success, the reality of Tony's situation would have been recognized immediately.

To define success, the teacher establishes a clear mental picture of what satisfactory work means in terms of the particular task being assigned. Degrees of failure and the myriads of reasons for failure are of no interest at all. From all the possible results of his effort, what requirements must be met in order for the student to fulfill the demands of this task successfully?

For every assignment made, the definition of success should be clearly stated as part of the process of making the lesson plans. What constitutes success, though decided solely by the teacher, should not be kept a secret from the student. If pupils understand the teacher's interpretation of success, they also know what their own goals must be. Thus, a clear understanding of success establishes guidelines for both the teacher and the students. Always, the goal is *real* success and nothing short of that will do.

In judging a pupil's work on a particular task, one question will clearly distinguish between success and failure: Did the child completely succeed in meeting the requirements of the assignment? Reasons, excuses, and extenuating circumstances will be considered later. At this point, the only allowable answer is "yes" or "no." Success means satisfactory work, done according to the directions, turned in on time. *Anything* less than this, no matter *what* the reason, is not success.

Discovering Patterns of Failure

Once a student's lack of success has been recognized, it's important to see how it relates to other aspects of his learning style. When a child fails to succeed on a particular task, there is almost always a thread that links it to other failures. This connection can usually be discovered by fitting the unsatisfactory performance into the broader picture of other assignments of a similar nature. This process is similar to finding a common denominator.

In actual classroom situations, the pattern of an LD student's failure is rarely glaringly apparent. Unless a child's lack of success is deliberately investigated, the common denominator that ties it to others is seldom detected. In dealing with one pupil out of a class of thirty, or a single student out of five full classes per day, teachers must not expect to recognize instantly these patterns as they develop. They seldom show up until someone starts snooping around.

After two years in a self-contained LD class, Harry was placed in a regular seventh-grade classroom. The junior high school's LD teacher provided the continued therapy he needed. She also worked closely with all of Harry's teachers. In every subject, the youth's work was adjusted so that success was realistically attainable.

Once a month all of Harry's seventh-grade teachers met together with the LD specialist. At these conferences, the youngster's progress was discussed, his difficulties analyzed, and any necessary corrective measures undertaken. Month after month, Harry was passing all of his subjects. The boy's teachers were delighted with his success.

Then, in mid-December, Harry's English teacher announced, "I don't think there's any way for the boy to pass my course this semester."

All of Harry's teachers gaped in stunned silence. Finally, one of them asked, "How is that possible? He's been doing fine for over three months."

The English teacher shrugged her shoulders and shook her head. "This late in the term, it's highly unlikely that he'll be able to make up all the work he has missed."

After a few minutes of general confusion, Harry's English grades were placed on the blackboard. Week after week the boy's work and attendance were satisfactory—except for Wednesdays. For the first four Wednesdays of the semester, the LD student had an F; on the last eight, zeros indicated that he'd been absent.

"What in the world do you do in there on Wednesday?" the science teacher teased.

"And how come he misses all your Wednesday classes and he never misses mine?" the math instructor queried with a very puzzled look.

Without responding to any of the individual questions, Harry's English teacher continued, "We have a quiz every Wednesday. It's our weekly test on spelling, vocabulary, and anything else we've been working on." She paused, sighed in resignation, then concluded, "And for weeks I've been giving Harry zeros, expecting him to come in for make-up tests."

Several of those present wanted to launch into an investigation of Harry's absences. Although it offered an intriguing opportunity for detective work, they quickly realized such action would be unproductive because it would involve trying to solve a problem by placing the blame on the child.

Everyone agreed that there was definitely something about the weekly English quizzes that made them impossibly difficult for Harry. Pressuring the youth to make up the work seemed pointless. It was decided that the English teacher would do the best she could to help the boy salvage the rest of the semester and to make sure he was in class on Wednesdays.

It was hoped that, with a little luck, Harry could pass his English course with a D −.

Things did not turn out well for this seventh-grader. Harry flunked the course. His failure was *not* inevitable—it was caused by an English teacher who did not recognize the significance of a series of zeros.

No one had become alarmed by Harry's situation in English because the problem was not interpreted as failure. Most of the marks in the grade book were zeros, not F's.

Right up to the end of the semester, the issue looked like a mere matter of making up work caused by absences. Harry's problem never got identified; thus it could not be corrected. If the requirements for success had been clearly defined, if the pattern of failure had been noticed and investigated, the seventh-grader's growing disaster would have been obvious. The youth needed to get at least a 70% on the weekly English quiz. Was he succeeding? No. Every Wednesday the simple truth could be seen as it was entered in the grade book: Harry was *not* successfully passing the weekly English quiz.

Sometimes the full failure pattern can't be uncovered without checking with the child's other teachers. Does he neglect *all* his homework? What kind of work does he do successfully in other classes? Former teachers and cumulative folders also offer important clues. Maybe this isn't the first year this child has failed to produce a single book report. In looking for patterns of failure, parents must not be overlooked as a superb source of information.

From September to Christmas, twelve-year-old Cal was one of my best students. His cooperative, cheery disposition made him a natural leader in my self-contained LD class. Despite his very severe learning disability, the boy could always be counted on to put maximum effort into all his schoolwork.

In early January Cal started horsing around in class and ignoring his work. Soon he began neglecting his homework. No matter what I did, his attitude continued to deteriorate. Something was terribly wrong. But I couldn't seem to figure out what.

The records showed a pattern of good grades fall and spring, bad attitude and lots of trouble every winter. I could find no clue as to why.

Cal's parents came in for a conference. As soon as I'd explained the strange difficulty her son was having in school, the boy's mother revealed the whole pattern. "There's nothing to worry about. It happens every year." She chuckled. "We're between seasons—and that boy lives for football."

Without his favorite sport to burn off frustration and energy, Cal was miserable. Fortunately, he used track as spring training for football. "Between seasons" lasted only from January to mid-March.

When track season started, Cal returned to being a pleasant, highly motivated student.

Most failure situations will not require massive investigations involving parents, other teachers, and cumulative folders. Usually, the teacher's own records will provide all the information required.

Analyze the Task

Defining success and finding patterns of failure lead to a clear understanding of a problem. In analyzing the task, attention shifts to finding a solution. This process breaks an assignment into its component parts so that it can be determined which specific elements must be altered in order for the student to succeed. By carefully studying the troublesome task, the teacher bridges the gap between investigative procedures and active corrective measures.

Ralph was a very bright eleven-year-old with a disability in writing and spelling. He did satisfactory work in a regular fifth-grade class and was excellent in arithmetic. I was surprised when the boy's teacher came in to tell me that Ralph was on the verge of flunking math.

"I can't get him to do his homework," Mr. Edmunds explained. "I've tried everything. I've kept him after school, I've called his parents, I've talked to that kid until I'm blue in the face. He's got a million excuses. . . ." The frustrated teacher pulled out his grade book and stuck it under my nose. "Look at that string of zeros!"

One-third of the final grade would be based on homework. Ralph was indeed in trouble.

Snapping the book shut, Mr. Edmunds continued, "The boy participates in class. He gets A's on all the tests. Ralph is one of my *best* math students. I *know* he can do the work. . . ."

Those words—"I *know* he can do it"—set off a warning bell in the brains of LD specialists. Automatically, my attention shifted to an examination of the pattern of the failure that was causing the difficulty. "What kind of homework do you give?"I asked.

The teacher shrugged off a casual reply, "Oh, the usual. You know—a page or two of problems, maybe six or eight story problems." It was apparent he thought this line of investigation was silly.

"The assignments that he did do," I continued, "what kind of problems were they?"

Mr. Edmunds referred again to his record book. After carefully running his finger along the column of scores, he looked at me with a puzzled furrow in his brow. "Story problems." The teacher paused, stared at the grade book in disbelief, then added, "Nobody likes story problems. Even the best math students have trouble with them." He shook his head. "Those are what Ralph does *well* . . . those and tests."

Shuddering at memories of my own years of inept struggling with airplanes and trains that just never wanted to meet in the right place, I forced myself to stick to the subject at hand. "What do tests and story problems have in common?"

Mr. Edmunds snapped his fingers and looked at me with mouth agape and eyes wide. "Writing! You don't have to do so much writing." Excited with his new insight, the teacher explained. "Two whole pages of story problems is never more than twelve examples, fifteen at the most. Two pages of practice problems— you're talking about at least thirty-five, forty, maybe over a hundred examples to be copied out of the book and worked."

Enthusiastically, I pointed out how this same reasoning applied to Ralph's success on tests. "There's no copying on tests. He does fine on tests because all he has to write is the answers."

We quickly realized that Ralph completed all his math assignments except the ones that required a lot of copying. With his writing disability, it would be a terribly long and painful process to copy rows and rows of problems out of the book. It wasn't that the boy didn't want to work the problems. It was just that he couldn't force himself to go through the agony of all that copying.

The solution to Ralph's dilemma was easy. We got him an old beat-up copy of the math text and let him write his answers right in the book.

When that common denominator is found and a child's failures are all neatly linked together, teachers sigh, "Oh, of course. Why didn't I see that before? It's perfectly logical— the kid fails every time he's asked to. . . ."

In analyzing a task, the teacher is looking for the aspects of an assignment that would make success impossible for a particular LD student. Once this element is recognized and isolated, that portion of the work will be altered.

It's always tempting to analyze the child, then blame him as the cause of the failure. In pursuing such an approach, the investigator gets trapped in nonsolutions. Creative, positive problem-solving technique is based on recognizing the child himself as given.

We can't change children directly. We can change assignments and books. Children alter their behavior in response to success and failure.

Chapter IV

Ask the Specialist

YEARS AGO I TAUGHT a regular fourth-grade class. Students were constantly pulled out of my room for band, safety patrol, student government, private counseling with the school psychologist, hall monitor duties, and so on. "There's *never* a time when I can teach my whole class," I'd protest through gritted teeth. Bolting the door to keep all the intruders from snatching my pupils was a frequent temptation. My reasoning told me that most of these activities were beneficial to the students involved. Yet, in my heart, I resented *anything* that removed even one of my children from my room.

It took years of classroom experience before I realized that my attitude was not unique. Most teachers feel a certain degree of possessiveness about their students. "I want *my* children in *my* classroom where I can teach them *myself*." Teachers rarely put it into words, but an outsider can feel their antagonism when he passes through the classroom door. (Once a spunky first-grade teacher actually did bar me at the door of her room. With a broad grin and playful tone of voice softening the deadly serious look in her eyes, she said, "Don't you dare come into *my* classroom." For three years she prevented me from "messing around" with her students. This lady was unusual only in that she openly expressed this element of possessiveness that all teachers feel.)

Anybody who enters a classroom for any reason is stepping into the teacher's territory. To those who enter her private domain, she issues the unspoken warning: "Don't you dare come in here and tell me how to run my class. You don't know as much about any of these children as I do. You

couldn't possibly care as much about these children as I do."
Her suspicious attitude forms a barrier to effective communication.

The teacher whose territorial instincts make it impossible
for her to open the door of her classroom to specialists, and
to open her mind to the kind of advice only they can give,
will *not* be able to give LD students the help they need.

Classroom teachers occasionally have contact with specialists from outside their own school system. But most
often, they will be working with LD teachers and psychologists who are part of the staff of their own school. Whether
a child is being helped by a private therapist, an outside
expert, or a specialist from within the school system, the
teacher should be able to develop a cooperative professional
relationship with the person involved. The expert will occasionally ask for information or request permission to observe the student within the regular classroom. For the most
part, however, specialists have much to offer and ask very
little in return. They have the knowledge that can make
classroom success possible for the LD child. Most of them
share this information freely.

In mainstreaming learning-disabled children, classroom
teachers need to confer with specialists for three reasons:
(1) solving problems that are preventing the student from
succeeding, (2) making major decisions about therapy, program, and placement, and (3) routine reporting of progress
and adjusting of program. Most of the exchange of information between experts and classroom teachers will take
place in conferences of one of the following types.

Types of Conferences

The nonconference or quickie

Teachers feel that conferring with specialists usually takes
three times as long as is really necessary. Experts aren't de-

liberately long-winded. They believe that educating the public is part of their job. Thus, for every two minutes of advice they give, they try to provide ten minutes of theory. In one of my schools, we had a standard joke: "Ask an LD specialist what time it is and she'll tell you how to build a watch."

For the sake of efficiency, classroom teachers need ways to get experts to present their advice so concisely that the conference takes five minutes or less. The nonconference can do exactly that. It is ideal for those common situations in which the teacher needs help with one specific student, the specialist knows that particular child, and there is one specific problem to be resolved.

The quickie has three basic rules: catch the specialist when she has only a few minutes, don't sit down, and state your question immediately.

The secret of success of the nonconference is to control very carefully the setting of the meeting. In the lunch line, over morning coffee in the lounge, while reading the announcements on the faculty bulletin board, when passing on the stairs—anywhere paths "happen" to cross, that's the setting for the nonconference. (It can work if the classroom teacher breezes into the specialist's room but does not sit down. It shouldn't be attempted if the specialist happens to be in the teacher's own classroom. That can lead to a situation best described as "trapped.")

When the timing and setting are right, the teacher should make a very direct approach. General openings such as "How's it going?" or "Do you have a minute?" should be avoided. They lead in the wrong direction and waste precious time. The idea is to dive right in. Name the child; describe the problem; ask for suggestions—in thirty seconds or less. "Jim Bolton is having trouble learning to multiply by two digit numbers. He says he gets confused about where to put the numbers he gets for answers. I tried the ones column, the tens column, and the hundreds column routine. It made things worse. Will you give me some ideas on how to help him get it straight?"

The chances are, the specialist will take a minute to offer three or four suggestions. And the nonconference will be successfully concluded.

There is, of course, the possibility that the specialist will say, "I don't have time right now." In mastering the technique of the quickie, teachers must guard against interpreting "Not now" as a brush-off. That reply should merely lead to one concluding step. "Will you think about it and give me some suggestions when I see you at lunch tomorrow?" The nonconference cannot conclude with "no" for an answer. It either ends with a solution or sets a time when the matter will be discussed.

The telephone nonconference

In getting advice from busy specialists outside the school, the telephone quickie can be a great time-saver. The trick is to catch the person whose opinion is wanted. Secretaries and messages can ruin the technique's effectiveness.

To make the telephone nonconference work, an introductory step must be added. "Dr. Stafford? . . . This is Mrs. Olson, Bobby Kline's teacher at Lake Hills Elementary School. You have Bobby on medication for his allergies. . . ." Before stating the problem and requesting help, the teacher must be certain she has clearly identified herself and the child in question.

Those who try the quickie over the phone will find that many experts will not give answers right off the top of their heads. In refusing to provide the instant information the teacher wants, they will politely say something like "Let me check my files and call you back." When faced with this response, the teacher merely moves to a concluding fourth step in which she and the specialist agree on when they will get back in touch with each other. The telephone quickie will almost always succeed in eliminating the need for a time-consuming formal conference.

The small formal conference

This conference is "small" in three ways: only two or three people will be involved, only a few problems will be discussed, and the time limit will be thirty minutes or less.

The beauty of this type of conference is its flexibility and somewhat casual tone. Though a formal, businesslike atmosphere will be necessary (applying all the techniques discussed later in this chapter), the teacher who requests the meeting will approach the specialist with an attitude of "I need a little advice."

The small conference has one unique advantage: it can be squeezed into any of a number of small time slots in the school day. The psychologist and LD specialist could join the classroom teacher for lunch in the teacher's workroom. A specialist and the teacher could confer in the classroom before the students arrive in the morning.

It is through the quickie and the small formal conference that the classroom teacher will get the routine expert guidance that can make her work with LD students successful.

The formal conference

The standard one-hour conference is appropriate for making a routine report on a student's progress over a whole semester or year. It is also appropriate for those times when there's a *big* problem. Any formal conference concerning an LD child will, of course, include both the LD teacher and the classroom teacher, as well as the parents. It will rarely involve less than these four people and will often include other teachers or specialists as well. Because they cover so many topics and involve so many people, formal conferences require strong, firm leadership. (The suggestions made later in this chapter will be especially useful to teachers participating in a formal conference.)

The major production

This conference is big and very official. It is called when radical action is needed. To settle major disagreements or work out large adjustments in the child's program, the major production is necessary. In some situations, this type of conference is required by law.

Major conferences almost always include several high-level officials from the school system, as well as the parents, classroom teacher, psychologist, LD specialist, and principal. It is not unusual for them to include also an assistant superintendent or two, lawyers or outside experts brought by the parents, a social worker, doctors, representatives from the special education department, and a host of others. It can get to be quite a crowd. Very rarely is the child's classroom teacher expected to provide leadership for such a large production. She will, however, be expected to be a very active participant.

Conference Guidelines

All of these conference situations will place new demands on teachers. They will have to learn to understand their role in such meetings, whether as leader or participant. And they will have to develop techniques that make it possible for them to communicate effectively with experts. The following suggestions should help.

1. Use and respect home court advantage.

Except in the case of a major production, the person who initiates a conference will usually assume the role of leadership. Even when acting for a large group (as in a formal conference involving psychologist, principal, specialist, parents, social worker, and classroom teacher), the one who makes the arrangements can assume she'll be expected to preside over the actual meeting.

The leader's first duty is to issue a clear, specific invitation, naming the child and giving the purpose, the time and place of the meeting, and the time limit. For instance, a classroom teacher would approach the LD teacher: "I need to talk to you about Bob Kline's math. Can you come by my room for about twenty minutes at three o'clock today?"

At the conference itself, the one in charge must open the meeting by restating its purpose and time limit, then see that things progress smoothly toward that goal. The advantage of having initiated the conference lies in the fact that the leader gets to bring up the topics she wishes to discuss. The other participants will be allowed time, but not equal time.

Obviously, the classroom teacher will not always be the one to request or set up a conference. When that is the case, she must respect the other person's right to assume command of the situation. In the role of participant, the teacher will be expected to bring appropriate records and materials with her to the conference. As an example: if Amanda Miller's problem with spelling is to be the topic, the teacher should bring the spelling book, the grade book, and samples of the girl's work. She should also bring the material needed to explore some of her own concerns about Amanda.

Whether acting as leader or participant, the teacher should employ creative problem-solving techniques as discussed in the previous chapter.

2. Talk about a specific child.

Even in meetings set up to discuss a particular child, experts sometimes end up presenting a broad general explanation of their particular field of special education. This is fine for a lecture, but is not appropriate for a conference. Teachers who seek general knowledge can read a book, attend a workshop, or take a course.

To keep discussion centered around a particular student, teachers should ask questions about *only* that student. Don't ask: "Why do LD children get mixed up when given a whole page of questions to answer?" Do ask: "Why does Joe get mixed up when he has to do a whole page of math problems?" It is up to the conference leader to keep the topic clearly focused on the one student whose problems are being considered.

3. Ask specific questions.

Teachers also ought to ask specific questions that deal with a particular point in the child's behavior. Experts cannot help in the problem-solving process unless teachers supply them with clear explanations of a student's difficulties and show examples of the work involved.

The following types of questions force specialists to talk in general terms: "How do I get Billy to do his math?" "Why does Billy have so much trouble doing routine spelling homework?"

Specific questions give experts an opportunity to produce truly creative solutions suited to a particular child: "Billy has trouble with several types of exercises routinely assigned as spelling homework. Here are two of his papers showing the difficulty he has when told to break words into syllables. Here's one of his typical unsuccessful attempts at alphabetizing. . . ." Notice that in asking for help, the teacher specifies the areas in which she feels it is most needed. It is her judgment, her evaluation of the situation, that acts to direct the expert in a productive direction.

4. Ask for *many* possible solutions.

Specialists are famous for coming up with brilliant solutions that are totally impractical. They often appear to have little knowledge or concern about the teacher's tight schedule and heavy workload.

There is a very simple way to avoid this problem: never ask an expert for *the* solution to any problem. To be on the safe side, it's best not to ask questions that even imply that only one solution would be acceptable.

Sample I

Teacher: "You've explained why Joe's spatial disability makes him get confused and lost when confronted with a whole page of questions or math problems. What do you suggest I do to make it possible for Joe to succeed?"

Specialist: "I recommend that you assign him the exact same work, but present it to him in a different way. If the class is doing a reading worksheet, give Joe the same worksheet—but have his cut up so that he sees only one question at a time. If the class's assignment is a page of arithmetic, have Joe do the same page and number of problems. But have his problems cut out of the book or written on file cards so that he looks at only one at a time. . . ."

At this point the teacher decides this expert is a crackpot not worthy of her attention.

It's not that the solution proposed above isn't superb. It is ideal—appropriate to a one-to-one tutorial school charging $12,000 a year. A classroom teacher in a public school needs a solution that is less time consuming. But any teacher who tries to tell the specialist this is squaring off for a real battle. The secret to the solution is in rephrasing the question.

Sample II

Teacher: "You've made me understand why Joe's spatial disability makes him get confused and lost when confronted with a whole page of questions or math problems. Would you suggest five or six things I might try in order to make it possible for Joe to succeed?"

Specialist: "You might try taking a file card and cutting a 'window' in it about the size of a postage stamp. On a page of math problems, Joe could use the card to reveal just one problem at a time. It would take a little experimentation with the size of the hole and getting him to use it effectively—but it could work.

"Or, you could try ways of folding his paper so that everything but what he's working on is folded back out of sight."

(By now, the teacher is furiously taking notes.)

"Or maybe get him to put a ruler under the row of problems he's doing and use a blank piece of paper to cover the part he's already done.

"Another approach would be to assign Joe a partner. One of your really good students could probably get his own work done while still helping Joe.

"For instance, with math: Let's say you're going to allow the class twenty minutes to do a sheet of problems. Since you know Joe's partner can easily do the work in ten minutes, you get him to help Joe while he does his own problems. Give the partner a stack of file cards. Have him copy a row of problems, one to a card, for Joe. While Joe works the first row, his partner does the same on his own paper. And so on.

"Or give the partner a piece of carbon paper to go with the stack of file cards. As he copies the problems for himself, he can make a copy for Joe—one to a card. . . ."

At this point the teacher is totally confident that she can indeed help that child. And, more important, she's armed with several good new ideas.

Most experts can produce an incredible number of marvelous solutions for every problem that comes up. Teachers should encourage them to do exactly that. A wide variety of possibilities allows the teacher to choose the one she believes most practical for her. Also, it leaves several ideas to fall back on if the one selected doesn't work out.

It's important to note that both samples above involved the same expert. When asked for "the best way," "the right way," "the recommended way," or even just "a good way," most specialists will come up with *one* idealistic solution. When asked for "five or six ideas," "a list of suggestions," "several possible solutions," they'll usually generate a string of suggestions, at least one or two of which will be practical.

5. Get answers in a language you understand.

The more highly trained and narrowly specialized the expert is, the less likely it is that she'll speak simple English. Those in the field of learning disabilities employ terminology from psychology, neurology, psychometry, linguistics, and so on. LD specialists not only speak in this language; they *think* in it. Because it's the accepted lingo in their department, campus, or clinic, it's the language they work in. Unless they've had a lot of recent experience with regular classroom teachers, they think their jargon is understood by every person in the teaching profession.

No matter how profoundly wise the expert's advice is, the teacher who can't understand it can't use it. The minute a teacher gets lost in a specialist's terminology, she should tactfully ask for a translation. A simple "Could you explain that in more simple terms?" or "Would you explain what you mean by that?" will usually suffice.

Specialists are often *not* very good at discussing their subject without the use of highly technical terminology. But when encouraged to do so, most can do a reasonably good job of presenting their ideas in plain English.

6. Get answers that are practical rather than abstract or theoretical.

Experts often speak in very broad terms, expecting their listener to fill in the details or apply the basic concept to reality. Teachers must learn to beware of abstract answers that sound useful because they're phrased in simple English.

Specialist: "Be sure all of Joe's work is presented to him in such a way that he sees only one question or one problem at a time."
Teacher: "Could you give me some examples of how I can do that?"

In fighting abstractions, the key word is *examples*. When lost or in doubt, ask for examples.

7. Know the classroom teacher's role in helping LD students.

When a learning-disabled child is diagnosed, given remediation, *and* kept in a regular classroom, his progress is a *group project*. The psychologist offers advice and supervision based on tests and other forms of formal evaluation. The LD teacher uses specialized instructional techniques to remediate the child's specific basic deficits. The classroom teacher, guided by the psychologist and the LD specialist, helps the child succeed in her classroom in spite of his learning disability.

The specialists help the LD youngster overcome his limitations. The classroom teacher accepts the LD student as he is and works around his limitations. By adjusting the work and not the child, she strives to teach him the skills and subject matter offered in her class. To be effective, she must think of herself as part of a team and view her responsibilities accordingly.

Chapter V

Ask the Child

WHEN FRUSTRATED by a child's lack of success, adults tend to ask questions like "Who told you to do it that way? . . . What did you do a dumb thing like that for? . . . Where on earth did you get that crazy idea? . . . When are you going to learn to do this the right way? . . . Why didn't you follow the directions? . . . How many times do I have to tell you? . . ." Unanswerable questions force the child to accept blame. They prevent him from seeking real solutions. The confession, "I did it wrong and it's all my fault," settles the issue. It closes the door to further exploration.

Within each student is the information that can explain the failure. The youngster himself knows more about his problems than *anybody* else. A technique must be developed to unlock this rich source of information. When a student fails at a particular task, the frustrated teacher needs to ask questions that encourage the child to participate in the search for the cause of the failure.

Preventive Questioning

Every time a teacher can prevent failure, she saves herself time, energy, and exasperation. Thus, before assigning a task that might cause an LD child difficulty, the teacher should take preventive measures. The files, the LD specialist, and past experience can all supply guidance. Often it's easiest to consult the youngster himself. (This should be done in private, of course.)

After years of teaching eighth-grade English, Mrs. Roberts knew which aspects of her course created problems for learning-disabled students. When Scott, an LD fourteen-year-old, was assigned to her class, she immediately began using preventive questioning in order to help him avoid academic disasters.

On Friday of the second week of school, the year's first vocabulary list was assigned. As the students filed out of the room, Scott was asked to remain after class.

Mrs. Roberts held out a copy of the week's vocabulary words as the puzzled student approached her desk. "I just want to take a minute to ask you about the vocabulary list," she explained. "Can you read these words?"

After glancing at the paper, Scott answered hesitantly, "Yeah . . . some of them."

"Let me see how you can do. Read the first five for me."

The boy tried but needed help with each of the five. When he finished, he let out a sigh of relief.

The youth's valiant effort made Mrs. Roberts smile with approval. "Tough ones, huh?"

Scott nodded.

"How good are you with a dictionary?" the teacher asked.

The boy shuffled his feet and stared at the floor. "Well . . . not very good," he muttered.

"Have you got a dictionary at home?"

"Yes."

"Scott, I don't want you to try to do the whole assignment tonight. How about if you do the first five words. . . . Do you think you could look up that many?"

Scott swallowed hard, then mumbled, "Yeah, I guess so."

That wasn't the positive response the teacher was seeking. "How many do you think you can do?" she asked.

The youth stared at the list in silence.

To help her student analyze the requirements of the task, Mrs. Roberts repeated the directions she'd given the class. "You'll have to find them in the dictionary, break them into syllables, and copy down the first definition for each."

Still Scott did not respond.

"How many of those words *can* you look up all by yourself tonight?"

Reluctantly, the boy replied, "Two or three?"

"Two at fifty points apiece, or three at thirty-three points each—which will it be?"

"Three. I'll do three."

"Okay." The teacher nodded as she wrote that number on her note pad. Looking back up at her pupil, she asked, "Do you want to pick them? Or do you want me to?"

"Read me the first five words again," the boy requested.

Mrs. Roberts complied.

"I'll take *exuberant* and *mediate*," Scott announced. "I like the sound of them." Looking at his new teacher, he grinned. "You pick the third one."

"Okay, I'll take number five, *intuition*. That's an important word to know." The teacher checked the three words they'd chosen, then handed the list to Scott. "What are you going to do with those three words tonight?"

"I'm going to look them up, break them into syllables, and write down the first definition."

Mrs. Roberts glanced at the clock, then drew the discussion to a close. "You've got two minutes to get to your next class. I'll give you an excuse in case you need to stop at your locker or get a drink."

Note in hand, Scott waved from the door. "I'll see you tomorrow—*with* my three words."

(Including the time it took Scott to struggle through reading the five words, this discussion took less than three minutes!)

In using preventive questioning, the teacher has a particular assignment in mind. She is seeking three pieces of information *before* making the assignment: (1) Is the student capable of doing work at this level of difficulty? (2) Can he handle the amount of work involved? (3) Can he and will he complete the assignment? She never takes anything for granted. Not only is her attitude one of "Can you do this?" She frequently asks, "Show me."

All three of these elements stand out clearly in the example of Scott's first vocabulary assignment. (1) The teacher found that the words were far beyond the boy's reading level. (2) Since she wanted to give him the challenge of trying them anyway, she reduced the assignment to an amount *he* believed he could handle. (3) Not considering hemming and hawing and shuffling feet as positive responses, she kept negotiating until the boy said "Yes, I can do that." The teacher did not stop until the student made a firm, confident commitment.

If the preventive questioning worked, Scott would succeed in looking up three vocabulary words each night, he would pass the weekly test covering the words he had studied, and there would be no need for further investigation. Lack of success on the homework *or* the test would make it necessary for the teacher to apply problem-solving techniques.

Questioning to Solve Problems

Every time failure materializes, an analysis of the situation is essential. Teachers will sometimes wish to pursue their investigation alone, in the manner described in previous chapters. Often, however, it is wise to include the student in the problem-solving process.

To incorporate the child as a full participant in an investigation of his own failure, the teacher must establish the appropriate tone and provide strong guidance. It is her responsibility to lead the student step by step through the process of analyzing the task that gave him difficulty.

To open the discussion, the teacher needs to state the problem and ask the child a specific question that will lead into an investigation of the elements of the failed assignment.

Example A "Scott, you didn't pass the vocabulary test. You got a 60%. What in the world went wrong?" Here we have an honest opening statement of the problem. But the question that follows is unanswerable and vague.

Example B "Scott, you did so well on the vocabulary test. Sixty percent is almost passing. What do you think we could do so you can do even better next time?" Here we have failure covered with syrupy praise to make it look like success. Such statements encourage a child to hide from the truth and prevent even the most superb problem-solving techniques from being truly effective.

Example C "This week's vocabulary test didn't work out so well. You needed ten more points to pass. What were the things that made the test hard for you?" Here we have an honest statement of the problem without any attempt either to criticize the student or to gloss over the lack of success. The well-phrased opening question should lead to a productive search for the cause of the difficulty.

Since the teacher is to guide the analysis, she must be careful to keep the search progressing until *real* causes are found. Children often prefer to take the blame ("I didn't study enough") rather than admit a cause they're ashamed of ("I couldn't read the words").

After three years of intensive LD therapy, Stewart confidently launched into his first year of high school. The fifteen-year-old was optimistic about his new school and his chances of success in its college preparatory program.

Although his previous academic problems were documented in his records, Stewart and his parents hoped his new teachers would not discover the fact that he had a learning disability. The ninth grade was to be the time when Stewart stopped being "different."

The first few weeks of school went beautifully. Stewart used all the tricks and gimmicks his LD therapist had taught him. He worked diligently to be sure he didn't get behind. He carefully double-checked all his work for errors. The youth's efforts paid off handsomely in all his classes but one.

Halfway through the first marking period, Stewart's parents received a notice warning them that their son was failing algebra.

When asked about the situation, Stewart snorted, "The teacher's a creep. She wears her hair in a bun and has these funny little glasses. And she always wears the same ugly brown dress." He shuddered dramatically. "I can't stand to go in her room."

Astonished, the youth's father asked, "Are you going to flunk algebra because you don't like the teacher?"

"No. I want to drop the course," Stewart replied.

The family could not seem to get to the bottom of the issue. Every time the subject was brought up, the failing student went off into a tirade about "that disgusting teacher."

Stewart's parents had a conference with the algebra teacher. From what they could see, the lady seemed normal enough. She felt the problem was in Stewart's attitude. "He did his homework for the first two weeks of school, found it difficult, and quit trying," she explained.

Looking surprised, Stewart's mother asked, "You mean the problem is that simple?"

In slow, even tones, the algebra teacher said, "Students who don't work don't learn." Casually pointing to her grade book, she summarized the facts. "Stewart hasn't completed a single assignment successfully since mid-September. He hasn't passed any tests since then, either."

Although the conference lasted more than an hour, Stewart's algebra teacher was of no help in identifying the failing student's problem. The parents had to look elsewhere for assistance.

After calls to the high school principal, the school's guidance counselor, and their son's former LD therapist, Stewart's parents enlisted the help of Mrs. Pratt, the high school's LD teacher. Once the details of the boy's difficulty had been explained to her, she agreed to check into the matter.

Mrs. Pratt had a brief chat with all of Stewart's teachers, checked the records and his cumulative folder, conferred with his former LD teacher by telephone, asked his mother a lot of questions, then called the boy himself in for a conference. Mrs. Pratt introduced herself to Stewart and quickly made him comfortable with the fact that she was going to help him straighten out the problems he was having in algebra. "I've talked to everyone else involved; now I want to hear what you have to say." The woman stared straight at Stewart and, with a no-nonsense attitude, asked, "What *is* going on in algebra?"

"I'm flunking, I guess," the boy replied.

"I'd say that's a pretty fair summary of the situation." Mrs. Pratt nodded. "And can you give me any clue as to *why* you're flunking?"

"Cuz the teacher's a jerk. . . ." Stewart paused, then added, "and I don't do any of the work."

"So I've heard." Again the LD teacher nodded calmly. "I understand you have no trouble getting homework done for your other classes. How is algebra different?"

The pupil snapped, "I like all my other classes."

Ignoring Stewart's flippant remark, Mrs. Pratt pursued her questioning. "Is it that you forget or just never get around to your algebra homework?"

While staring at his thumbnail and rubbing it with his forefinger, the student responded in a very soft voice, "No. I just don't do it." Stewart gave a heavy shrug of his shoulders and shook his head. "There's no way to please her—so why bother."

"No way to please her?" Mrs. Pratt repeated the youngster's phrase in a questioning tone.

Stewart did not elaborate.

Faced with the student's silence, Mrs. Pratt tried a different approach. "Can you do the problems?" she asked.

With instant certainty, Stewart answered, "Yes, I sure can." He paused to stare intently at the LD specialist before adding, "I made a B – in pre-algebra last year."

Staring earnestly into the youth's face, Mrs. Pratt asked, "Without any difficulty?"

"Without *any* difficulty!" Stewart nodded emphatically. "I did all my work. I did good on tests. I got good grades." As an afterthought, he added, "I even *liked* it."

"What's so different this year?" the LD specialist asked.

As the student paused to reflect, the enthusiasm drained out of his face. Stewart sighed heavily, then responded flatly, "The teacher."

Since the youth kept coming back to this subject, Mrs. Pratt decided to pursue it. "How does the teacher stop you from succeeding?"

Stewart sneered, "I could do the work if she'd let me do it my own way."

"What's wrong with the teacher's way?" the LD teacher probed.

The volume of Stewart's voice intensified as his frustration mounted. "The way she makes us do it, I get mixed up," he said.

Mrs. Pratt countered, "What are some of the things that make you get mixed up?"

"All kinds of stuff." The agitated student used little choppy gestures to emphasize his words. "She's got her own way of doing algebra—and it doesn't make sense!"

From the increasing level of Stewart's excitement, Mrs. Pratt knew she was on the right track. "What kinds of things do you have to do to do it "her" way?"

The pupil blustered and muttered a second, then started again. "She's got a lot of dumb rules about how your paper has to be set up. She's got rules about everything. No talking. No gum. No leaving the room. Everything has to be just so. . . ."

The LD teacher cocked an eyebrow, tilted her head to one side, and queried, "So right answers aren't enough?"

"For this crazy lady, getting the right answer is just the beginning. Then you have to move it over and put it in her stupid 'answer column.'" Stewart snorted with outrage. "The woman is so lazy she won't look to find your answers right there where you worked the problem. Oh, no, she's got to find all the answers in a nice neat little row down the side of the page. . . ." Sputtering and huffing with fury, the boy snarled out a few vulgar names, then set his lips in a rigid straight line and fell into glowering silence.

"Getting the answers into the answer column gives you trouble, huh?"

"Gives me trouble?!" The student's eyes narrowed, his back

stiffened, and his fists clenched. "That woman and her ———
——— answer column is driving me crazy. I *hate* her. . . ."

"What happens when you do a page of algebra?"

"I get it all wrong."

"Why?"

"Because I forget to copy the answers into the stupid idiotic answer column. . . ." Stewart's voice trailed off.

In a gentle whisper, Mrs. Pratt asked, "Or you copy them down wrong?"

As though confessing a ghastly atrocity, Stewart replied, "Yes . . . " then closed his eyes and let his head drop down onto his chest.

"And then you feel foolish . . . and stupid . . . "

"And embarrassed," Stewart muttered without looking up.

Knowing that they had finally gotten to the bottom line, Mrs. Pratt gently explained that the inability to copy accurately was a common problem for the learning disabled.

Gradually Stewart calmed down. He found it very reassuring to see that someone understood just how frustrating it was to make mistakes with a task as simple as copying.

Before choosing some possible solutions, the LD specialist asked one last question. "If you didn't have to be bothered with the answer column, what grade would you get in algebra?"

Grinning with hope and confidence, Stewart replied, "I could get a B easy." He winked, clicked his tongue, then answered again, "I could pass for sure."

With an understanding of the problem, Stewart's teachers were finally in a position to start working on some real solutions.

Leading a student through an analysis of a situation never follows any neatly organized script the teacher might have had in mind. Real children give surprising responses that make it impossible to pursue any preplanned sequence of investigation. If the teacher will persist in asking leading questions, she can keep the search moving in a productive direction.

Including the child in the problem-solving process helps

the student as well as the teacher. It fosters a healthy relationship of mutual trust. By working together as partners, the pupil and the teacher assume joint responsibility for the student's progress.

There are times when this "straight from the shoulder" approach is ineffective. Teachers need to be wary about *forcing* a youngster to face the facts about his learning disability. The attempt to impose an attitude of openness and honesty drives children away.

This is especially true of adolescents. To a teen-ager, it is so important to blend in and look like everybody else that almost all special assistance will be highly resisted or even rejected outright. If forced to make a choice, he will choose failure—to which he is accustomed—rather than allow himself to be singled out by any type of material or attention that is out of the ordinary.

By the time learning-disabled youngsters are thirteen or fourteen years old, the failure pattern is so deeply ingrained that they can't *imagine* themselves succeeding in school. Any teacher who insists that it is possible for them to achieve academic success will simply not be believed. Thus, in working with junior and senior high school students, it is frequently necessary to be discrete to the point of subterfuge.

The "straight from the shoulder" approach is also inappropriate for students who have not been officially "identified" as learning disabled. Classroom teachers are in no way qualified to diagnose or categorize those whom they suspect of being LD. Yet, it is their responsiblity to recognize a pupil's learning style and make the kinds of adaptions that will make maximum academic achievement possible.

Adjustments will often have to be made without ever discussing the matter openly with the student. Rather than seeking feedback directly from him the teacher must monitor closely his level of success as a guide in making appropriate changes.

Chapter VI

Ask the Parents

THE PARENTS are in the key position that determines whether or not an LD child will find success. Teachers, doctors, psychologists, specialists—they come and go. Only the mother and father have responsibility and influence all through a youngster's schooling. They can undermine all the professionals struggling to help their child. They can also create a home environment that is so rich and rewarding that no amount of professional ineptness damages their offspring. A teacher who does not fully appreciate the role of the parents will not be able to do much lasting good for a learning-disabled child.

Teachers' traditional attitude toward parents is that the farther they stay away from the school, the better. Teachers who apply this approach to parents of LD children are depriving themselves of a very valuable resource.

Mothers and fathers rarely use fancy terminology or refer to standardized test scores. Yet to the teacher who will listen, they can provide a vast amount of useful information. A particular student's problems may be new to this year's teacher. But they're not new to his parents. "He never could understand borrowing and carrying. If he uses his fingers, that sometimes helps." Parents may not know much about educational theories, but they almost always have a pretty good idea of what will work with their youngster.

There are two dangers involved in seeking the advice of parents: (1) they'll tell the teacher more than she ever wanted to know about their child, and (2) they'll try to get the school to make special adjustments that are totally impractical. However, these obstacles are not insurmountable.

Through careful management of conferences, a teacher

can gain the information she needs from parents *and* avoid becoming entangled in situations that prevent cooperation and communication. The following recommendations will help teachers use conferences as an effective means of working with parents.

Deal with both parents.

Mothers are almost always able to come to the school for a conference. Unless there are big problems, fathers rarely are asked to appear.

One-parent conferences put the attending parent in an awkward position. And they cheat the nonattending family member out of desired information. No one can go to a meeting on someone else's behalf. It's impossible for others to explore fully all the questions that are of particular interest to someone who isn't present. It's impossible to give a full report that adequately describes all the topics that were discussed. The teacher's attitude, the appearance and atmosphere of the classroom, and other such impressions can only be gained by being there. It is not fair to expect one parent to act as the family's sole representative in dealing with the school. If two parents live in the home with the child, then two parents should come to the school for conferences.

In order to get both parents to attend a conference, teachers must (1) make it clear that the presence of both of them is strongly desired, and (2) be available at whatever time is convenient for the parents to come to the school together. Any parent willing to give up his lunch hour or take time off from work is entitled to the full cooperation of the teacher. It will sometimes be necessary to reschedule an entire school day in order to free a teacher for an important conference. Such things as swapping gym or library periods with some other class, getting an aide to supervise lunch, or trading free periods with a teacher who's willing to act as a substitute can create the free time the teacher needs while still providing a creative, well-supervised environment for her class.

Speak plain English.

Technical terminology intimidates parents. Jargon confuses them. Even simple words such as *structure* and *reinforcement* are terms with specialized meanings among educators. Leave the lingo to the Ph.D.'s. To talk with parents about real children use real words.

Set a time limit.

A professor once gave me the following warning: "Keep in mind, in conferring with parents, you'll be talking about one of their favorite subjects—their child. With just the slightest provocation, they'll whip out the baby pictures and tell all about how cute he was on his third birthday." Experience has proved this to be true.

Parents of LD children are especially prone to go on for hours describing all the trouble they've had getting help for their youngsters. Accounts of their agonizing struggles deserve patient understanding. A time limit, however, helps keep these situations from getting out of hand.

The time limit should be clearly established in the note or conversation used to schedule the appointment. It is wise to mention it again at the beginning of the conference. Then it is the teacher's job to set a pace that will allow discussion of all the desired topics within the time allotted.

In cases of a conference on the phone, the time limit should be specified before ever bringing up the subject that prompted the call. "Mrs. Watson? . . . This is Miss Carling,

John's teacher. I need to talk to you for about five minutes. . . . John is having a problem with his math homework. . . ." If a longer conversation is desired, use the time limit to make sure the call is not causing serious inconvenience. "Mrs. Watson? . . . this is Miss Carling, John's teacher. Do you have time to talk for about fifteen minutes? . . . "

In addition to giving the teacher a certain degree of control over the situation, the time limit helps create the businesslike tone that is essential in all conferences.

Establish an atmosphere of mutual respect and trust.

In every conference situation, the teacher's first goal is to develop effective communication. This is achieved through words and actions that make parents feel comfortable and optimistic. They need to be led to an understanding of their role as full partners in a project concerning their child.

Conferences are almost always held in schools. That is the teacher's territory. Inside these institutions of learning, principals and teachers are in charge. They are powerful authority figures.

Very few adults *ever* get over their fear of teachers. They come to school as full-grown adults—successful, even rich and influential—yet they are afraid they will be criticized and condemned for some flaw in the way they're raising their child.

When my own son, Alex, reached his senior year in high school, he had the legendary Mrs. Spalding for physics. The lady was notorious for being a tough, no-nonsense teacher who could make the most unruly eighteen-year-old cower in terror.

Daily, Alex regaled me with accounts of what went on in physics class. He didn't seem to be afraid of Mrs. Spalding. But he and I were both fascinated with the methods she used to tyrannize students.

A typical incident involved a boy suspected of breaking the dress code.

"'You got a tie under that sweater?'" Alex squawked in imitation of his teacher.

Pausing, my son explained, "Jeff *had* a tie on. You just couldn't see it under his sweater. He *knew* he wasn't going to get in trouble. . . . But, before he could say anything, old Spalding grabbed him by the front of his shirt and shoved him up against the wall."

Pretending to have Jeff by the throat, Alex set his face into a stern, menacing glower. "Then she shoves her nose right up into his face and says, 'You forget to wear a tie to *my* class and we'll have to play house—you'll be the door and I'll slam ya.'"

I gasped. "That woman is definitely tough!"

My son shrugged. "Nah, most of it's just words."

My eyes were probably as big as saucers as I shook my head and warned Alex, "Listen, kid—if you ever get in trouble with that woman, I am not coming to the school and try to bail you out." I was deadly serious.

Realistically, I knew that starchy teacher couldn't hurt me. But, deep down inside, I wanted to avoid meeting her at all costs. Whatever opinions she might have had about me as a mother, I definitely did not want to hear them.

During that entire year, I never set foot in Alex's school. If Mrs. Spalding had called me in for a conference, I'd have been terrified.

Parents must be treated gently. It must be understood that they enter the classroom feeling nervous and apprehensive. They are afraid they're going to be scolded or blamed for something they're doing in the upbringing of their child. They fear they will meet resistance instead of cooperation, condemnation instead of help. Until the teacher demonstrates otherwise, she is thought of as an adversary. Thus, it is up to the teacher to express and demonstrate clearly her confidence in their ability to work together as equals in the best interest of the child.

By understanding the advantage given her by the mere fact that she is "the teacher," it becomes possible for her to find ways to put parents at ease.

It is wise for the teacher to go to the door to meet parents as they enter the room. This makes them feel they are respected and welcome guests in her classroom. It is appropriate to greet them in the formal businesslike manner of shaking hands and addressing them by surnames. The parents will need time for a moment of light chitchat and some browsing around the room. As they scan bulletin boards and other display areas, they enjoy hearing about interesting projects—especially those that involved their child. Most parents like to be shown their youngster's desk. Some even like to take a look inside. Even after previous successful meetings have established an attitude of mutual trust, the teacher should begin every conference by allowing five minutes for the parents to survey the classroom and become comfortably familiar with the environment.

The seating arrangement is vitally important. Sitting behind a desk is like sitting on a throne: it is a position of authority. Those who must perch on small uncomfortable chairs pulled up alongside are made to feel like underlings. The teacher who conducts a conference from behind her desk adds all possible weight to the idea that she is the superior in charge here. Unless there's some reason to "keep parents in their place," it's best to arrange the seating in such a way that everybody feels like an equal. This can be achieved by pulling together a cluster of student desks. Conferring around a work table can be effective provided the family and school personnel don't sit facing each other like two opposing teams. At all costs, the feeling of "us" versus "them" should be avoided.

The larger the conference, the harder it is to set up the seating so that the parents don't feel "ganged up against."

In a big major production, it is likely that the classroom teacher and the LD specialist will be the only ones with whom the parents are acquainted. A room full of strange faces usually makes the mother and father feel pretty badly "outnumbered." In such situations, those who are known and trusted by the family should be seated near them. Since she is the one most deeply involved with both the parents and the child, the classroom teacher is always the one responsible for making her student's family as comfortable as possible in conferences.

As soon as all the participants have arrived and the parents have been given a few minutes to get acclimated, the teacher should get everyone seated and assume the role of discussion leader. The first order of business is to state the purpose of the meeting and the time limit. The stage should then be set by naming the issues that need consideration. Having a list of specific questions ready at hand is essential.

Teacher: "There are three things I need to talk over with you: the weekly vocabulary tests, math homework that isn't getting done, and some behavior problems John's been having in the lunchroom."

Mother: "We want to talk about that math homework, too. Nobody in our house can ever seem to figure out the directions."

Teacher: "Then John has been trying to do it?"

Father: "Trying? We've *all* been trying it. But those directions. . . ."

Teacher: "Yes, they are sometimes confusing. Once John *does* understand what he's supposed to do, does he have any more trouble with the assignment?"

Mother: "Not usually. At least if he does, we don't hear about it until he's done and shows us his finished paper."

Teacher: "What happens when nobody can figure out the directions?"

Father: "Oh, that's a mess. John usually gets so upset he goes in his room and locks the door."

Mother: "If he gets really riled up, he ends up not doing any of his homework."

Teacher: "That explains several things that have been puzzling me. I can see that the math has really been causing some problems."

Father: "Not as many problems as we got with his older brother. Now, Paul. . . ."

(At the *first* opportunity, the teacher brings the talk back to the subject.)

Teacher: "Well, let's see if we can figure out a way to solve John's difficulties. His learning disability makes it hard for him to understand and follow directions."

Father: "Maybe you could write out an explanation of the directions for *us*. Then, once we know what he's supposed to do, we can explain it to him."

Teacher: "I think it would be better for John if we could find a way for him to do his math homework by himself."

Mother: "You mean you're going to try to get us out of the homework business?"

Teacher: "Absolutely. You've already passed the fifth grade. Now it's John's turn."

Father: "Maybe if you'd go over it with him one extra time before he leaves school. . . ."

Teacher: That sounds like a good idea. I can take a minute to go over the directions with him. I could even have him work the first problem to be sure he understood. . . . Do you think it would help if I wrote my home phone number in the front of his book? Then, if he forgot what he was supposed to do, he could call me."

Mother: "That's a great idea. That would get us out of math entirely."

Teacher: "Then we agree: I'll give John some extra help with the directions, and from now on, if he has trouble with his math, he's to call me."

Father: "Right. And we'll keep out of it."

Teacher: "Now, as to the difficulty with the vocabulary tests. So far this semester, we've had four weekly tests. John has succeeded in passing only one. . . ."

Parents need to be given a clear description of what their child would have had to do in order to succeed. "Every Friday the children get twenty minutes to do a matching test with their vocabulary words. They have to get a grade of at least 70% to pass." At this point the wise teacher will show the parents the test in question. Once the mother and father see the actual work that caused their youngster difficulty, they can usually come up with some very helpful insights.

It is important to notice that by being specific and honest, the teacher keeps control of the conference. She accomplishes this by (1) knowing exactly what she wants to discuss, (2) stating the problems clearly, (3) explaining what would be needed to achieve success, and (4) keeping conversation focused on the desired subject.

Think of several possible solutions.

After the cause of the difficulty has been discovered, the teacher *and* the parents need to explore many of the possible ways the problem could be resolved. Then, from this list of possibilities, one can be selected that is mutually agreeable.

Parents do not have to take the needs of an entire class into consideration. The teacher does. It's up to the teacher to see to it that all special commitments made are practical and reasonable for the child *and* for his classmates. Sometimes, in the process of exploring a problem, parents come up with unworkable suggestions (as did John's parents, who asked the teacher to send them a special explanation of the directions to his math homework). These need not cause alarm. In any problem-solving session, most of the proposals will be discarded. They are merely part of the thinking process. Unrealistic solutions are never given further consideration after a practical and effective solution is found.

Give the parents a turn.

Longer conferences should allow time for parents to bring up subjects they wish to discuss. The teacher needs to turn the floor over to the mother and father with a clear statement of her intentions. "We've discussed all the topics that have been concerning me. We have about ten minutes left. Are there any things you want to talk about?" Notice that even here, the time limit is issued right along with the invitation.

Parents often have an amazing awareness of how their learning-disabled child's mind works. Psychologists and specialists can offer knowledge gained in a few hours of intense formal testing. The mother and father can offer the knowledge gained through the hard knocks of years of experience.

Section Three

TEACHERS FREQUENTLY COMPLAIN that learning-disabled students are unmotivated. "Turned off," they say. "Can't reach them." It's true, most LD children tune out teachers and turn off to school. That's the natural result of repeated failure.

When students attempt the impossible, failure is inevitable. Failure kills motivation. Repeated failure kills interest and confidence. But motivation and interest can be created by reversing the process. If students attempt only what is possible, success is likely to follow. Success stirs interest. Repeated success builds confidence. Continued success motivates.

In making adjustments to help a learning-disabled child, the teacher's objective must be twofold: (1) to decrease frustration and failure, and (2) to increase success. This goal can be achieved by always following one guideline: never ask the impossible.

Chapter VII

Developing Creative Child Management Techniques

THERE ARE TWO STANDARD STYLES of discipline: old-fashioned strict and modern permissive. Neither is effective with the LD child. Rigidly following traditional rules and enforcement procedures does not acknowledge and accommodate his differences. Strict disciplinarians hurt him with harsh inflexible controls that offer no understanding or compassion. Yet, giving the learning-disabled child complete freedom to pursue his own basic nature does not recognize his special need for strong, firm guidance. If the classroom teacher does not create a setting that puts limits on the LD pupil, he will not make up for the lack by imposing control on himself.

The learning-disabled student needs a "structured environment." Yet the art of establishing one is generally unknown. The highly organized classroom got sacrificed back in the 1920s as part of the process of shifting to our modern, flexible style of child management. Most of our present-day educators have never been exposed to the carefully controlled schoolroom. The techniques involved in creating one have not been passed on through instruction or example.

In this chapter and the next one, we will explore ways to develop a structured environment. Through proper discipline and careful classroom management, the teacher can get the LD student to be cooperative and attentive. Only then can he learn.

Prevention Is the Key

Effective child management is based on prevention and praise. When a teacher thinks ahead, a crisis is not allowed to develop. By carefully setting up the conditions, a teacher can trick the child into good behavior, which is immediately recognized and rewarded. Really bad conduct can almost always be predicted and counteracted before it materializes. Danger can be foreseen by knowing the child as an individual, recognizing types of situations that lead him into trouble, and keeping attuned to his varying moods and attitudes.

A psychologist was called in to observe Jimmy, a learning-disabled second-grader. His teacher suspected that his "compulsive behavior" might be a sign of an emotional problem.

For more than an hour the specialist sat in the classroom waiting to see Jimmy do something "compulsive." The child did nothing that could even be classified as strange. He stayed in his seat and kept to himself. He didn't get much of his work done, but he didn't cause any trouble either.

By the time Jimmy's reading group was called up to the front, the psychologist had about given up on observing anything significant. It didn't seem likely that anything noteworthy would happen, but she did want to hear him read.

Jimmy grabbed a chair in the middle of the reading circle. After the usual commotion of getting seated and organized, the lesson began. Starting at the left, one by one, the children took their turn reading orally. Jimmy had his book open and followed along. With each new reader, he sat up more rigidly in his chair. As his turn drew nearer and nearer, he began to fidget. He shuffled his feet and glanced about at the other children. The little girl on his immediate left began on her page. Jimmy was next.

With no warning at all, Jimmy jammed his elbow into the ribs of the boy sitting beside him. In the quick scuffle that followed, the victim's chair flipped over backward.

Leaping to her feet, the teacher shouted, "Jimmy, go back to your seat and stay there." Then she bent over to comfort the youngster who had been attacked.

Jimmy did as he was told. Once back to his place, he put his head down on his desk and remained in that position until reading period was over.

In talking to the psychologist later, the teacher said, "See what I mean?! He does something like that in the reading circle every day!"

"Can he read?" the specialist asked.

"How should I know?" the teacher snorted. "He always gets in trouble before I get to hear him."

This seven-year-old child was outwitting his teacher daily. She was failing to prevent the continual disturbance he was causing. And, worse yet, in handling his bad behavior, she was rewarding him instead of punishing him. Getting out of that reading circle was exactly what Jimmy wanted. He hated oral reading.

Many preventive measures were possible in this situation. All of them would have saved innocent children from injury, spared the teacher the time and energy needed to resolve the daily crisis, and gotten Jimmy to do his reading. The youngster's oral reading could have been done privately one-to-one. Or he could have been called on first to spare him the mounting anxiety of waiting. He could have been required to participate in all the activities of the group except reading aloud. Or he could have been seated at the end of the row with an empty chair separating him from anyone he might harm with disruptive behavior. Or he could have been allowed to select his passage in advance so he could practice it before reading it aloud in the circle. He could have been put in a group that used a book he could read more easily. The possibilities are all but endless. Rather than trying to stop Jimmy's bad behavior, the teacher needed to focus her attention on preventing it entirely. She needed to change the situation into one in which the boy could succeed. Jimmy would still have been different. But he'd have felt proud of his satisfactory reading and good behavior. His teacher's praise would have been a pleasant reward. And the vicious cycle of failure and misconduct would have been reversed. Jimmy would still be getting special attention. But now it would be positive and satisfying.

Call students by name

Prehistoric man believed that his own name was magic. The person who knew his name had power over him and was feared.

Deep down inside, we humans still feel that way. We will do rude things to strangers that we would never consider doing in front of someone with whom we are even remotely acquainted. It's not safe to break the rules in front of even one disapproving person who can find us later for criticism, punishment, or revenge.

There is safety in anonymity. As long as no one knows who we are, we can get away with almost anything.

Believing that one person gains power over another merely by knowing his name sounds like primitive superstition. It's not. It's a basic and simple part of human nature. An example will make this obvious.

Some neighborhood children had been using my apartment building for war games. Ducking in and out of corridors and doorways to shoot at each other with BB guns, they had turned the place into a battle zone.

The tenants who caught the culprits in the act yelled, "Go play somewhere else," or lectured that "those guns are dangerous. You could put somebody's eye out." Such encounters didn't discourage the invading armies.

I'd been out of town while most of this was going on. When I returned home, my neighbors told me all about these horrible teen-agers who had invaded our building.

The following week, several boys were on the front porch of my apartment house when I came back from doing some shopping. Although I knew they didn't live in the building, I felt no suspicion about this blue-jeaned bunch of twelve- and thirteen-year-olds. Most of them scampered off the porch as I approached with my first load of groceries. One darted into the stair well and bounded up the steps; his partner stayed at the bottom and peeked around the corner of the open door. Held up close to his chest in a ready-to-fire position, the boy standing guard had a pellet pistol. And I knew him.

As I fumbled to get my keys out of my purse, I looked the make-believe soldier sternly in the eyes and said, "Richard, you take your friends and your guns and get out of here."

He didn't say anything. Only his eyes told me he'd heard me as he turned and raced up the stairs.

I didn't say anything more or take any further action.

In the time it took me to unload my car, the youths peacefully departed. The war games in my building never resumed.

The power of the name—out of five or six children, I knew *one* by name. I knew where he lived. I was acquainted with his mother and his sister. If he didn't cooperate, I had the ability to find him. My knowing who Richard was meant his friends couldn't remain safely anonymous either. If informed of the group's behavior, Richard's mother and sister could have gotten on the phone and shared the news with the families of the others.

No threats or actions were necessary. I had the power to make all their lives very unpleasant. Knowing that one name gave me power over the whole group!

The official use of legal identification is based on this same principle. When the highway patrol pulls a car over, the first thing said is, "Let me see your driver's license." The nature of the offense is not emphasized until after the driver's identity has been established and called in to headquarters. Always, anyone in authority acts to remove the safety of anonymity before taking further action. Passports, application forms, references, automobile license plates, dog tags, check-cashing policies, library cards, social security numbers, credit cards—the power of the name is a very active principle among us. If I've got your name, I've got the edge. No matter what you do, you can no longer be certain of getting away with it.

Smart teachers make it the first order of business to learn each student's name during the opening days of school. It is the basic requirement behind all effective systems of child management and discipline.

When understood and used wisely, the ability to call every student by name is more than a protective device. There is strong positive magic associated with the use of a person's name. It gives that "personal" touch that communicates caring and intimacy and love. Any child who is addressed with "Little boy with the blue shirt in the back row" knows for sure that his teacher can't possibly understand him or care about him. She doesn't even *know* him. It is impossible to feel that other people really know us in the fullest positive sense if they don't know our name.

A great deal of social etiquette is concerned with proper use of a person's name. Titles show respect. Use of surnames is businesslike; it maintains distance and formality. Calling someone by his first name shows familiarity. It implies, "We are friends." We are all very sensitive about what we are called or not called. Children get very upset when someone calls them names. So do adults. Ph.D.'s become irate when not called "doctor." The way a person uses our name has a powerful effect on us.

LD children frequently have trouble remembering my name. As often as not, they call me Stevenson instead of Stevens. Sometimes I correct them. Usually, I just let it go.

I once had an eighth-grade student who called me Stevenson as a deliberate form of disrespect. With defiant eyes and a malicious grin, Carl would say, "Good morning, Mrs. Stevenson," as he brushed by my desk on the way to his seat.

Always, I politely replied, "The name is Stevens."

Without even looking at me, Carl would grunt, "Right."

It was like small skirmishes in a war. Every day the youth would take a shot at me. He started every class with a little victory at my expense.

One day I thought of a way to return the fire.

Carl's last name was Kudlinski. Most people found it difficult to pronounce. It had never caused me any trouble. When Carl entered the room that day and shot out his customary greeting, I retorted with a broad, sweet smile, "Good morning, Mr. Kudlinstovich."

My improvising with the last two syllables of *his* name did not set well with Carl at all. He fumed in silence for most of the class period.

I don't know if the youth ever forgot about it or forgave me, but he never played games with my name again. Hearing his own name deliberately mispronounced had been a painful insult.

What a teacher does with pupils' names sets the tone for their whole relationship. If allowed to remain nameless, students are forced to remain distant. No bond of trust can be developed. Children are expected to remember and correctly use their teachers' surnames as a form of respect. It causes resentment and hostility when the teacher does not extend the same courtesy in return. It is illogical for teachers to expect cooperation and respect from students whose names they have never bothered to learn.

For those who teach self-contained classes, getting to know 30 pupils is not a particularly difficult task. For those who have five or six classes a day, mastering 150 to 200 names is an awesome undertaking. For those who teach music, art, or physical education to from 300 to 500 different students each week, the assignment seems impossible. And for those who do substitute teaching, the task seems downright ridiculous. Yet, with increased numbers of pupils, the importance of being able to call each one by name increases. Art, music, band, and physical education classes are the ones that most often turn into a "zoo." That's not merely because they are less structured. It's also a result of students who are allowed to remain anonymous. Any teacher carrying such a massive student load cannot know them all by name and, therefore, is forced to forfeit control.

Name tags, seating charts, and place cards solve the problem easily. For physical education teachers, a carefully kept record of batting order and position played will serve the same purpose. Seating charts are not conspicuous and do not inconvenience the children. But they do impose a certain degree of regimentation on the class. Name tags allow for a freer-flowing, less structured environment, but students sometimes dislike wearing them. Place cards taped to hang from the front of the desk offer a reasonable combination of flexibility with little inconvenience. Most students will cooperate with a system based on name tags or place cards *if* they are allowed to make their own as an expression of their personality and creativity.

Some teachers prefer memory courses, get acquainted games, or other devices. Any gimmick is fine. The object is always the same: to get to know the students and be able to call each one by name—*fast*.

Make realistic demands

Everyone has his limitations. The perfectly rounded person, capable of fulfilling every expectation, simply does not exist. There are grown men who can't sit still, and perfectly normal mothers who have trouble remembering where they put the grocery list. Teachers have pet peeves, subjects they hate to teach, responsibilities that require the use of skills they don't have, and days when they're sure that there must be an easier way to make a living. No one can live up to all the ideals and hopes of self or others.

In establishing the code of conduct that will be imposed on their students, teachers must set high *but achievable* standards. Totally unrealistic goals do not inspire; they overwhelm and kill motivation.

By demanding only what is possible, old-fashioned strict discipline can be tempered by our modern respect for the child as an individual. In setting up reasonable expectations, the teacher must make the student's uniqueness the main consideration. Yet, once the rules have been established, the disciplinarian's firm enforcement methods provide the consistency upon which a structured environment is founded.

Setting standards is an especially difficult task when dealing with the learning disabled. It's very hard to tell just exactly what is impossible for them. Things they can't do usually look like things they could do if they really tried. This is further complicated by their on-again-off-again pattern. Things they could do yesterday are not necessarily possible for them today. Teachers find it a constant challenge to try always to recognize an LD student's limitations and make appropriate adjustments.

It is vitally important that the standards of behavior demanded of LD children be totally realistic. They become overwhelmed very easily. They handle frustration poorly. Expectations that they cannot meet will produce dramatic and devastating effects. For them, it must be one day at a time, one small success at a time, gradually building and growing from one accomplishment to another. They can achieve our loftiest goals if we lead them forward just one step at a time.

An unruly, self-contained LD class of fifth- and sixth-graders always wanted to play football during their physical education period. But they couldn't run more than a few plays before someone started a fight which erupted into a free-for-all.

When the fists and foul language started flying, they were brought back into the classroom to sit out the rest of the period in silence. The longest lecture they ever got was "You may play football. You may not fight."

After a series of these abruptly abandoned games, the boys asked permission to set up rules to prevent the fights. They wanted to stay outside for the full time allowed for physical education.

The self-imposed regulations improved the situation so that fighting broke up their game no more than two or three days a week.

The children had one simple goal: to get that full gym period.

I had only one objective: no fighting.

The boys revised their rules and struggled to referee more justly. Their increased determination gradually produced acceptable playground behavior almost every day. By January, individual outbursts did not trigger both teams into a brawl. The no-fighting rule was enforced by assigning offenders two to five minutes in the penalty box. Flashes of anger grew rare. We often went a whole week without having even one student forced to sit out a part of the game. Day after day, the boys refereed their own game and settled their differences peaceably as I sat on the sidelines taking a siesta.

During the February slump, we started a behavior mod program to perk up classroom performance and study habits. The boys needed to find a realistic reward to buy with the points they would be earning. The first suggestions were the usual jokes of "How about a color TV?" and "You could take us to the beach for a week." Then, one by one, the class came to agreement. They wanted to be allowed to go out and play football for the last part of their twenty-five minute lunch period.

I protested immediately. "That means I'd have to give up part of my lunch time to come out and supervise."

"No, you wouldn't. We can take care of ourselves" came a chorus of reassurances.

I reminded them that in September they had been the only class in the school that couldn't make it through five minutes of football without getting into a fight and being brought in. Despite their changed behavior, there was still a long list of logical reasons why twelve rowdy boys would end up in trouble if left unsupervised on a playground full of children.

They held their ground. They were willing to work for the privilege, but they wanted a chance.

The behavior mod plan was so demanding, it seemed unlikely that the prize could be attained in the three months left of the school year. Just to be on the safe side, the principal's permission was requested. A brave but wise man, he advised, "Be sure they've really earned it, then let them give it a try."

With a juicy reward as an incentive, the program began. February and March flew by. The boys' class performance and behavior were fantastic. The points mounted rapidly. The magic number of the goal was reached before the end of April!

When the day arrived to begin the big payoff, I shuddered as my class headed out the door. It was all I could do to finish my lunch and head calmly toward the classroom. My mind kept flashing pictures of blood and mayhem. I could just see some angry teacher charging down the hall dragging one of my boys by the scruff of the neck.

But nothing happened. My students did just fine. They raced back to the classroom the minute the green flag appeared in the window to signal them. With proud smiles of satisfaction, they hurried to their seats and prepared for work.

For six solid weeks the class earned the privilege of going outside after lunch every day. Never once did they abuse it. It was such a remarkable accomplishment that the principal himself complimented the boys on their outstanding behavior.

They had achieved something very special—one tiny step at a time.

There had been no lofty hopes of making these LD boys models of good sportsmanship. All of us had goals that were short-sighted and totally selfish. I was determined to eliminate fights during gym class. They simply wanted to stay outside and play.

By aiming at a level of behavior that *could* be attained, these LD youngsters worked their way from one small victory to the next. Each new objective was difficult but possible. Every small success had a desired reward. At the end, totally by accident, they stumbled into achieving what had originally been impossible.

LD youngsters will turn themselves inside out to accomplish the possible. They crave success. No ultimate objective is too high *if* they are convinced they can succeed with the step that is required today.

For teachers—have your impossible dreams. But keep them to yourself. Tell the child only that part of your goal that he can achieve today.

Don't ask senseless questions

In a classroom, the teacher is in charge. At the moment when a student's behavior needs correction, this authority must be communicated. This is easily achieved through body language. The teacher raises herself to her full body height, squares her shoulders, sets brow and forehead into an expression of sternness, levels her unflinching gaze at the offender, and speaks the official word.

If the disapproval is expressed as a question or in a questioning tone, the air of authority is destroyed.

"John, will you please put that cap gun away and get back to work?" What if he says "No!"? Such questions give the child an option—will you do as I ask, or won't you? Good behavior is *not* optional. Good discipline does not give the student a choice about whether or not he will live within reasonable standards of conduct. If rephrased without the "will you," the request stated above can even be delivered in a very gentle tone of voice and include the word "please" without compromising the teacher's position of authority.

Unanswerable questions are a still more destructive form of teacher communication. They kill the effectiveness of discipline the moment the words are spoken. They remove the tone of authority *and* make the student intensely uncomfortable. "John, why are you still playing with that cap gun when I told you to put it away ten minutes ago?" How can the child possibly respond to that without getting himself into further trouble? There is no acceptable answer. The child is caught in a power play designed to humiliate him. There's a huge variety of these cruel, unanswerable questions available. All of them should be considered unethical. They are meant to trap a youngster and make him feel ashamed. Children resent them bitterly.

David's year in the ninth grade got off to a very bad start. He wasn't getting as much special instruction as he needed for his very severe learning disability. The classroom teachers at his new school didn't understand how to work with him. Although he'd been the hero of his junior high football team, his new coach didn't appreciate his talents and disliked his attitude. As his frustration mounted, the youth's allergies flared up and forced him to miss a lot of school. Daily trips to the doctor for immunization shots made him miss most of his first-period class every day. By early October, things were a mess.

Accustomed to working closely with her LD son's teachers, David's mother repeatedly called the school to request conferences. But her pleas fell on deaf ears.

The situation grew steadily worse. David gave up all involvement in sports, took up with a new crowd, and began causing serious discipline problems at home. He hated the world and everybody in it. His frantic mother knew the whole problem stemmed from her son's extreme frustration in school. But, try as she might, she could not get any cooperation from administrators who had the authority to help.

In midwinter David got arrested. The offense was quite serious, but the juvenile court was merciful because he was a first-time offender.

At David's trial, it came out that he had a severe learning disability and that the school had refused to cooperate with his mother's request to bring a private specialist to confer with his teachers. The judge probed to get all the important details, then issued a stern order to one of the court officials: "You call Mr. Paloman, the lawyer for the school system, the minute we're finished here. You tell him to get in touch with this boy's principal to get a conference set up within the next twenty-four hours—or I'll see him here in my court tomorrow."

After so many months of useless attempts, David's mother was going to get a conference with his teachers by court order.

The meeting was well attended. Crowded around two conference tables were principal, assistant principal, guidance counselor, the high school's LD teacher, two high-level administrators from the school system's department of special education, several other administrators, David's probation officer, the youth himself, his mother, and an outside LD specialist. Only one teacher came!

For more than an hour, the educators took turns defending the system and blaming the youth for his lack of success. From their point of view, everything possible had been done to help the boy; all the problems and failures were his own fault. Over and over, David was told, "You have a bad attitude. Until you change your attitude, there's just nothing we can do. . . ."

The condemned teen-ager sat there in silence. When accused of chronic and deliberate tardiness, he did not defend himself. Yet every one of his thirty-six tardy reports was later found to have a doctor's excuse.

After everyone had thoroughly berated the boy, it was decided that the school didn't need to make any changes on his behalf.

The principal had sat through most of the meeting with narrowed, glaring eyes and firmly set lips. At this point, he took the floor to lead the conference to its conclusion. A hushed silence fell over the room as, with the cold tone of a powerful authority, the man talked with his troubled student. "David," he began, "I want you to look around this table at all these people here."

The boy glanced up briefly, then returned his gaze to stare rigidly at his hands.

After a long pause, the principal continued, "Son, there are a lot of people here, busy people who have important work to do and very full schedules. . . . All of these people had other things they could have been doing this afternoon—but they're here." Again the school's official leader paused.

The color was rising in David's face. He did not look up.

The principal leaned on the conference table to stare contemptuously at his pupil. "David, I want you to answer one question for me: Why are all these people here? You think about that for a minute, then tell me: Why are we all here today?" With the repetition of his question, the man sat back in his chair and let the room fall into a thick, uncomfortable silence.

All eyes were on David. His face was glowing red. As he slumped forward with a bowed head, the muscles of his cheeks bulged and twitched with the energy holding his jaws clenched and his features rigid. He knew exactly what he was supposed to say. But he couldn't bring himself to do it. He didn't dare speak the truth either.

Instead of shouting, "You're here because the court said you had to be here," he drew his fingers into a tight fist, lowered his head still further, and said nothing. When the principal repeated the question and forced a response, David said, "I don't know."

It is impossible to describe the hatred that boy feels toward the man who relentlessly tormented him with that unanswerable question.

Whenever a student is asked a question, it should be mutually understood that the response will be heard open-mindedly, then given genuine consideration. Questions should be used only to lead, guide, and help. They can be a great tool in developing understanding.

Avoid lectures

Learning-disabled children are especially immune to lectures. They live in the world of the senses. They are action-oriented. Avalanches of words just roll right by them. Many LD youngsters get lost in long speeches regardless of their intentions. Logic, analysis, reasoning, looking back at the past, abstractions presented verbally—none of these fit with the way their minds work. Lectures turn them off. Any method of child management that relies on long verbal explanations is not likely to work with LD children.

Long, logical, complex monologues which eloquently explore the significance of the rule that has just been broken are a form of punishment. They are boring. For most children, boredom is very unpleasant. But it doesn't produce changed behavior. Most children think of the lecture as "paying the price." To them, it's like an agreement: "I'm willing to listen to your speech in return for getting to do what I want."

Gentle, soft-spoken Miss Blackham did her student teaching in my self-contained LD class. She had never been around children before. All of her ideas about them came from books. Miss Blackham really believed that she could manage an LD class without ever raising her voice or putting her foot down. She thought the only truly effective method of child discipline had to be based on developing understanding. In a discussion, she told me, "Correcting bad behavior is merely a matter of getting a youngster to understand why some action is offensive. Punishment should never ever be necessary." The young lady shook her head emphatically and concluded, "Once a child knows *why* he's supposed to act in a particular way, he'll do it on his own."

It made a great theory.

In practice it didn't work so well. Miss Blackham was very conscientious about applying her method of child management. Yet the children walked all over her. They didn't take her discipline seriously at all.

One morning I was grading papers in the back of the room while Miss Blackham was teaching the reading lesson. She and the students were playing a phonics game that she had spent weeks designing and making.

From her position in the front of the room, the student teacher couldn't see that Marty, one of the boys in the back row, was busily mutilating one of the exquisite players' cards she had crafted. I walked over to the youngster to investigate. He didn't notice my approach.

Putting an arm around his shoulder, I leaned over Marty and the ragged game card in stunned silence.

The boy looked up at me, rolled his eyes, shrugged his shoulders, and whispered, "Boy, am I going to hear about this one, huh?" We both paused to think about what the student teacher was going to say.

Marty already *knew* he was doing wrong. As far as he was concerned, the detailed explanation Miss Blackham was going to give him was nothing more than a boring lecture.

As a means of rewarding success or good behavior, the lecture doesn't work very well either. Praise that is too lavish makes children feel embarrassed.

Elaine, an intern, was working one-to-one with fifteen-year-old Jack. The boy was extremely self-conscious about his poor reading and needed lots of encouragement. His young teacher tried to recognize all of his small successes and reward them.

But Elaine thought praise had to be in the form of a long, gushy speech. "Jack, I'm so proud of you. You just read that page with almost no mistakes. Your reading has gotten so much better. It's really wonderful to see you make all this progress. . . ." The intern poured out paragraphs of approval.

Each extravagantly applauded success made Jack more uncomfortable. With a look of sheer agony, he would slink down lower into his chair and glance at me out of the corners of his eyes.

Even if I hadn't been there, the long lectures would have been terribly embarrassing to the teen-ager. Success was actually causing Jack pain!

Whether correcting or praising, it's wise to use as few words as possible. Keep it specific and brief. Success needs to be recognized and appreciated. "Paul, that was excellent lunchroom behavior. You stayed in your seat, kept your voice low, and ate like a gentleman." Corrections are best made with similar exactness and brevity.

Avoid threats and promises

We've always been told, "Don't make a threat if you don't intend to follow through." That's decent advice. But it's only a partial truth. Yes, if a specific threat is made and a child persists in the objectionable behavior, it is important to carry out the pledged action. Promises must be honored in the same way. If a student is promised something as a reward, the teacher must follow through regardless of how much she regrets having made such a foolish offer.

Since the teacher's word must be treated as a sacred bond, it's better not to make any threats or promises in the first place.

I had gotten tired of my students slouching, clomping, shuffling, weaving, shoving, tripping, stumbling, and straggling down the halls. No matter what I tried as an incentive to get them to change, they continued to look like some ragtag band of thugs.

One day, after an especially ghastly procession back from the lunchroom, I exploded. Snorting and steaming with fury, I concluded my tirade by giving up on them in disgust. "I quit," I shouted. "It's hopeless. You guys *can't* walk down the hall like gentlemen. I give up. If you're ever going to learn to walk like gentlemen, the army will have to teach you. . . ."

The students had a surprising reaction to my belief that they were hopeless cases. Although they all still looked guilty and ashamed, most of them drew up taller in their seats and squared their shoulders.

After a long silence that brought each boy to rigid attention, spunky Bobby looked me right in the eye and asked, "What'll you give us if we can?"

"Nothing," I snapped. "Because you *can't*! Even if you really *wanted* to look sharp in the halls—you guys don't know how!"

I was being deliberately insulting, but the class ignored it completely. Bobby cheerfully pursued his idea of striking a bargain. "A trip to the Soda Shoppe to get one of those $6.00 twenty-three scoop sundaes?" he asked.

"I wouldn't buy you slobs an ice cream cone," I sneered.

Following Bobby's lead, Larry took over the negotiations with a revised proposal. "Next Friday, after one week of A+ in the halls—you take us to the Soda Shoppe. We pay the $6.00 ourselves."

They were wheelers and dealers.

But it was pointless. I was totally convinced that outside of the four walls of our classroom it was not possible for them to act like gentlemen. My anger was gone as I honestly gave them my opinion. "It'll never happen—A+'s in the halls. You guys are kidding yourselves. You've never even been *decent*. What makes you think you can act *excellent*?!"

With wide, questioning eyes, Larry nodded at me and asked, "Deal?"

"It'll never happen," I protested.

Bobby grinned. "Maybe we'll have a miracle—Deal?"

Smugly certain of their failure, I nodded, "Deal."

There's no need to describe the gory details. For one solid week those twelve-year-old monsters were angels. Other teachers commented on their fantastic behavior. The principal even noticed their superb conduct in the lunchroom and halls. I wanted to wring their adorable, well-mannered little necks.

They brought money. They brought permission slips. They knew I'd keep my word. And they knew I'd hate doing it.

Despite the fact that I felt very foolish, I had to explain the situation to my principal and get his permission to take my class off the school grounds. After telling him how I'd gotten myself into such a mess, I concluded, ". . . I climbed out on this limb and they are in the process of gleefully sawing me off."

The principal chuckled, then offered a piece of wisdom based on his years of experience as an educator. "There is a certain perversity in children that makes them delight in watching teachers eat their words." Then he kindly gave our outing his blessing.

I was too embarrassed about our frivolous field trip to ask anyone to help with transportation. It took all afternoon Friday for us to walk to the distant ice cream parlor and back.

Living up to rashly made promises is more than a simple inconvenience. It makes students lose confidence in their teacher by proving she can be manipulated. Children always think they can outwit the teacher. But every time they do so in reality, they lose respect for her.

Threats are equally dangerous. They do damage even if they never have to be carried out. The teacher undermines her own authority every time she gives dire warnings of just exactly what will happen if some particular behavior continues. Since she is reacting with words and not action, she is postponing. Putting something off until later communicates weakness. It implies that the person in charge prefers not to deal with this problem at all.

Threats often include references to a higher authority. "One more crack like that, young man, and you're going to the principal's office." This is a doubly destructive tactic. The hope is that the misbehaving youngster will be impressed by the power of the person who will be called upon later if the need arises. But the main message is, "I can't make you behave." An authority who has that attitude will not be taken very seriously.

Threats produce some very subtle negative side effects.

They show that the teacher doesn't really expect good behavior. And they give the youngster a clear-cut choice. By announcing the penalty in advance, the teacher indicates her belief that the offensive actions might possibly continue. In dealing with children, it's very dangerous to make them think bad behavior is being expected. More often than not, they live up to our expectations.

Threats and promises weaken the teacher's position by shifting the power of choice to the child. If the student knows the cost of his actions in advance, he can make his own decision about whether or not he'll cooperate. Acceptable conduct has been made optional. By foregoing the trip to the Soda Shoppe, my class could have continued to clomp around the halls in their preferred sloppy fashion. Suppose Todd is sitting in the back of the room playing with a rubber band, and the teacher tries to correct him by saying, "Young man, you stop making those noises or you'll get an extra row of math problems added to your homework." For only ten extra minutes of homework, Todd could buy the right to disrupt the class by twanging his rubber band. To him, it might be worth it. For a few minutes, he'd get the added bonus of having control over his teacher. All he has to do is give the signal, and he can stop the math lesson and throw his teacher into a tizzy. Promises and threats are intended to trap the child. Usually they put the child in control and trap the teacher.

Make rules broad

To make a child-management system effective, it is essential that *all* the rules be enforced vigorously. This requires constant vigilance and determination. Because of the human limitations on time and strength, wise teachers make as few regulations as possible. They conserve their energy. They do not waste their ammunition on minor irritants. Either an issue is important enough to warrant strong, consistent action, or it's insignificant enough to be ignored. Teachers need to pick their issues carefully and establish only those regulations that can be wholeheartedly enforced.

By defining major categories of conduct, it's possible to set up very broad, easily understood, and totally enforceable rules for classroom behavior.

One major area requiring firm regulation concerns property rights: if you don't own it, don't touch it without permission from the owner. This plain statement covers all those awkward situations where students protest, "I was only going to borrow it," or "I didn't mean to lose it," or "It was already cracked before I got it." This one rule eliminates the need for a whole list of smaller ones such as: you may not go into anyone else's desk; you may not take anything from another person's locker; you may not get materials out of the cupboard without permission; you may not remove anything from the teacher's desk; you may not borrow anything without asking the owner's permission first; you may not use the tape out of the supply closet; and so forth. Without very strict, very broad guidelines governing respect for others' property, teachers can run themselves ragged playing policemen.

Another needed category of rules centers around the necessity of maintaining a quiet classroom atmosphere. Students must understand that they will not be allowed to prevent others from getting their work done. This can be attempted through a set of regulations covering spit wads, whispering, humming, roaming the room, using the pencil sharpener, throwing paper airplanes, slamming books and tops of desks, calling out to the teacher, and so on. Or it can be viewed as one rule: no one has the right to disturb his classmates.

The single regulation approach allows the teacher to determine the areas in which she will concentrate her energy. And, by strictly enforcing basic rules, teachers can back off on matters of less significance. There is no sound reason for the guilty conscience caused by letting a child get away with something. Some issues are better ignored. Teachers often disturb their whole class in the process of correcting some student who wasn't bothering anybody. Classroom tranquility should not be broken by loud calls of "Harry, get back to work." The child who is snoozing or quietly amusing himself does not require immediate correction. Unless a student's actions are already causing a disturbance, teachers are wise either to ignore the infraction altogether or to postpone criticism until it can be whispered to the offender privately.

Praise must not be neglected. Broad categories of rules are especially good for providing increased opportunities for praise.

Chuck was the bully of the entire school. He was famous for blackening eyes and bloodying noses. The big, muscular youth with the bad temper was in my eighth-grade LD group.

At the beginning of the year, the students set up regulations to govern class conduct. The rule forbidding fighting and punching merely said, "I will respect the physical well-being of others." I wasn't at all sure Chuck would abide by such a gently stated regulation. Teen-agers like him are usually thought to need a somewhat tougher discipline policy.

On the last day of school before Christmas vacation, one of the other boys in the class made a really nasty crack about the shirt Chuck was wearing. The remark was both crude and totally uncalled for.

Chuck and I both responded immediately. He leaped to his feet with his fists clenched. I called to the youth who had offended him, "Joe, I will talk to you in the hall." Not sure what Chuck would do, I walked to the door and held it open—waiting.

Joe's eyes darted back and forth between his infuriated classmate and me. A minute or two of electric silence filled the room. Then, Joe turned and walked toward me at the door. Chuck let him leave unmolested.

After the issue was totally settled, apologies sincerely offered and accepted, I kept Chuck outside for a brief private exchange.

Anybody with Chuck's quick fists could have found dozens of ways to get back at Joe. But they all fell under our one broad rule. It was with real pleasure that I complimented the notorious troublemaker. "Thank you for respecting the physical well-being of Joe. I know you could have taken him apart. I'm glad you didn't."

The big, burly youth grinned. It was probably the first time in his life that he'd been praised for *not* punching.

In selecting the broad categories of rules that will govern their students, teachers make a commitment to enforce a basic code of conduct strictly. But they also free themselves from getting excited over nit-picky misdeeds that don't really matter. For most classrooms, effective child management can be maintained with ten rules or less.

Wide-coverage regulations are especially useful when the teacher is adjusting expectations to govern the conduct of LD children. If it is a cosmic law that all students must stay squarely seated at their desks, the hyperactive youngster cannot obey. If the rules emphasize not disturbing classmates, the overactive child is free to kneel, stand, crouch, lounge, or perch as long as his movement doesn't bother others. Broad regulations based on categories give the teacher and her pupils the latitude to accommodate individual differences while still living strictly by the rules. This type of child management system provides the unusual blend of extra structure and extra freedom that learning-disabled students need.

Imaginative rewards and threats

By strictly adhering to a system of preventive measures, a teacher can get children to abide by a few broad rules. But merely avoiding anonymity, impossible demands, senseless questions, lectures, and threats is not enough. The teacher needs new weapons. She must have surefire tactical maneuvers that put authority into her words. Day in and day out, the teacher needs to communicate: "I am in charge of this class. If you misbehave, you have to answer to *me*."

It's much easier to get a child to "want" to behave than it is to "make" him behave. Thus, the mainstay of the teacher's disciplinary arsenal should be incentives, reminders, and motivators that focus on the positive. Rather than warning about the bad, talk about the good. Don't caution: "Anybody who starts a fight on the playground will get sent in." Emphasize what is desired: "Children who cooperate and play according to the rules will get the bonus of a pleasant smile from a happy teacher." Through properly devised motivators, children are reminded that it *is* possible to please the teacher. They are told how to do it in the given situation. And they're given a reason for wanting to cooperate.

Through the offer of ridiculous rewards, teachers can add a new depth of honesty and strength to their positive incentives. Children find it fun to hear, "Good lunchroom behavior will get you your very own Saturn V rocket for the weekend." The outlandish promise really says, "You'll do it because I say so." But it says it nicely, with good humor, and no head-on confrontations. It eliminates the need for bullying or pressuring. Children fully understand the "real" message intended. The outrageous prize doesn't confuse them. They know the teacher has offered them something that's fun to dream about but far too fantastic ever to expect in reality.

I was always very strict about homework. Every student had to do all his homework every night. Failing to complete the nightly assignments was simply not allowed.

Every once in a while, some student would pester me about my firm policy, asking, "What's in it for me?"

I never bored such protesters with a truthful "You get an education, you get my approval, you get a check in the gradebook, you get the acceptance of your classmates, you get to feel good about yourself. . . ."

In response to the proverbial question, "What'll I get if I do my homework?" I'd respond enthusiastically, "You'll get a trip to Europe."

Offering a ridiculous reward is usually a two-step process. First, state the *real* goal clearly and simply: "You act like gentlemen during the assembly, with no horsing around in the auditorium, and . . . " Second, tack on some wildly extravagant prize: ". . . your tickets to the Super Bowl will arrive in the next mail." In the daily routine of child management, this technique can be used regularly. It should be considered a powerful preventive disciplinary measure.

But it's not always possible to focus on the positive. Sometimes a situation is too grave for the offer of any type of reward. When disaster appears imminent, it's time for the ultimate weapon: The Fonz Technique.

Fonz is the smallest of all the youths in his TV gang. Yet he always gets his way.

He never hits. He never whines. He never bullies. Yet his friends will do anything for one small sign of his approval. Everyone, adults and teen-agers alike, treats The Fonz with the utmost respect. Everybody wilts at the slightest indication of his disapproval.

How does he do it? What gives him absolute control over all those around him? It's the product of honesty, consistency, and the power of the outrageous threat.

No one *ever* crosses the Fonz and gets away with it. He is never too busy to stop everything and demand respect. He always stands firmly on his own authority. He never looks to someone else to protect his personal interests. The Fonz would never say, "If you do that again I'll tell your mother." Every time his rights are threatened, he acts instantly with "Whoa. That ain't the way you're gonna treat The Fonz."

At times that require really firm action, he relies entirely on wildly absurd threats such as "How would you like to see the parking lot upside down?"

This technique has been known for years. It never seems to be taught anywhere. Those teachers who discover its effectiveness are usually operating on pure natural instinct. Some teachers have tried everything else and turned to this method in desperation. The outrageous threat is especially useful with children who don't respond well to logic. But since everyone has a sense of the absurd, the technique is equally effective with all children. It is ideally suited to the learning disabled.

To adults, these threats sound humorous to the point of being downright silly. But students of all ages take them very, very seriously. Despite the fact that I never laid a hand on students, my pupils all believed that I had left a trail of little corpses behind me in my previous years of teaching.

Some people complain that this tactic could be emotionally damaging. As long as the wild threats are not graphically ghoulish and are balanced by equally enthusiastic—but real—praise when appropriate, youngsters will not be harmed. I used to think of myself as an ogre. Yet love notes and presents constantly poured in from my fiercely loyal students. Parents frequently called to express delight over their child's new love of school. Children who are being mistreated don't feel such affection for their tormentor.

If the outrageous threat damages a teacher-child relationship, it's being used incorrectly.

My first wild threats were used on a regular self-contained fourth-grade class. Throughout the year, I worked to perfect the technique that was making such an amazing difference in the behavior of my students. As a beginner, I made a few mistakes.

Jack was horsing around and ignoring his work as usual. The great big tough farmboy was preventing three reading groups from getting their seatwork done. His antics were also distracting me and the youngsters working with me up in the front.

As one group returned to their seats and another prepared to come forward, I walked over to Jack's desk. The boy was so engrossed in his own activities that he didn't notice me approaching. Out of the blue, he heard his teacher's voice snarling, "You stop disrupting this class or I'll rip off your arm and beat you with the bloody end of it."

Stunned, Jack turned to me, gaped for a second, then burst into tears.

Although I apologized to that boy immediately, my conscience still bothers me. My lesson was learned the hard way at a child's expense. The object is to stop bad behavior, not shock and terrify children. Go gently. Don't employ surprise attacks. Avoid blood and gore.

Miss Green was an absolute master in the use of the outrageous threat. This loving lady was always in total control of her exceedingly difficult class of thirteen- to fifteen-year-old LD students. Nothing escaped her notice. Her students couldn't get away with anything. She was equally lavish with wild threats and real praise.

In walking by the door to Miss Green's room, my class and I overheard an open confrontation between this fantastic teacher and a student recently assigned to her class. The big gangly youth was angry about something. In his rage, he had squared off in preparation to attack Miss Green.

The large, statuesque lady raised herself up to full height and glowered into the boy's face. "Honey, you hit me and there'll be two of us on the floor—" Pausing, she cocked her head and narrowed her eyes. "And I promise, *I'll* be on the top!"

The student dropped his fists, stared at the ground for a second, and returned to his seat.

*   *   *

Miss Jennings had spent years as a teacher's aide working with all types of exceptional children. She had the outrageous threat down to a science.

While she was supervising a small group of LD children on the playground, one of her charges tried to force his way into another class's kickball game. Tom's loud curses and brazen challenges terrified the thirty players and their teacher.

"Tom, quit bothering that class," the aide called.

The youngster stared at her hatefully and stood his ground.

Not one to take no or nonaction as an answer, Miss Jennings strode toward the infield. Tom got to give the second baseman one shove before the teacher's aide nabbed him.

The troublemaker pulled free from the aide's grasp and shouted, "Don't touch me!"

Miss Jennings did not attempt to grab hold of her charge again. Instead, she stared him straight in the eyes and said, "You come with me or I'll touch you all over."

Obediently, the boy followed her off the playing field.

*   *   *

Theft is a common problem in all schools. Most teachers guard against it by locking up their purses and other valuables. There is an approach that's much less bother.

It's traditional to announce the ground rules on the opening day of school. In the brief speech of do's and don't's, I always included one wild threat: "Don't ever touch my desk. That is *my* property. You touch my desk and thunder and lightning will strike you dead!"

Once or twice a year the warning would need repeating as some student's hand hesitantly reached forward to borrow a pencil or piece of tape. "Touching that desk is very dangerous," was always enough of a reminder.

This one simple outrageous threat produced a wonderful string of benefits. For years my purse hung casually on the back of my chair without anyone ever touching it. Stop watches, keys, Red Cross money, and other objects of interest to children remained safe while in open view on the top of my desk. The students adopted the same kind of strong respect for private property among themselves. No one ever went into another person's desk. Among the students in my class, there was always great trust. They took tremendous pride in the fact that there were no thieves in our class.

All of this grew out of a ridiculous threat that affected students' behavior as if they took it seriously. What would I have actually done if some child had deliberately ignored the rule about the sacredness of my desk? I don't know. In seventeen years of teaching, it never happened!

Outrageous threats must be recognized as more than a mere warning. They do act to caution the child against continuing a specific activity. They also make it clear that the misconduct is not going to be tolerated further. And, for most children, wild threats carry such a strong message of disapproval that they actually function as a form of punishment.

Like most people, children are afraid of anger. They do not want to see what might happen if the teacher lost control of herself and flew into a real rage. Those who paddle, send notes home, and expel students from class are usually the least effective disciplinarians. Those who use outrageous threats reveal a tiny corner of themselves that serves to remind students that an angry human being can be very un-pleasant.

For most situations, a swift, simple "No, you may not do that" is sufficient. For those occasions when a blockbuster is needed, the crazy wild threat can be tremendously pow-erful. Extravagant threats and promises are extremely effec-tive methods of communicating an attitude of total confidence. The words and body postures are merely ways for the teacher to act out her own inner conviction that she does have the power to manage this class. Such inner cer-tainty is the solid foundation of effective discipline.

Enforcement Procedures

No matter how carefully practiced, preventive measures will go only so far. The unexpected will happen. Children are going to misbehave. There will be times when the teacher must take *real* action. In applying disciplinary measures, there is always a threefold purpose: (1) to stop the child from persisting with his offensive behavior, (2) to punish the youngster for his present misconduct, and (3) to prevent recurrence of the misbehavior.

It must not be assumed that punishment changes behav-ior. Disciplinary procedures do encourage a youngster to stop using some unacceptable pattern of action. But they do not teach him more appropriate behavior. New habits are established through success and praise. Thus, true child management goes far beyond merely setting up rules and enforcing them through punishment. It must also include the positive aspect of leading a child to adopt new patterns of conduct. Good discipline does not eliminate bad behav-ior—it replaces it with good behavior.

To be effective, the punishments and rewards that comprise good discipline must be administered in accord with the following four rules.

Punishments and rewards must be immediate.

Discipline must be in full operation at all times and places. A child's bad behavior must be recognized, stopped, and punished immediately.

When faced with a misbehaving student, the good disciplinarian does not have a choice about whether or not to take action. There are no options about when or where to make a firm corrective move. The time is always *now*, at the moment of the misconduct. The place is always *here*, at the scene of the crime. All youngsters know that there are certain situations in which they can get away with almost anything. If there's ever a time when children will do something obnoxious, it will be in a public place where the teacher would be too embarrassed to take action. Or it will be at a moment when the teacher is too busy to take action. On such occasions, children feel it's safe to ignore the usual rules. If punishment is immediate, such carefully timed misconduct will not happen more than once.

For public misbehavior, the immediate part of the discipline involves getting the offender to a private place. The long arm of the teacher could tap the pesky child on the shoulder and guide him toward an exit. "Step out into the hall," could be quietly whispered. The message could be delivered silently by motioning with the hand. There must be no shouting. No scene. The offender must be removed so that his problem does not become a problem for others. In this way, the disciplinary action begins immediately. It will be completed outside the room.

The same principle holds true for rewards. If a child is trying to establish a new pattern of behavior, his first successes must be recognized and applauded no matter when or where they occur. The praise does not have to be elaborate, but it does have to be genuine and specific.

There is a tricky aspect of praising immediately. If not timed carefully, the reward can interrupt the desired behavior and stop it from continuing. Generally, it's best to hold the compliments until the new good conduct has reached its natural limit.

Rick hated arithmetic. He was working so far below grade level that even the slowest students in his class were ahead of him. For years the boy had failed to develop any skills with numbers. While his classmates worked problems and watched the teacher do examples, Rick amused himself by drawing and daydreaming. It was a long-established habit: Rick never paid attention during math class.

At the beginning of the ninth grade Rick's learning disability was finally recognized and diagnosed. A therapist began working with him on his math. After so many years of tuning out any work that had to do with numbers, Rick was unable to pay attention even when working one-to-one. He said he wanted help, yet his mind drifted off constantly. He'd be copying an example out of the book and suddenly fade off into his own little world. The tutor would be explaining something and he'd suddenly turn lifeless and blank. Any enthusiasm he did show during his lessons always involved conversation on topics other than arithmetic.

At first there was no way to praise Rick. He couldn't concentrate at all. His private lessons were a continuous series of corrections. Over and over, his therapist had to draw his attention back to the work at hand. "Your mind is wandering. Bring it back to this subtraction problem." Constant criticism was the only thing that worked.

After weeks of intense effort, the boy got so he could keep his attention focused on arithmetic for about thirty seconds.

And there progress stopped.

Immediately punishing his unacceptable behavior made Rick get back to work. But it didn't help him establish a new pattern of concentration. The LD specialist had to find a way to reward instantly the short bursts of attention that were possible for her student so that he could be taught to recognize what the desired behavior felt like.

With a stopwatch and a file card, Rick's therapist devised a method of immediately rewarding his successes. Every time the youth started an activity, his tutor started the stopwatch. The second his spurt of attentiveness ended, the youth checked the watch and recorded the elapsed time that measured his period of concentration.

In addition to providing a natural opportunity for immediate praise, the stopwatch system taught Rick to become aware that his thoughts were drifting off. It also provided him with a record of his progress, which made the learning process a mature type of challenge.

It took months of LD therapy before Rick was ready to try to begin paying attention in his regular math class. At first it was agreed that he would attempt staying focused for just a few minutes at the beginning of every class period. Rather than stop at the end of some specific number of minutes and say, "Rick, you can stop now.," the math teacher merely noted the time when her LD student quit paying attention. She reported this information to him privately at some convenient moment during the first half of the class. "Not so good today. Only seven minutes. Keep trying." Gradually the time increased until the daily comments were almost always raves. "Congratulations. Sixteen minutes! Nice work."

By the end of the year, Rick was able to keep his mind on math for more than twenty minutes at a time. For him that was a great victory.

Through immediate praise, Rick managed to change a long-standing failure pattern.

Rewards must be pleasant, punishments must be unpleasant.

Youngsters are often rewarded with things they would normally try to avoid. Old-fashioned teachers used to say,

"You be good and get all your work done, and I'll let you sit up here with me during story hour." Little children found that very appealing. But the offer struck terror into the hearts of all youngsters beyond the third grade. Older students carefully guarded against being too good lest they face the embarrassment of actually having to sit on the teacher's lap. The teacher's idea of a reward affected most students as sheer torture.

Lots of things done as punishment don't seem even mildly unpleasant to children. Mothers hiss at youngsters who wiggle in church, "You sit still and be quiet." When the fidgeting continues, the child is taken outside. The kid wins! He was misbehaving because he didn't want to be trapped on a hard pew in a stuffy room listening to a boring sermon. He wanted out. What did his unacceptable behavior get for him? It got him exactly what he wanted!

It's not at all unusual for teachers to misjudge a situation and end up rewarding bad behavior.

A small group of fifth-graders was working with me in the LD resource room. Surprisingly, they found the day's lesson difficult and boring. Their usual cooperative attitude disappeared. Wiggling, snickering, and horsing around replaced any serious attempt at paying attention. Unable to get them back on the right track, I finally gave up in sheer frustration. "Break time. We're going outside for ten minutes. After everybody has run off all the wiggles, we'll come back in and try this again."

The little group bounded gleefully out onto the playground. The time off felt good to me, too. Smelling sweet spring air was infinitely more pleasant than struggling to teach syllabication rules.

We returned to the resource room refreshed and free of tension. As the students took their places, the real significance of our delightful break dawned on me. Wisely, I had bailed out of a losing lesson plan. But, foolishly, I had rewarded my students for bad behavior.

Discipline does not have to be physical in order to be unpleasant. It's possible to administer a truly ghastly penalty without ever laying a hand on a child.

When I was in high school, there was a Spanish teacher who hated gum-chewing. Every year she warned her students of the bizarre fate that would befall them if they chewed gum in her class.

Those few students who got caught with gum in Señora Lepley's room became the laughingstock of the school. For weeks they would be reminded of how foolish they looked as the Spanish teacher marched them up and down the halls meting out her version of just desserts.

Armed with a paper bag and supersharp pencil, the rule-breaker would be led to each of the dozens of drinking fountains in the building. The criminal used the pencil to spear those awful wads of used gum that collect around the drains of public drinking fountains. One by one, from fountain to fountain, the gooey blobs were stabbed and dropped into the bag.

That feisty little Spanish teacher couldn't have been more than five feet tall. But her crusade against chewing gum humbled even the toughest teen-agers.

Señora Lepley's gum-spearing expeditions were unusual because they horrified everybody. There was never a youth who found the activity even mildly tolerable. Very few punishments are considered unpleasant by all students. Little girls don't particularly mind sitting still; for most little boys it's agony. Overweight, unathletic types hate running laps. The agile or hyperactive think such strenuous exercise is fun. Those who are good at amusing themselves can even get pleasure out of sitting alone in the cloakroom. For most youngsters, being shut in a large closet would be so terrifying that the teacher could be accused of child abuse. One child's delight is another child's torture.

All-purpose rewards and penalties are not nearly so effective as those specially selected for a particular child. In choosing an appropriate disciplinary action, the child's typical behavior patterns should be taken into consideration. Something intended as punishment must not end up providing fun time. To have the desired affect, penalties must be easy, safe, and definitely *not* enjoyable to the child involved—and rewards must bring pleasure.

Discipline must be consistent.

Discipline that is on-again, off-again encourages a child to analyze the situation and adjust his conduct accordingly. With haphazardly enforced standards, the youngster does not develop an attitude of cooperative consideration for others. He becomes devious. He becomes one of those clever little brats who size up the teacher to figure out just how much they can get away with. Sneaky children are not born that way; they are created by adults who enforce discipline inconsistently.

Children are persistent. If there's the slightest chance of getting the payoff they desire, they'll keep trying. But they're not stupid. If a particular action *always* results in an unpleasant experience, they quickly give up and move on to something else.

Youngsters never persist in tempting the law of gravity. As toddlers they fall off the couch a time or two. At five, climbing trees or riding bikes produces a few more falls. Before they even enter school, painful experience has proved beyond any possible doubt that gravity is always in effect. Like all humans, children are earthbound. And they totally accept that fact.

Consistent discipline is extremely effective. Any action that always produces unpleasant results is quickly abandoned. Nature teaches this way.

Parents and teachers usually apply such absolute enforcement techniques only in areas of their own pet peeves.

Gum-chewing has never bothered me. But most schools have rules forbidding it. Year after year, I compromised with the system by revising the regulations to fit standards that I could rigorously uphold.

Discrete, nonoffensive use of gum was allowed in my classroom. Nothing messy, noisy, obnoxious, or damaging to property was tolerated. The preferences of administrators and other teachers were respected. Any student who happened to be chewing gum in my class dropped it into the wastebasket before leaving the room. Its use was allowed only within the four walls of my domain.

My tolerance for gum-chewing had one strange limitation. I find the sight and aroma of purple gum repulsive. I can smell the stuff clear across a room. Students weren't allowed to bring grape gum into my room at all. The only child who ever tried it was immediately whisked out to the hall to dispose of the offending wad plus the rest of the pack he had stashed in his pocket.

The appearance of my students and classroom gave clear evidence of the type of policy that was strictly enforced. There were no gooey blobs stuck to the bottoms of seats and desks. No one blew bubbles or made cracking noises. The aroma of artificial grape flavoring was never present. Yet it was not unusual to see one or two sets of jaws rhythmically working on a piece of gum. The rules that were consistently enforced were obeyed.

Being consistent about praise requires some careful maneuvering. It is vitally important that the child's success always be recognized. But the way achievement is rewarded should vary. As a youngster first starts behaving in a new desired way, he should get something special for every success. The first time a student actually does his homework he could get something like a star on a daily chart or an extra two minutes of free time. As the new conduct grows into a habit, the reward should be decreased in size and frequency but still used for encouragement. Retiring the stars and chart, the reward could shift to something weekly like five minutes of extra free time for every five days of satisfactory homework. After the new pattern is firmly established, the routine recognition given anyone else for the same behavior will be enough—with an occasional added word of praise.

All children who are doing what is required and expected should be frequently rewarded with praise. Students who faithfully do their homework night after night should get a public pat on the head every once in a while. As Fred turns in his assignment for the 103rd consecutive day, a comment to the entire class is appropriate. "Fred still has a perfect record! Never ever has he failed to do his homework." Simple recognition does a great deal to maintain desired behavior.

Adults rarely provide punishments and rewards with absolutely relentless determination. If total consistency were applied to all child management measures, the results would be revolutionary.

Discipline must be understood.

When students accidentally do something good, they're likely to get complimented, "Wow, kid, that's terrific." With no notion of whether the praise was for their sunny smile, neat paper, cooperative attitude, good posture, correct answers, or the teacher's good mood, they grin sheepishly and mutter, "Thanks." By not understanding what they did that was so good, they have no chance of deliberately repeating the satisfying experience and earning another pleasant reward.

The same thing happens with punishment. "Stop that!" carries almost no information. Most LD students could probably stay out of trouble if they'd just stick to amusing themselves quietly at their desks. Very few of them ever figure that out. It never occurs to them that most of their problems are caused by continually disrupting the class. And teachers never tell them. What seems obvious to the adult in charge is often not even faintly apparent to the child.

Eleven-year-old Penny had emotional difficulties in addition to a severe learning disability. Everybody disliked her constant whining and complaining. Both at home and at school, this thoroughly unpleasant little girl was a discipline problem and had no friends.

Penny's parents had taken her to counselors and clinics. Over the years, the youngster had been exposed to tennis, swimming, dancing, horseback riding, tap dancing, cooking, sewing, rock collecting, and rock climbing. She had been given lessons in piano, guitar, clarinet, crafts, and art. At various times she had been a member of the "Y," girl scouts, 4H, church choir, and school band. She had been sent to camps and special schools. None of these activities suited Penny. Always she dropped out within a month.

Just when it looked as if Penny was destined to spend the rest of her life watching TV, eating, and having tantrums, some neighbors went on vacation and asked her to baby-sit with their guinea pigs. Reluctantly, the girl's parents agreed to let her try it.

Much to everyone's amazement, Penny was totally conscientious about caring for the guinea pigs. She did the feeding, watering, and cleaning of cages without even being reminded.

During their last week in her care, one of the females produced a large litter. Since the young baby-sitter was unprepared for such an event, she had to consult the library and pet shop for advice. When the neighbors returned to reclaim their furry little rodents, Penny proudly presented them with a healthy and greatly enlarged group of pets.

As a reward for a job well done, Penny was given a pair of guinea pigs from the litter born while under her care.

Gradually Penny's attitude began to change. Her compelling interest in guinea pigs gave her something to be proud of and something to talk about. She found that other children would listen to her. Some of them even seemed to like her. For the first time in her life, Penny had friends and playmates.

There was an equally dramatic improvement in the situation at school. Penny's attitude toward her work and her classmates showed a marked change. The girl's new confidence helped her gain increasing success in every area.

In January, Penny's growing collection of pets was featured in a newspaper story. In the aftermath of all the excitement caused by the article, the young celebrity commented to her parents, "Now that I have guinea pigs, everybody wants to be my friend." The girl did not understand the real reason for her new popularity.

Wisely, Penny's mother and father began a program of praising their daughter for the cheerful, cooperative attitude that was making her so attractive to all those around her. Every act of outstanding kindness or generosity was recognized and praised. At every reasonable opportunity, Penny was made to see that she now had friends because she had learned how to *be* a friend.

At fifteen Penny's interests shifted from guinea pigs to boys and a more mature social life. But the lessons she'd learned through her pets remained unchanged. With or without guinea pigs, Penny had become a charming, attractive, thoroughly pleasant young lady.

Teachers need to be careful that a student sees a clear connection between his behavior and the punishment or reward that results. This is easily accomplished through one statement of very few words. With direct eye contact or use of the child's name, the broad category that covers the present conduct should be named specifically. "Bob, you are disrupting the class," or "Carol, stop that whining," or "Lester, thank you for being so helpful." It is usually appropriate to add a brief description of precisely what the child did to prompt the teacher's reaction. "Ted, you are disturbing the class with your humming." "Jeff, you were very helpful in art class today. Thank you for cleaning all the brushes." Whether positive or negative, the statement should be specific and brief. Prolonged praise is embarrassing. Lectures about bad conduct are boring. The object is to see that the child understands that there is a cause-and-effect relationship between his action and the praise or punishment that follows.

An organized system of punishments and rewards can lead youngsters through a change of behavior. For this to happen, children need teachers and parents to go before them, clearing the way, marking the course, directing movement on the path. They count on us to see potentials and possibilities, then set them up as goals. They rely on us to make the objectives clear, then break the task into sequential steps that can be faced as challenges one at a time. They look to us to monitor their progress so that they can make the adjustments that lead away from failure and toward success. And then, at the end, as they smile in victory, shouting, "Wow. See what I did!" they need us to confirm their success.

Chapter VIII

Adjustments in Classroom Management

ONE LEARNING-DISABLED CHILD can keep a classroom in a constant uproar if nothing is done to counteract his trouble with attention, organization, time, and social acceptance. In these areas the youngster does not have the ability to control and change his own behavior. Teachers will have to deal with these problems by adjusting his environment. Careful classroom management can prevent the LD student from becoming a strongly disruptive influence.

In a carefully controlled atmosphere, the learning-disabled pupil has his best chance for successful learning.

Distractibility and a short attention span are major causes of the LD youngster's classroom disasters. The child who is not paying attention to his work is usually doing something else. And as often as not, that something else will produce noise or movement that disturbs the rest of the class.

Thus, the teacher's first objective is to establish firm limits on the LD student. His difficulty with focusing attention must not become the entire class's problem.

Seating

Regardless of age, the LD student usually has an attention span that is significantly shorter than that of his classmates. Because his periods of concentration are so brief, he frequently looks up from his work and checks on what's going on around him. If there is something interesting nearby, it will capture his attention so that he never returns to his work.

Claude was an extremely bright, extremely active first-grader. He loved school; he loved people. He was curious about everything. The child bounded with energy and enthusiasm for all the wonderfully interesting things around him.

First-grade work should not have been terribly difficult for Claude. His learning disability was quite mild, he was getting excellent therapy, and he very much wanted to learn.

But in the classroom, the youngster never got his work done. He barely even got started on most of his schoolwork. "He's off in the clouds," his teacher complained. "Staring off into space. He just won't get down to business. The boy doesn't even try."

The LD specialist spent a morning in the classroom observing Claude. Just as had been recommended, the boy was seated at the end of the front row next to the teacher's desk. Unfortunately, this ideal location placed him right beside an aquarium and a row of windows that provided a fabulous view of a very busy playground.

Claude wasn't "off in the clouds." Every time his attention broke and he looked up, there was something fascinating going on in the fish tank or out on the playground. Always, something drew his attention away from his work.

It took several moves to find just the right spot for this wide-eyed first-grader who found everything interesting. One seat provided a neighbor who enjoyed fooling around with him. Another was so close to the door that he kept watching the activity in the hall. Finally, when seated off to the side by a blank wall, with two studious little neighbors and no interesting animals or vistas nearby, Claude found his ideal location. His surroundings were so boring that schoolwork was the most interesting thing available.

Everything in the LD child's environment competes for his attention. And extreme distractibility makes his focus of attention very fragile. Even among highly motivated LD students who do develop adequate study skills, difficulties with concentration are typical.

For the teacher, the trick is to seat the LD pupil where

there will be as few distractions as possible and where there will be little of interest to hold his attention when it's not focused on schoolwork. A seat in the front of the room is usually best. This limits what's in the student's line of vision. Instead of seeing a whole room of interesting bulletin boards plus thirty active children, he sees only the front third of the room, the blackboard, and a few classmates. If the pupil is situated on the extreme left or right side of the front row, the potential for distractions can be cut to a minimum. However, front-row corner seats present special problems which must be taken into consideration. Areas of heavy traffic and frequent activity should be avoided. If the teacher's desk, waste basket, and pencil sharpener are on one side, the LD child should be on the other. When this does leave a choice between near the door or near the window, the door is usually the less distracting of the two.

Some LD students should *not* be placed in the first row of a classroom. For those who are hyperactive, or those who have serious behavior problems, being seated in front of an entire class makes them actors with an audience. In limiting the distractions that disturb them, they become the distraction that disturbs *everyone* else. This must not be allowed.

The overactive child, whether learning disabled or not, is going to wiggle, bounce, tap, twist, hang out of his chair, wander around the room, and race to the teacher's desk. Most of the time, he will be playing with something in his hands. Almost always, he'll be in motion. It is pointless to try to limit his level of activity. The most effective approach is to limit his territory.

A hyperactive child usually is least disruptive if seated at one end of the back row. Also, in this location he can be allowed the extra amount of physical freedom he needs. Rather than waste her time and energy trying to keep him in his seat, the teacher can concentrate on confining his activity within reasonable but specific bounds. It is effective to give the youngster an adjusted set of rules: "You may move freely about this area of the room, provided you do your work, don't do anything dangerous, and don't disturb others." The exact limits of his territory should be made *absolutely* clear. With young children it may be necessary to mark off their space with a chalk line or strip of tape so the student knows exactly where his boundaries are. This approach enables a teacher to exert a reasonable amount of control over a hyperactive pupil. But it will work only if all parts of the adjusted rules are *strictly* enforced.

LD students who cause constant discipline problems should also be seated in the back. With them, the teacher's objective is to protect the rest of the class from the disturbance they create. Situating these youngsters in a corner or the back row has the effect of separating them from the other children. No one has to watch their antics, and there is only one neighbor to be disturbed.

For more complete separation, a disruptive boy can be surrounded by girls who will not interact with him. He should *not* be given the enlarged territory allowed the hyperactive child. And he should *not* be placed in some remote corner that isolates him entirely. (Although such a measure may occasionally be necessary, a teacher should not take this type of action without first consulting the LD specialist or psychologist.)

Always, in selecting the ideal seat for a learning-disabled student, the teacher needs to look for a quiet spot, with little traffic, limited view, and few neighbors.

The neighbors can be as important as the location. The LD child should *not* be seated near children who pick on him or tease him. Talkative students or those who fool around a lot should be avoided. Distractibility is bothersome enough without having noisy children nearby to make it worse. A short attention span causes enough difficulty without having the class clown nearby to provide entertainment for every break in concentration. A seat beside a pleasant, quiet, good student can have a very steadying effect on an LD pupil.

The "Good Neighbor"

"What page are we on?" "What row are we supposed to do?" "What were the directions?" The learning-disabled pupil has many such questions. Traditional classroom rules force him either to figure out such things for himself or to go to the teacher for help. Figuring them out for himself seldom leads the LD student to successful completion of an assignment. Asking the teacher would be fine, if the situation didn't occur so often. Constantly trotting up to the front of the room embarrasses the child and becomes an inconvenience to the teacher.

The LD child's routine questions about an assignment can almost always be answered by any good student in the class. By choosing the right neighbor and carefully controlling an adjusted set of rules, the teacher can see to it that the learning-disabled pupil has a ready source of information available right there at his elbow.

The teacher, the LD child, and the special neighbor must all have a clear understanding of the special arrangements they're making to create a "good neighbor plan": (1) The two children will be allowed to talk openly and freely, but quietly, during class. (2) The LD student will not pester his neighbor needlessly or use the conversations as an excuse for socializing. (3) The "good neighbor" will maintain a cooperative, understanding attitude. (4) In order that the children may understand the difference between a "good neighbor policy" and a partnership, the teacher must establish clear and specific guidelines. The youngsters must know what kinds of questions the LD student may take to his special neighbor. "What does this word say?" or "How long did the teacher give us to do this?" would probably be allowed. "What's the answer to number six?" would definitely not be an acceptable type of question. The two youngsters would also have to understand exactly what kind of help the neighbor may provide. Is he to copy arithmetic problems from the book? Does he supply basic information such as "How much is 14 take away 6?" Is he responsible for reminding the LD child about capital letters and punctuation? There would also have to be a clear understanding of special situations where their talking will not be allowed. Does the policy remain in effect even during tests? Does it apply only in this classroom, or anywhere in the school?

Most LD children ask two questions repeatedly: "What's that word?" and "How do you spell———?" They need to know where to turn for answers to these questions no matter what the situation. Most difficulties can be avoided if the full details are settled at the time the original agreement is made.

By the fifth grade, Mike had overcome almost all of the problems caused by his learning disability. In most areas he was a good student. He was especially patient with himself about his poor spelling. Whenever he got stuck on a word, he would quietly go to the teacher and ask for help. But Mike did not deal with his copying problem so effectively. His difficulty in copying things off the blackboard caused him serious problems. Every time he made a mistake, he got terribly upset. Erasing and correcting his errors made him furious. It got to the point that Mike caused at least one ugly scene every day.

In mid-November, a new boy, Tim, was enrolled in the fifth-grade class. For no particular reason, the teacher gave him a seat next to Mike.

Immediately, Mike took it upon himself to help the new student get into the routine of the class. In hushed tones, he answered questions about the way the teacher wanted things done. He told Tim where to find materials and supplies. He helped his new classmate adjust to the weekly schedule. Throughout the school day, the LD child and the new boy conferred and consulted together frequently. Quickly, the two became friends.

Sometime in December, the teacher realized that Mike no longer had problems copying things off the board. He hadn't had one of his temper outbursts in weeks. She had no idea what had caused the change in her LD pupil. She assumed it had something to do with sitting next to Tim. The two boys sometimes spent too much time talking, but overall she felt that they were a good influence on each other.

By Easter, Mike and Tim were frequently in trouble for whispering in class. When routine punishments didn't help, the teacher threatened to separate them.

One afternoon, right in the middle of a social studies test, the teacher caught Tim handing a note to Mike. Positive that the two boys were cheating, she snatched their papers away, demanded that Mike give her the note, and dragged the two criminals out into the hall.

On the little scrap of paper that Tim had given to Mike, there was only one word written: "democracy." Waving this final piece of evidence, the teacher challenged sternly, "Other than cheating, I can't imagine any possible reason for this one-word note!" Her eyes flashed as she glared first at one boy then at the other. "I will give you gentlemen one minute to explain exactly what this note means."

Gulping and stammering, both boys tired to talk at once. "I asked him how to spell democracy," Mike muttered at exactly the same time that Tim said, "He asked me how to spell democracy."

Since it seemed unlikely that two children would tell the exact same lie simultaneously, the teacher heard her two students out. Their stories fitted together perfectly. And their explanations clarified several things that the teacher had found puzzling.

Mike and Tim had developed their own version of the good neighbor policy.

Tim explained simply, "Mike don't spell so good, so I help him sometimes."

"And he copies stuff off the board for me," Mike added. Shrugging, he confessed, "That's how come I don't mess up and get so hoppin' mad anymore."

The teacher's broad smile made it easy to see that she approved of the system that these two friends had devised. Her curiosity led her to ask her LD student one final question. "And what do you do for Tim in return?"

Before the learning-disabled pupil could reply, his friend cut him off. "He don't have to do nothin' in return. It's okay. He's my friend."

In his own crude way, that eleven-year-old boy stated the whole theory behind the "good neighbor policy": When given an opportunity, most children will gladly help a classmate without expecting anything in return.

Selecting just the right child to act as a helping neighbor can be very difficult. It's often wise to let the LD student himself take a part in the process of choosing a likely candidate. Sometimes a rotating team of good neighbors is most practical. With that system, the LD pupil has a regular seat, and one desk immediately beside him is reserved for his special neighbor. Week by week, or month by month, students rotate in and out of the good neighbor's seat. Regardless of the system used, only students who are willing or anxious to be an assistant should be considered for the role. Recruits have the wrong attitude. They tend to see their role as a chore rather than a privilege.

Time Limits and Schedules

Not all LD children are dawdling slow movers, but for most of them time does tend to just slip through their fingers. Whenever they're allowed out of the classroom, it's unlikely that they'll be seen again soon. A two-minute trip to the bathroom takes them five minutes. For a short errand to the office or library, they'll be gone twice as long as seems reasonable. Much of this must be expected and tolerated. A few gimmicks can help to some extent.

Many teachers impose a time limit on students who leave the classroom for a trip to the lavatory, locker, drinking fountain, and so on. This is usually done with a sign-out sheet on which students record their name and the time they left the room. Since most LD children (of all ages) have trouble reading a clock, this standard method won't work for them. Yet, more than most students, they need something to force them to hurry along on their errands.

The sign-out approach can work for learning-disabled students if it's based on an hour glass or cooking timer instead of a clock. When leaving the room, the student takes the hourglass or timer from a shelf near the door, starts it running, and places it on his own desk. If he returns before the sand runs out or the bell goes off, he merely puts it back on its shelf and returns to his seat. If he's late, he suffers some standard penalty that is part of the system. For grades one through twelve, with *all* types of students, this method gives the teacher a way to enforce reasonable rules governing how long pupils may be allowed out of the classroom. It has two distinct advantages: it's no trouble to the teacher at all, and it does not single out LD children for special treatment. The rule and time limit applies equally to all. (For those children who are repeatedly late with the timer, some other system would have to be devised.)

Brian was a chronic slow mover. If allowed out of the classroom, this pleasant eighth-grader just lost track of time altogether.

In my second-floor classroom, the bathrooms and drinking fountains were right across the hall. All of my students could visit both places and be back before the three-minute timer ran out of sand.

That is, all but Brian. I tried using the five-minute timer to allow for his slow, shuffling pace. I tried having him carry a cooking timer with him so that he could see the time running out. I even sent students with him as an escort.

Nothing worked.

Always he came dragging back shamefaced and at least two minutes late.

Much as the other pupils liked Brian, his delayed returns always prompted a few comments from his classmates.

"Out there watchin' the girls, ehhh, Bri?" someone would tease.

"What'd you do, man, use the sink to wash out a few things?"

The jokes about what took him so long embarrassed the youth terribly. They were much worse than any punishment I'd have ever thought up.

In desperation, I gave up. Unless it was a real emergency, Brian was not allowed out of the room.

The stalemate continued until a January day when Brian had a legitimate reason to leave the room and I had an equally valid reason for insisting that he be back in no more than five minutes. On a sudden inspiration, I pulled my pocket calculator out of my purse, set its timer for four minutes, and shoved it into Brian's hip pocket. "When that beeper goes off, you drop whatever you're doing and run back to this room," I warned.

The boy grabbed a hall pass and scurried out the door as though carrying a bomb in his pocket. He completed his mission and made it back to the class before the alarm even went off. I guess Brian didn't want to deal with the embarrassment of having people see him with beeping noises coming out of his jeans.

It takes a tremendous amount of patience and energy to work around the LD child's nonadjustable pace. For Brian, the pocket calculator developed into a real solution. In most situations, the only available answers are compromises that work around the problem.

Whenever the teacher takes her students outside the classroom, it is necessary to guard against the LD child's problems with pace. Like most other youngsters, the learning-disabled child will push and shove to get to the front of the line. Yet, once the group is on the way to its destination, that same LD child will lag behind. If he's at the end of the line, he may get left behind altogether. This is particularly troublesome on field trips.

There are no surefire cures for this problem. A sturdy name tag (giving address and phone number for both home and school) is a necessity for any young LD child being taken off the school grounds. A buddy system can also be effective in such situations. At any time, it is *not* wise to let a learning-disabled youth be the last one in the line.

As a part of their difficulties with a nonvariable pace, most LD youngsters have trouble shifting from one activity to another. "It's time for music," "Turn in your sentences and get out your dictionary," "Put away your math and go wash for lunch" . . . the school day is full of abrupt changes. Some students develop a habit of pleading, "Just let me finish this one last sentence," or protesting, "I'm not done yet." LD students are particularly prone to cause trouble when concluding one activity and beginning another. In the first place, they frequently fail to complete their work within the period allotted. Also, their faulty concept of time makes it difficult for them to gauge how many minutes they have left for a particular activity. For them, "Turn in your paper" comes as a total surprise. If LD children are not mentally prepared, they balk. Instead of an agreeable, efficient change from math to reading, they keep right on with math, or begin horsing around, or stare off into space, or get angry and rip up their paper. Orders that come like a bolt out of the blue do not produce the desired responses from learning-disabled students.

A system that involves regular use of a five-minute warning can work wonders. Within the classroom, a simple "Five minutes left for the health project" will help the entire class get into the right frame of mind for the coming change. On the playground or in the lunchroom, the teacher can signal by holding up five fingers. Such advance notice sets the stage. When the moment arrives, everyone knows the time for action is NOW. No excuses will be accepted. The five-minute warning makes it possible for a teacher to impose the added structure needed in order to get LD children to live within some kind of schedule.

Controlling Distractions

Modern electronic equipment offers some amazing new alternatives in controlling the distractions in the LD student's learning environment.

Ed was taking ninth-grade algebra in an individualized program with an open classroom type of environment. His extremely short attention span and high level of distractibility made it impossible for him to concentrate. Most of his class time was spent chatting with his neighbors.

When assigned a page of easy problems, Ed would ask permission to put on a headset and listen to rock and roll while he worked. The music helped him concentrate. Despite some skepticism, Ed's teacher agreed to the arrangement. As long as the youth had rock and roll blasting through his headset, he was attentive and productive.

Ed's teachers tried to think of a way to extend his new success into other areas. But the youth could study to rock and roll only when the assignment involved easy, routine, mechanical work. The pleasant sense of isolation produced by the headset then made it possible for the young student to tune out distractions. But if he had to read or do a lot of thinking, the loud thumping rock music proved to be a terrible distraction. The boy's teachers searched for some kind of music that would be more compatible with concentration while doing reading activities. Several types of soft, repetitive, nonintrusive music were considered. Finally, one of the teachers discovered a recording of the ocean. As long as this tape played, the listener heard only the rolling breakers and crashing surf. The cyclic ebb and flow sounded so realistic that you could almost taste the salt in the air.

Ed loved it. And he loved what it did for his concentration. He carried a cassette recorder around with him from class to class. Other students heard about Ed's special background music and began asking to try it out. By the end of the semester, at least a dozen students were using a tape recorder and headset as a means of improving concentration.

Through the use of a headset, the auditory level of a student's environment can be almost completely controlled. Distracting noises in the classroom can thus be masked by neutral, nondisturbing sound.

The microcomputers now found in many homes and classrooms increase attentiveness while also providing instruction or drill. Because they engage the student kinesthetically and tactily (in addition to visually and auditorially), desk-top computers have tremendous potential as an aid in improving concentration among the learning disabled.

Avoiding Social Problems

Any student who takes more than his fair share of the teacher's time . . . any pupil who ruins the peaceful atmosphere within the classroom with strange or disruptive behavior . . . any child who gets away with ignoring rules, schedules, and assignments . . . any youngster who keeps the entire classroom in a turmoil will be resented and rejected by his classmates.

Thus, prevention must be the teacher's first line of defense against the LD child's social problems. Through careful classroom management and all the special adjustments discussed in this book, the teacher must help the learning-disabled student succeed with his schoolwork. If he can do his math, he won't have the tantrums that make the other children think he's weird. If he can finish his assignment and hand it in on time, the others won't grow angry because they're constantly waiting for him. Everything that makes it possible for an LD student to function satisfactorily within the classroom makes him more acceptable to his classmates.

While using this indirect approach to achieve long-range goals, teachers also need to be on guard against issues that require firm, direct intervention. "I don't want to sit next to him." "I don't want him on my team." "Does he have to be on our committee?" Statements like these hurt. But learning-disabled youngsters often feel a much stronger level of rejection than is intended. As long as there is no name-calling or open ridicule, the issue is best treated as a "social snub." For the offender, the routine lecture about "A classroom is not a social club containing only a select group who choose to be together" is appropriate. Then the matter should be dropped.

Rejection that includes name-calling and cruel teasing needs to be treated as a major offense. Just as a teacher will not allow anyone to call a black student a "nigger," an oriental student a "slant," an Italian student a "wop," or a Jewish student a "kike," it must not be tolerated when children call a learning-disabled child "stupid" or "retard." Such name-calling requires strong, immediate corrective action.

Teachers need to keep in mind that children "mirror" the attitudes and behavior of the adults around them. If the teacher hounds and scolds a child constantly, the students in the class will tend to do the same. If the teacher shows a lack of patience, understanding, or respect for a student, the other children will follow her example.

Harold came to the LD resource room with a small group of his classmates from Miss Johnson's fourth grade. The freckle-faced youngster was energetic, cooperative, and very eager to learn. He had the short attention span typical of learning-disabled children of his age. The child acted just about like the other little boys who came with him from Miss Johnson's class.

But the other children treated Harold as though he were different. They criticized him constantly.

"Harold, stop tapping your foot."

"Harold, quit jiggling the table."

The other students often corrected the boy for some small disturbance even when I felt that he had done nothing wrong.

The situation was very puzzling.

It was likely that the boy's homeroom teacher knew why the other children picked on him. But Miss Johnson and I couldn't seem to get together for a conference. While waiting for the meeting date we finally agreed upon, I struggled to find the reason for my fourth-grade group's strange behavior.

A day or two before the conference, as the class recorded a dictated paragraph, Harold did something that irritated Betsy. (It was so slight that I didn't even notice it!) The little girl slapped her pencil down, scowled at Harold, and snapped, "Can't you see I'm trying to get my work done? You just stop all that disruptive behavior."

"Disruptive behavior?" I gasped to myself. "Since when does a fourth-grader talk like that?" As I stared at the cute little girl who'd just used such an unexpected expression, the realization dawned. "That's an adult expression. She heard that somewhere. . . ." Suddenly the whole picture became clear: the children treated Harold the same way their teacher did!

At our meeting, Miss Johnson was very open about her feelings toward Harold. Her voice edged with frustration, she told me what her days were like. "All day long, it's 'Harold, get back to work. . . . Harold, why aren't you in your seat? . . . Harold, quit pestering Melissa. . . .' I get so sick of trying to get that kid to behave I could just scream. . . ." Miss Johnson stopped abruptly, looked earnestly at me, then asked, "Have you ever had a student you just plain didn't like?"

"Yeah," I nodded. "Every few years there's one that just rubs me the wrong way." Grinning, I added, "But I prefer to call it a 'personality conflict.'"

Miss Johnson was too upset to appreciate my attempt at humor. With a heavy sigh and a look of deep shame, she concluded, "Every day on my way to school, I hope Harold will be absent."

Whether positive or negative, children will adopt attitudes similar to those of the adults around them. Thus, to improve the relationship between a child and his classmates, the teacher must start by changing her own relationship with the youngster. It is the teacher who takes the lead in developing an atmosphere of acceptance toward an LD student.

Any person who does not really know what the learning-disabled child is up against will find it very difficult to be sympathetic and patient. The classroom teacher involved with an LD student is faced with a two-step process: first she must learn to understand and accept the child herself; then she must lead the class to do the same. The key is in developing the understanding.

Chapter IX

Adjustments in Texts, Materials, and Assignments

LEARNING-DISABLED STUDENTS sometimes have trouble with math, usually have trouble with reading, and almost always have trouble with writing and spelling. It's not that they can't think or understand. They can usually learn the material being presented. What they can't do is read the regular book or do the routine writing required on assignments, reports, and tests. By altering texts and materials used with LD students, teachers make it possible for them to learn successfully despite their weakness in some of the basic skills.

Using the Regular Text

It is often possible to adapt a student's work in such a way that he gains enough efficiency to use the standard texts and materials with ease and speed. Such alterations enable the LD pupil to succeed with "regular" work.

Math workbooks and worksheets

Many learning-disabled students have trouble copying math problems out of a book. Through workbooks, sets of ditto masters, and hand-copied worksheets, teachers can eliminate the need for copying while still providing the child with the arithmetic practice he needs. If the LD student is in a regular math group, it's best to use the worksheet approach with the entire group.

Old copies of textbooks

Most LD students have trouble writing out the answers to questions that routinely appear at the end of each chapter in textbooks. To avoid the need for extensive copying and writing, the student can be provided with an old text which he is allowed to mark up. Thus, instead of writing out the answers to end-of-the-chapter questions, the pupil can record the number of the page on which the answer can be found in the book, and circle the information where it appears in the text.

An extra set of books

"Forgot to take my book home" sounds like just another excuse to get out of doing homework. Yet, for those LD children who are poorly organized, constantly forgetting books can be a very real problem. Having a duplicate set of texts at home can save everybody a lot of trouble.

Steve was in Mrs. Phipps's tenth-grade American literature class. To help the LD youth work around his difficulty with reading, his literature teacher very carefully adjusted and adapted all his assignments. The young lady did everything in her power to give Steve a chance to succeed in her class. Yet by mid-October the youth was headed toward certain failure. He rarely did his homework, never brought his book to class, and usually slept through most of the period.

In analyzing the situation, the teacher realized that Steve had a pattern. Day after day he began class by requesting, "Can I go to my locker? I think I left my book there." When Mrs. Phipps did let him go, the boy would miss the first ten minutes of class. And, as often as not, it turned out he'd left his materials at home anyway. The youth had had the same difficulty for years.

All Steve's past teachers believed his real problem was lack of motivation. But Mrs. Phipps was young and idealistic. She discussed her student's situation with the LD specialist, the school psychologist, the youngster's parents, and the boy himself. None of them offered either suggestions or encouragement.

In a conference, Steve's father tried to get Mrs. Phipps to see his son in the same way everyone else did. "Steve don't like school, and he ain't gonna study," the man explained with simple honesty. "The boy's just waitin' to hit sixteen so he can drop out." Shrugging his shoulders and waving his hands in resignation, the boy's father tried to get this nice young teacher to understand that it would be much better for everybody if she'd just give up and let the boy remain the poor student he was destined to be.

Mrs. Phipps did not argue. But she didn't give up either. She was absolutely determined to make Steve's last year in school a profitable one.

With no one to help her in her crusade, she got a stack of material on learning disabilities from the library. A week of reading gave her only one good suggestion. But it was an intriguing idea.

In an article by a learning disabilities expert, Mrs. Phipps read, ". . . it helps if the LD youngster can be assigned a duplicate set of textbooks for use at home. . . ." Because of his parents' attitude, it was unlikely that Steve would study at home. But the availability of a duplicate copy of the American Literature book offered a solution for the youth's problem.

Mrs. Phipps arranged for Steve to keep his own personal second copy of the literature text in the school library. (The original copy stayed in the classroom.) The boy gladly agreed to have his daily study hall moved to the new location where his literature materials were kept. Doing assignments was such a new experience for Steve that he actually got a kick out of sneaking around doing them in secret.

The youth did not tell any of his friends what he was up to, and the success did not spread beyond American literature. But, for two straight semesters, fifteen-year-old LD Steve got a B in American literature. They were the only passing grades in his final year of school.

Many learning-disabled students will gladly do their

homework if someone will just help them keep track of their books. A duplicate set of texts can make it possible for these youngsters to do their assignments. Being prepared for class is often the deciding factor in whether a student passes or fails.

A reading partner

A reading partnership can provide the LD student with a person to read *with* him, while still requiring him to do at least some of the reading for himself. The partner could be a "good neighbor," a classmate specially chosen for the job, an older student, an adult volunteer, or a teacher's aide. Although the learning-disabled youth and his reading partner take turns reading the assignment aloud, they do *not* have to divide the material equally. It is perfectly acceptable for the partner to do the majority of the reading.

Reading partnerships do not have to be limited to just two people. An adult can easily read with two or three children at once. The teacher should *not* be an LD child's reading partner.

A reader

A "reader" can supply the LD child with a person to read *to* him. When the helper acts as a reader, the LD child's role involves following along in the book and paying close attention. But he is *not* expected to take a turn reading aloud or silently. This method is ideally suited for those occasions when the reading level of an assignment makes it too difficult for the child, yet no adjusted material is available.

Twelve LD seventh-graders had their language arts instruction from me. We worked on reading, writing, spelling, grammar, punctuation, literature, and composition for two hours every day.

As a special project, this group of seventh-graders adopted the learning-disabled youngsters in our school's third grade. Twice a week each of my students spent thirty minutes with the child assigned to him. In nooks and crannies all over the building, the teen-agers huddled up to work with their little partners. Sometimes they helped with a test or worksheet. Usually they acted as readers. By having their own special assistant, the little children could do the regular class work just as quickly and easily as their classmates.

A recording

A cassette tape recording of the text provides the LD pupil with a reader, while also allowing him to maintain a degree of independence. If thirty students are reading silently to themselves and one or two students are intently listening to a voice on the headset of a tape recorder, then an entire class is actively involved in completing the same assignment. Using a cassette tape player within a classroom need not cause *any* disturbance. Headsets and earplugs make its operation silent to all but the intended listener.

There is rarely any problem concerning the operation of the tape player. LD children tend to be good with mechanical things. And, in our gadget-oriented society, even very young children are usually familiar with the operation of stereos, color TV's, and so forth.

Some school systems have collections of tapes on which all their adopted texts are read aloud. Many LD teachers are in the process of building such tape libraries.

Mrs. Nettle was a dedicated specialist assigned to run LD resource rooms in three different schools. Since most of her fifth-grade pupils had trouble using the regular social studies text, she spent one summer reading the entire book aloud onto cassette tapes.

When school opened in the fall, Mrs. Nettle made the tapes available to all her students and all their classroom teachers. Many of the children used the recordings during their time in the resource room. But not one of the teachers ever requested cassettes for an LD pupil to use within her room. Their explanation was always something like "It's too inconvenient to make the arrangements. And, besides, it wouldn't fit in with my regular program."

Since these teachers didn't know how to take advantage of an unusual opportunity, it passed them by. Unfortunately, their LD students suffered for it.

Through the LD teacher and the special education department, audio-visual equipment is usually readily available for use with learning-disabled children assigned to regular classrooms. An ample supply of blank cassettes is usually on hand, as well. Caution: Classroom teachers should *not* take on large taping projects. There will be times when the teacher will want to make a tape or two, but it should not be a routine part of her regular class preparation.

In junior and senior high schools, LD students who use recordings of their texts need these special materials readily available during study halls. Keeping the entire collection stored in the LD resource room or the library makes this possible. Even a system of very careful control will not prevent loss of tapes if they are taken outside the classroom, LD room, or library. At all ages, the learning disabled are usually very bad about losing things. Without strict rules, entire tape libraries disappear among the junk at the bottom of cluttered lockers.

Adapting the Regular Text

Sometimes a student's assignment within the regular textbook is altered to fit his personal level of skills. In this type of arrangement, the child is expected to use the regular material; however, the kind or amount of work assigned him is different from that required of the rest of the class. Many learning-disabled students read well enough to deal with regular texts yet have no chance of success unless the amount of material is adapted to fit their slow reading speed. With schoolwork that involves writing, LD children will almost always need their assignments adapted.

It is possible to adapt a child's assignments in such a way that the youngster gains the ability to study independently. The simplest such changes involve altering the size of assignments. If the other students do twenty-five addition problems, the LD student might be told to do the first ten, every other one, every other row, the last three rows, the last one in each row, etc. If the other children read fifteen pages in their library book, the learning-disabled youngster might be told to read five in his. If the class learns twenty spelling words a week, the LD pupil might be required to master ten. Some types of assignments can be easily cut down in size without sacrificing mastery of the skills being presented at that grade level.

It can be very difficult to adapt reading assignments in subject matter courses such as social studies, science, health, history, and so on. Having a student read only a portion of the material almost always means he gets only a portion of the information. And most of the systems for selecting the parts to be read are either complicated for the pupil or time-consuming for the teacher.

There are four basic techniques that *can* work. Sometimes one of them can be useful in making the most of an otherwise impossible situation. Sometimes one provides a truly ideal solution.

1. Instruct the student to read only the bold face type,

italics, and certain crucially placed paragraphs. He can then skip over the less important material. In precisely organized texts with a clear format, this type of adapted reading system would enable the student to get the overall concept, plus definitions and other significant details.

2. Get the pupil to read the questions at the end of the chapter *before* reading the text. He can then scan the material in search of the answers. Thus guided toward the key passages that discuss the issues suggested by the questions, he can find the important parts and read them.

3. Give the student assignments in terms of time to be allowed rather than numbers of pages required. On a twenty-minute reading assignment, the LD pupil would read just like everybody else, and when his time limit was up, he'd quit. Whatever number of pages he read would be considered sufficient. This time limit tactic can be especially helpful when the student is required to do skimming, scanning, or selective reading of some specially designated segment of the material.

4. Get someone to mark the key passages in the student's text. The teacher can then allow him to skip over the un-marked, less important material. With this approach, the youngster reads to get general concepts and main ideas. This technique sounds terribly time-consuming for the teacher. It doesn't have to be.

Ralph's learning disability made twelfth-grade World History extremely difficult for him. He could not read twenty to thirty pages per night.

The teacher, Mr. Deal, had taught the course for a number of years. His own copy of the text had all the important passages underlined. Mr. Deal and Ralph both realized that the teacher's well-marked text offered them a solution to the boy's problem with slow reading. If the student read just the material the teacher had underlined, it would be possible for the boy to cut his reading assignments in half without skipping over any important material.

For a while they tried having the student borrow the teacher's book. That didn't work very well. It deprived Mr. Deal of his text at just the times he needed it to prepare for the next day's class.

The teacher tried marking his pupil's book so that it matched his own. When Ralph had his very own copy of the adapted material, the youth's book became useful for study and reviewing for tests, as well as for nightly reading. This system was great for Ralph but too demanding on Mr. Deal. With the responsibilities of his heavy teaching load, it was just not practical for the teacher to take on the job of underlining one student's text.

The learning-disabled youth tried marking his own book. His difficulty with copying made the task an impossible chore. Ralph could read and understand the material, but he could not copy underlining accurately.

By early October, Ralph was so discouraged that he wanted to drop World History. The boy's parents were frantic. They were afraid their son wouldn't graduate. Only Mr. Deal believed that his student's problem with slow reading could be solved.

Although Ralph had never had any contact with the high school's LD teacher, it was agreed that she would be called for advice. The student and his history teacher went to see her together.

The LD specialist quickly recognized Ralph's dilemma and made a string of suggestions. "Have you got anybody at home who could take Mr. Deal's book for a weekend and copy out *all* the underlining?" she asked.

The boy thought a moment. "Nahh, my folks both work. . . ." Pausing, he reconsidered, then added a bit more optimistically, "I could maybe con my sister into doing it. . . . But she's at college and won't be home 'til Christmas vacation."

"No aunts, uncles, cousins . . . ?" Mr. Deal asked.

Ralph shrugged. "Our whole family lives up north."

The specialist looked at Mr. Deal and grinned. "How about you? Got anybody who owes you a big favor?"

"Not that big." The teacher chuckled.

"Okay. Let's see what we can find here within the school, paid or free." The LD teacher's eyes lit up as her own word "free" registered. "That's it," she announced, energetically jabbing at the air with one finger. "We have two volunteers here at this school. A couple of mothers come in twice a week. They are both assigned to help out with special education. Mostly, they grade papers and do bulletin boards. . . ."

"But I'm not in special ed," Ralph protested.

"Ahh, but technically you are," the specialist corrected, her voice full of enthusiasm. "You are a recognized and diagnosed learning-disabled student. Whether or not you are presently getting therapy with the school's LD specialist has nothing to do with it. You are entitled to all the services the special ed department has available."

The history teacher and his pupil were both delighted. The LD specialist made the necessary arrangements. Within a week a mother/volunteer got Ralph's World History text completely underlined for him. For the rest of his senior year the boy kept up with his history assignments with ease.

All four of the above techniques have the LD pupil read only a portion of the regular assignment. But they allow him to do his reading independently. Although he never makes up the parts that are skipped over, he is expected to learn the details and finer points through class discussion and oral instruction.

Substituting Alternate Materials

Whenever a student is given a specially selected book appropriate to his personal level of skill, his material is said to have been adjusted. Under such an arrangement, the pupil is *not* expected to deal with the regular text at all. Classroom teachers who hope to work effectively with LD students will have to learn to make many routine adjustments in materials.

Rob was a fifth-grader with a very severe learning disability. In history, his class was studying Egypt. With reading skills at the low third-grade level, Rob found the regular textbook far too difficult.

Since the teacher wanted the boy to be able to work independently, she found several library books on Egypt that were written at his reading level. Every time the rest of the class had a reading assignment in the textbook, Rob was given a reading assignment in one of his library books. When the class had a written assignment, Rob prepared a brief oral report. Like all his classmates, he participated in discussions, did a project, and took a test (oral, in this case) at the end of the unit.

Rob's teacher adjusted his social studies material by making one trip to the library. Sometimes making such an adjustment is not that easy. Teachers who are trying to locate and select altered materials will find the LD teacher a valuable source of assistance. Whenever a radical adjustment is necessary, the LD specialist *should* be consulted.

In reading, spelling, and math, appropriately adjusted books are vital. These three areas are so crucial that the classroom teacher should expect the LD specialist to take an active role in the selection. The expert understands an LD student's special limitations and needs. Also, she is usually well informed about special materials that are available. (As in all problem-solving conferences with an LD specialist, the wise teacher will get several suggestions rather than just one. From several equally suitable sets of adjusted material, the teacher can then select the one most practical for her classroom and teaching style.)

Pete was a very bright sixth-grader whose spelling was at high second-grade level. He could not even *read* the words in the regular spelling book, so his teacher put him in the low group with the fifth-grade book. Pete couldn't read those words either, but it was the book being used by the lowest group in the class.

Week after week, Pete failed his tests. His teacher kept cutting down his list, hoping that if he had only a few words, he would succeed. But instead of improving, he experienced more and more difficulty. The boy quit trying altogether.

In desperation, the teacher put Pete in a spelling group all by himself and gave him a third-grade book. He hated the whole idea. He was constantly losing or forgetting "that baby book." It embarrassed him to be seen with any of the adjusted spelling materials his teacher worked so hard to provide. In addition to continued failure and lack of effort, the youngster's attitude became defiant and surly.

Finally the LD specialist was consulted. By that time the situation was such a mess that radical action was necessary. Pete's daily sessions in the LD resource room were changed to coincide with the period when his regular class had spelling. The specialist took over the responsibility of teaching the boy all his spelling.

Pete's teacher was wise enough to know that he needed adjusted material in spelling. But she made a bad situation worse by trying singlehandedly to solve a problem beyond the average classroom teacher's area of expertise. In adjusting materials, teachers should not hesitate to ask the specialist for help.

Parallel reading

It's nearly impossible to find an adjusted textbook for an entire year's study of a particular subject. Parallel reading designed to fit each separate unit is the most practical approach. Rob's teacher provided him with books written on the third-grade level to blend with a fifth-grade unit on Egypt. Because of the advanced vocabulary, a tenth-grade biology text could never be replaced by a fifth-grade science book. The student can learn the general principles from the easier books; the fancy terminology would be learned orally in class.

Paraphrases and condensations

High school courses in literature and history seem specially designed to make LD children suffer. Even after successful therapy, most learning-disabled students are still very slow readers. *Huckleberry Finn*, *Oliver Twist*, and *Uncle Tom's Cabin* are difficult reading for teen-agers who are good students. For LD students they are a nearly impossible chore.

But all school systems have certain "classics" built into their program. And nobody gets through without reading them. In such cases the LD specialist or a good librarian can help the teacher find a suitable paraphrase or condensation. Many of our culture's literary masterpieces are available in a variety of paraphrases. There are a few sets on the third- or fourth-grade level, many different editions from the seventh-grade level on, and even a series or two done in a comic book format. The *Reader's Digest* has produced a variety of condensations that are readily available.

When an entire class is reading a particular piece of literature and the child with disabilities in reading must do the same, a pharaphrase appropriate to his reading level is best. For those who are adequate but slow readers, a good condensation is ideal.

It must not be pretended that a paraphrase or condensation is of the same aesthetic value as the original. In order to produce a toned-down, easier-to-read version, at least some of a masterpiece's rich vocabulary, complex plot structure, exquisite characterization, broad sweeping grandeur, and elegant use of language must be sacrificed. But for the LD child who could never struggle through all fourteen hundred pages of *War and Peace*, a good condensation allows him to savor at least some of the elements that make the work a literary classic.

Materials designed for the blind

From *The Canterbury Tales* to the poetry of e e cummings, almost all the great literature is available on tapes and records. Anything that is studied for a junior or senior high school English class is likely to be available on records obtainable through the public library. Some of these sound productions are designed for anybody interested in hearing plays, poetry, or other literary works read aloud. Many of them, however, are part of the "talking books" series designed for the blind. Learning-disabled students are eligible to use the extensive "Books for the Blind" collection. (For information, get in touch with Talking Books, care of your local library, state library, or the Library of Congress.) The student will be required to have his doctor sign a certificate stating that he is learning disabled. That's the only red tape involved. Once it's been established that he qualifies, he'll be allowed to use freely anything in the large catalogue they will provide for him. If a record-player is needed, one will be supplied free of charge.

If it's *Hamlet* every February for all tenth-graders, the teacher should get an LD student set up with a source of recordings before Christmas. It won't always be possible to get the adjusted material *for* the youngster. But it is the teacher's responsibility to help the parents make whatever arrangements are necessary to see that the special material is *on hand* when it is needed.

Changing Writing Assignments

Almost all learning-disabled children have extreme difficulty presenting their ideas in writing. Most have problems with spelling, punctuation, and handwriting as well. Yet only a few have any trouble expressing themselves orally.

Adapting materials and assignments to allow for an LD student's problem with writing must be a major area of concern to the child's classroom teacher. Whenever possible, the requirements of written work should be cut down drastically in size or changed to oral assignments. With older students, it must be remembered that trouble with writing often makes note-taking impossible.

Several types of adaptions can decrease the amount of writing required to fulfill the purpose of a given assignment in *any* subject.

1. Eliminate copying. Writing down the question as well as the answer is usually busy work, a nicety, not an essential element of the material being studied.

In all grades, assignments are usually written on the board so that students can note subject, chapter, page, numbers of problems or questions to be done, the specific directions, and date due. It's part of the normal routine. And for LD children of all ages, it causes problems. They can't copy accurately, they write very slowly, and they get frustrated very quickly whenever they have a pencil in their hand. Thus, even the way the assignment is made needs adapting!

The "good neighbor" can be a valuable tool in making the necessary changes. First, the LD child will always need someone to verify that he has copied the numbers and instructions down correctly. Also, when his slow writing makes it impossible for him to complete the task in the time available, he'll need someone else to do it for him. Usually one of the helping neighbor's main jobs is making duplicates of routine classwork that must be copied from somewhere. When the LD student asks his good neighbor, "Will you make me a copy of that?" the teacher need not even get involved (except to see that the two students don't run out of carbon paper).

"Copy the question out of the book" or "Write your answers in complete sentences"—for learning-disabled students, both are needless torture. For them, getting the correct answer onto the paper is enough of a challenge. If the student's answer is satisfactory, it can safely be assumed that the question was adequately read and understood.

Research for reports is supposed to teach a student how to take notes. Copying long difficult passages from an encyclopedia onto file cards takes a learning-disabled youngster an incredible amount of time. With the use of a copy machine, scissors, and glue, note taking requires no writing. To use the cut-and-paste research method, the child merely finds the information needed, writes down the page numbers, gets the pages photocopied by office secretary or librarian, cuts out the key sentences and paragraphs, and attaches them to file cards. These become his note cards. Research using old newspapers and magazines allows cutting directly from the original material.

Defining vocabulary words found in a dictionary or glossary is primarily a copying activity. Partnership arrangements are usually the most logical solution. Using basically the same type of system discussed under reading partners, the LD student takes an active part in finding the words, reading the definitions, and selecting the one that best fits the requirements of the assignment. The partner (with carbon paper, if it's a classmate) does *all* the writing.

With older students, teachers ask that they "make a final draft in ink." Younger children are told, "Now go back to your seat and write this neatly." Either way, it's a copying assignment. The rough draft is full of repaired errors, erasures, crossed-out words, spelling corrections. It's the original, and it's perfect—but it's a mess. In making his final finished copy, complete with his very best handwriting, the LD child usually makes so many copying mistakes that the paper is no longer satisfactory.

Helping an LD youngster produce an acceptable final copy of a report is *not* a job for an amateur. This is a major tears-and-tantrums-type task requiring *close* supervision by a trained professional. Without the assistance of the LD teacher, classroom teacher, or a trained aide, the learning-disabled student cannot be expected to complete the job satisfactorily, and the assignment should be radically adapted. A pupil who completes a satisfactory rough draft can read it aloud to his teacher, to the class, or onto a cassette tape as his way of producing an acceptable final copy.

2. Accept oral work as a substitute for written work. Although it would be ideal for the teacher to find a way to let the learning-disabled student present his work to her in a one-to-one conference, this is not realistic as a routine practice. A cassette tape recorder (provided by the school and kept within the classroom) is a valuable tool for recording reports and any other assignments that can be spoken instead of written. Thus, when the other members of the class turn in their papers, the LD student can turn in a cassette containing his work.

3. Accept illustrations as substitutes for written explanations. If a science question asks, "How does the human heart work?" the correct answer can be illustrated through charts, cartoons, graphs, diagrams, or other visual representations. If a comprehension question for a reading story asks, "What happened to Bob's new wagon?" a set of pictures like a comic strip can show the sequence of events

involved in the disappearance of the wagon. The teacher won't have to think up ways for LD children to illustrate their answers. If the pupil understands that he is free to use an alternate method of presenting answers, he'll figure out good, logical ways to do it.

4. Assign demonstrations and projects instead of large written reports. Most LD students learn best when dealing with concrete objects. In order to tell about different types of Indian dwellings, it is possible to use models, illustrations, or blueprints to give an adequate portrayal of their housing. For a report on teeth, it would be logical for the teacher to eliminate any need for writing. The student could make a large model or poster clearly showing a tooth and all its parts. Then, in a presentation to the class, he could explain everything he'd learned about his subject.

5. Accept the briefest possible written form of an answer. One good sentence or a list of separate facts often presents as much information as a paragraph. For learning-disabled students, all correct answers should be acceptable.

6. Never count off for spelling errors outside of spelling class. Messy papers with poor handwriting should be cheerfully accepted as long as the answers are legible. When an LD student's version of a word makes it totally unrecognizable, the issue is easily resolved by asking him, "What's that supposed to say?"

LD students can often fulfill the requirements of an assignment if they are allowed to deviate from traditional study methods. Teachers who allow such special accommodations for students' weaknesses are guided by the basic principle: forget the form, go for the content.

Writing Helpers

A "writing partner" can provide the learning-disabled child with someone to write *with* him. In such an arrangement, the LD student does all of the planning and thinking. He also records some of the answers himself (with the partner helping with the spelling). The assistant writes at least half of the work.

A "secretary" can supply the LD child with someone to write *for* him. Usually the person providing this service should be a teacher, aide, or volunteer from outside the class. The task is much too time-consuming for a "good neighbor." The secretary's sole job is to translate the child's spoken words into their written form. Pointing out errors or making corrections is *not* part of the task. The child does the thinking; the helper merely supplies the hand that records the words.

Kent had a very severe learning disability. Although he was extremely intelligent, at the age of eighteen he was only in the ninth grade. His disability in reading, writing, and spelling prevented him from succeeding in any of his high school subjects. His grades were a dismal series of repeated failures.

Glenda, a senior, was Kent's girlfriend. The couple often spent their evenings studying together. Gradually, the two developed a system whereby Glenda became her boyfriend's "reader" and "secretary." She read all of Kent's assignments to him aloud, then recorded what he dictated for his written answers and assignments.

Tests were very difficult, but most of them required little writing. As long as Kent didn't have to write essay-type answers, he got by in spite of his extremely poor reading and spelling. By January he was doing better than he'd ever done before.

During the second semester, the youth's English class was taught by a student teacher. This young lady quickly realized that Kent could pass tests when allowed to give his answers orally. With his girlfriend acting as his "secretary" at home, and one teacher making special adaptions, Kent made the honor roll!

Unfortunately, the boy's father found out about the homework arrangement and didn't approve. Glenda graduated and went off to college. And Kent returned to his failure patterns.

Classroom computers now make a whole new set of alternatives available to teachers who are trying to adapt assignments in accord with an LD student's impaired skill in writing. From routine worksheets to quizzes and major tests, all can be programmed into a microcomputer so that the learning-disabled pupil does not have to write anything more than a few letters to indicate his choices. And, for those large writing tasks that have traditionally produced hysteria in the LD student, frustration in the teacher, and failure for everyone—a word processor offers an entirely new chance for success. Children proofread and make corrections with ease as they get the computer to delete, insert, rearrange, or otherwise alter the words displayed on the screen. Producing a perfect final draft is a breeze—just push a button marked "print out."

Producing written work with a word processor has several unique advantages: (1) It circumvents the panic LD children feel when handed a pencil and faced with a blank piece of paper. Taking the pencil out of his hand tends to unblock the LD youngster so he is really free to think. (2) It removes the element of criticism and impatience generated by human teachers. (3) It involves the child's thought-processing on four major levels (visual, auditory, kinesthetic, tactile), thus heightening interest and enhancing concentration. (4) It usually produces a feeling of enthusiasm and optimism. Most children think of working at a computer as a pleasant, challenging adventure.

By adjusting materials and adapting assignments to fit the limitations of learning-disabled students, teachers make it possible for these youngsters to learn in spite of their problem. The LD specialist and classroom teacher work together toward two separate goals. Through special instruction in the basic skills, the LD teacher tries to make the youngster "literate." Through special alterations in materials and assignments, the classroom teacher works to teach him the subject matter that makes him "educated."

Chapter X

Adjustments in Teaching Techniques

LEARNING-DISABLED CHILDREN learn best when experiencing concrete reality. The following hierarchy guides the choice of instructional methods to use with such youngsters.

- Rather than have him read about it, tell him about it.
- Rather than telling him about it, show it to him.
- Rather than showing it to him, let him touch it, handle it, observe it, feel it, build one, work one, or do one.

In a class where instruction is based on experiments and demonstrations, the LD child is likely to excel. He needs a "hands on" approach to learning. Such methods of instruction allow him to combine his high level of curiosity with his unusual powers of observation and his talent for dealing with three-dimensional objects. He'll reason out what's going on, draw his own logical conclusions, and not forget the concept presented. That's good learning.

In a class where instruction is based on reading the book and answering questions, the LD child is likely to be bored and unmotivated. Such teaching techniques force him to rely on areas where his skills are weak. With his slow, labored reading, he forgets what was said at the beginning of the paragraph before he gets to the end. Misreading and skipping over hard words give him only a garbled hint of the concept being presented. Rather than wade through masses of words explaining some abstract theory, he will use his high level of curiosity to investigate the freckles on the backs of his hands. That's also good learning. But he's learning about freckles, not the topic being presented.

Teaching techniques that are appropriate for the learning disabled are appropriate for others as well. Anything done to help an LD pupil become more attentive and better organized tends to have the same effect on the entire class. Special instructional methods adopted to help an LD child frequently result in better learning for all the students and increased efficiency for the teacher.

After his second unsuccessful year in the seventh grade, Fred was diagnosed as learning disabled by the largest child development clinic in his state. Since there was not a single LD specialist in the boy's small hometown, the clinic where he'd been tested agreed to send an expert to consult with his school.

In a series of after-school meetings, all of Fred's teachers were given the kind of guidance they needed in order to work effectively with the LD youth.

As the semester progressed, Fred's teachers got discouraged. With each monthly visit, the consultant found that another teacher or two had given up.

"All he wants to do in class is socialize," Fred's science teacher complained. "If he'd pay attention, I could help him. But all he does is talk and fool around."

"I can't get him to do his homework or bring his materials to class." The boy's English teacher sighed. "It's gotten to the point that he just sits there and looks out the window—and I let him."

Fred's reading teacher didn't like his attitude. She gave up when he failed to produce a book report after repeated warnings and postponements. The youngster's math teacher remained optimistic until midsemester. For her the final blow came when a routine notebook grading revealed that Fred was at least a month behind.

One by one, all of Fred's teachers threw their hands up in disgust.

All but Mr. Ward—the history teacher. At every monthly meeting he discussed the problems he was having with Fred and asked the LD specialist for new suggestions. With the quiet patience of a wise, experienced teacher, Mr. Ward listened to the advice he was given, then went back to his classroom to put it into practice.

The eighth-grade history teacher used tremendous ingenuity in working to solve his LD student's classroom problems. With insight, flexibility, and creativity, Mr. Ward made many radical changes in his own teaching techniques. All of the alterations paid off handsomely for Fred, for his classmates, and for Mr. Ward.

The following list describes a few of the adjustments devised by Mr. Ward:

1. Instead of lecturing from notes he'd written on file cards, Mr. Ward changed to outlining his lectures on ditto masters. Every morning he ran off about a dozen copies of the day's material. One copy automatically went to Fred. Others went to students who'd missed the class. Pupils who'd lost their own notes got replacements from the teacher's master file. Many youngsters requested sets of the mimeographed pages as a study guide for tests. By the end of the semester, Mr. Ward made his own lecture notes available in all of his classes.

2. In lecturing, Mr. Ward often gave names, dates, and other specific details that were not recorded in his outline. Since Fred was a very poor speller and made many reversals when writing dates, the teacher devised a two-part system. When first introducing an important name or date, Mr. Ward wrote it on the blackboard and on a file card he kept at his podium. The entire class was expected to record the information in a special section of their notebooks. As a backup measure for the learning-disabled boy who couldn't copy accurately, one of the girls in the class always used carbon paper to make a second list. At the end of each class, she gave Fred a reliable copy of all the material on the board.

As the second part of his system, Mr. Ward dated and filed the card he'd used to record the list of details. Students who had been absent or lost their own notes found the teacher's file of the daily lists useful.

Mr. Ward soon noticed that Fred's class was doing better work than any of the other history classes he taught. Oral reading and discussions went more smoothly. Fred's classmates had very little trouble pronouncing and remembering difficult names. Their test grades were consistently higher than those of Mr. Ward's other eighth-grade history classes. The daily information list was such an effective study aid that the teacher introduced this system also in all of his other classes.

3. During movies and film strips, Mr. Ward routinely jotted down the main ideas so that they could be discussed, reviewed, and included in tests. Normally, he expected his students to make their own record of the important facts. But Fred couldn't take notes. To help the LD student, Mr. Ward had to devise an altered system.

First, during the presentation, the teacher made his own notes on a ditto master. By running off duplicates, he always had a good set of notes available for Fred. Then, since he had the material already available anyway, the teacher went one step further and used it as a lesson in note-taking for the entire class.

Immediately after a film concluded, Mr. Ward would announce, "That movie had one major subject, three main points, and twenty-three important details. Check your notes and see what *you* have."

After the students counted up their record of the topics presented, the teacher led a point-by-point discussion.

"What was the major subject?" he asked.

Pupils volunteered answers until there was general agreement.

Mr. Ward continued, "What was the first main idea?"

After that was answered, he challenged, "There were eight important details about that one main idea. What were they?"

Students called out the points they had listed in their notes. Groaning over their defeats, proudly smiling with their triumphs, the students always made the discussion very lively. Even Fred participated actively.

At the end of the class, each pupil was given a copy of the

teacher's notes to compare with his own. No grades or scores were ever given.

What had started out as an adjustment to help one LD student survive became a technique that helped an entire class.

4. To get away from writing daily assignments on the blackboard, Mr. Ward handed out a weekly homework sheet every Monday. In addition to relieving Fred of the difficult copying task, it also allowed him to get a head start on long reading assignments that he couldn't complete in one night.

Major reports, tests, and projects were assigned well in advance. Week by week, the sheet reminded students to prepare for big assignments.

Mr. Ward found this technique to be such a time-saver that he immediately put all of his classes on a weekly assignment program.

5. Fred had a major problem with attention. His mind constantly drifted off into daydreams during class. To keep the youngster's attention focused on the work at hand, Mr. Ward saw to it that the boy took an active part in all discussions. If Fred's hand went up, he was always called on. If Fred's hand didn't go up, he was often called on anyway. (For some LD children, that would be a cruel torture. Since Fred loved to talk and knew a lot about history, it was an effective and reasonable technique to use with him.)

6. Once a week Fred and his history teacher had a fifteen-minute conference.

The time was mainly used as a way to keep Fred organized. He and his teacher looked over the assignment sheet and checked off the work he'd already done. Then he reported on his progress with special projects or preparations for a large test. Mr. Ward approved, advised, prodded, made suggestions, wrote a note to his pupil's parents, requested some special piece of material from the library—whatever was needed. He helped Fred organize the notes and lists that had accumulated over the last week. Anything that was missing was replaced from the file.

Mr. Ward did not start having weekly conferences with all of his eighth-graders. But he did find that if he left his room and his files open, many students came by to organize their own materials.

How is it that Mr. Ward succeeded where four other teachers failed? He was willing to change more than materials and assignments. He went to the core of his program and altered his teaching techniques. Most teachers are very reluctant to change their instructional methods.

"Teaching techniques" must not be confused with "teaching styles." There are many sound basic instructional techniques. They are easily adopted, adjusted, and discarded. Finding a new way to teach the same old thing can add an invigorating element of excitement and challenge to a class. Varying instructional methods helps fight boredom in both students and teachers. Creative teachers tend to have an open-minded, experimental attitude toward teaching techniques.

That is not the case with teaching styles. Personal teaching styles differ widely. But always, they are a reflection of the entire individual. When a teacher tries to imitate the words, behavior, and attitudes of some other person, she is likely to make herself and her students uncomfortable.

Julia was a highly intelligent college senior doing her learning-disabilities internship under my supervision. She was a very pleasant and agreeable person but definitely had an honest, up-front, straight-from-the-shoulder approach to life.

The first time I observed Julia teaching a one-to-one lesson, she used a variety of acceptable LD techniques. But her teaching style didn't fit her personality at all. In presenting material to her fourteen-year-old student, she treated him as though he were a baby. Smiling and talking in a little high-pitched voice, Julia praised his good work by cooing, "Oh, you did a wonderful job on that, Walter. I'm so proud of you. And it was hard, too, wasn't it . . . "

The intern's behavior puzzled her student. He glanced at me, rolled his eyes, and shook his head.

Not noticing her student's discomfort, Julia went on and on. ". . . As a reward for doing such good work today, I'm going to let you play this special game. Doesn't that look like fun? . . . "

I couldn't stand it. I left the room. The poor teen-ager had to stay and put up with it.

Later, when we discussed what I had observed during her lesson, I bluntly asked the intern, "Why were you doing all that gushing?"

Julia understood immediately. "I thought I was *supposed* to do that," she replied.

"You treated a teen-age boy like a seven-year-old."

The intern looked tremendously relieved. "You mean I don't *have* to do that?"

"Certainly not. Whatever gave you the idea that you did?"

"All the teachers I've observed treated their pupils that way. So I thought I had to do the same."

It turned out that Julia had observed in three LD classrooms. Two had been first-grade classes where the "oh-this-is-going-to-be-so-much-fun" attitude is common and acceptable. Within the clinic, the girl had observed one of our finest master therapists. Mrs. Collins was an old pro in her 60's. With a wonderful, warm smile and a deep Southern drawl, she addressed everybody as "Honey," "Dahlin'," "Sweetheart," or "Sugah." The director of the clinic, the psychologists, secretaries, and other therapists—Mrs. Collins gushed over everybody. It was just her way. From Mrs. Collins, the constant, effusive sweetness was real. Students of all ages loved it and responded well. From Julia, it came across as phony, and her student hated it.

Teachers who explore adjusted teaching techniques must guard against the tendency to revise their teaching style in the process. A new instructional method may feel awkward or strange for a while. But an altered instructing style that does not fit the individual teacher's temperament will feel uncomfortable always. When a teacher feels that she's putting on an act, she is probably using an unsuitable teaching style that does not allow her to express herself honestly.

Change the Form, Not the Content

In making adjustments to help LD students succeed in regular classrooms, teachers always apply the same general principle: change the form, not the content. To alter instructional methods, teachers change *how* they teach, not *what* they teach. Adjusted teaching techniques make it possible for the learning-disabled student to learn the content of the material without having to rely on weak skills in reading, writing, copying, and spelling.

Keep all directions clear and simple.

Rather than: John, today is the day we solve your problem with the numbering on your spelling test. Instead of numbering your paper before we take the test, I want you to try a new method. I really think it will help if you write down the numbers as we go along. That way you'll get the right number for each word. You won't get mixed up because all you'll have to do is write down what I say. I think this will be a lot easier for you. Don't you think it will help? . . .

Say: John, don't number your paper now. As I give the test, you put the numbers when you hear me say them. Today, you write the numbers, with the words, during the test.

Essentially, that's *one* message said three different ways: first as a command, then with the detailed instructions, and last as a summary. That's not a good conversational technique with spouse and friends. But, in the classroom, speaking to LD children, to give the same message in three different forms can be very effective. (It's important to notice that the child didn't get an explanation of "why." When he finishes the test, has all his numbers correct, and looks up at the teacher with the "Wow" of success, he'll totally understand why he was told to do it.)

Explaining the assignment is only the first step in a three-step process. At this point, words are used to tell the child what to do.

Working a sample for the child is the second stage. By doing this, the teacher shows the child what to do. (At the end of the example, the pupil is usually nodding and smiling. "I got it. I got it.")

To really imprint the idea on the student's memory, the third step requires him to do a sample for himself. The LD youngster often forgets what he hears and sees. But once he has done something for himself and gotten the feel of it, he usually remembers.

The LD student's organizational difficulties are overcome by clear and simple directions. His tendency to forget what he's supposed to do will be overcome by the three-step approach: *tell* him, *show* him, have him *do* it.

Avoid giving multiple assignments.

When presented with more than one type of study activity at a time, the LD youngster is likely to become confused. Directions for one segment get mistakenly applied to another. Much is merely forgotten.

If a learning-disabled student is required to do three separate worksheets, he needs to have them explained to him one by one as he does them. Even when all the work is totally routine, problems arise in shifting from one type of thinking to another.

Avoid techniques based on sequencing.

Many good teaching techniques are based on the fact that the human mind can remember a surprisingly long series of things—as long as they're always kept in a particular order. For most people, sequencing is a memory aid. Many of our most commonly used instructional methods help the student learn by taking advantage of this natural ability.

Ron was having trouble mastering long division. After working a few problems with him, his teacher gave him the standard gimmick that is supposed to help all children keep the process straight: "It's just five steps that you do over and over. It's divide, multiply, subtract, compare, bring down—divide, multiply, subtract, compare, bring down. All you have to do is get those five steps into your head, and you've got it."

Even at the junior and senior high level, LD students often have trouble remembering winter, spring, summer, and fall in the right order. How are *they* going to be helped by a trick that requires them to keep any five words in a particular sequence?

It's bad enough when a teaching technique is based on sequencing. Many times an entire lesson is based on this skill. For learning-disabled children, such a task provides no real chance for success at all. They are simply not able to keep a complicated series of directions straight.

Avoid using techniques based on directional patterns.

Once a youngster gets beyond the age of playing Simon Says, it is assumed that he understands directions like up, down, left, right, under, over, beside, and around. Teachers often take patterns of directional moves and label them with words. This method helps most children master a new task.

For teachers who want to teach long division without relying on sequencing, there is another common memory trick. It is based on the use of directional patterns. "It's really a matter of working circles or big loops," children are told. "Starting with the number on the far left, you divide it into the one on its right. Then the answer goes up above, is multiplied by the number below on the left, is written at the very bottom, and goes down further when you subtract. So, you loop through the problem like this—left, right, up, around, down, down, compare, bring down."

It's such a simple little sweeping formation. The gimmick of movement patterns helps most children master the complex system of maneuvers involved in long division. For a child who can't tell a file cabinet's left side from its right, a technique based on right-left directions makes a difficult task impossible.

Sometimes the only known way to teach a particular skill involves the use of descriptions of directional movements. In such cases, teachers can adapt the method by showing the pattern with arrows instead of describing it with words.

Teaching young children manuscript and cursive writing is usually based on directional instructions. The most common technique teaches youngsters to "talk their way through" the process of forming a newly learned letter.

"To make a cursive capital J, you start on the line. Go up and around to the left, down below the line, around, and back up and around." After demonstrating once or twice, the teacher tells the child, "Say it with me as we do it together." In unison they form the letter while saying, "Up, around, downnnnn, around, up, and over." It's an effective method for most children. For the learning disabled, it doesn't work. They get lost in all the words. LD specialists teach writing by telling the child where to start, showing him how to do it, then getting him to feel it. Sometimes they take the child's hand and guide him through the motions. Often they have him trace the movement pattern over and over. They rarely use words to explain the directions of the movements.

To teach a student to deal with maps, charts, graphs, football plays, gymnastics, dance steps, dissecting a frog, setting up a chemistry experiment, and a host of other activities, the standard method of instruction is based on verbally describing directional movements and patterns. This technique can be adapted by shifting away from telling and placing the emphasis on demonstrating. LD students can then learn the process through imitation.

Avoid instructional methods that require a great deal of independent work.

Within the regular classroom, the LD child seems an ideal candidate for the kind of individualized instruction in which all his work is specially designed for him. Teach him one-to-one. Have him work by himself on tailor-made assignments created specifically to meet his particular needs. It sounds wonderful. And, since individualized instruction is so much work for the teacher, we tend to think it is very good for the child. In the case of learning-disabled youngsters, that is not true.

Because of their problems with organization and attention, LD children almost always have trouble working independently. They do not do well with work that, although designed specifically for them, requires them to work unsupervised. Their minds wander. Often they never succeed in getting down to business at all.

On their own, learning-disabled students are usually not very productive. They need structure and firm guidance.

They thrive on the kind of close supervision that cannot be readily provided when their classwork involves a great deal of individualized instruction.

Spare the child the embarrassment of demonstrating his weakness in front of his classmates.

In classes other than reading, it is not necessary for all the students to read aloud. If an LD pupil volunteers to take a turn at oral reading, one of the shorter, easier passages is appropriate for him.

The annual spelling bee is usually unavoidable. Mercifully, learning-disabled students are almost always eliminated in the first few rounds.

Writing on the blackboard can be another awkward situation that is best avoided unless the youngster volunteers.

Publicly displaying their weaknesses makes LD children feel terribly ashamed. It also opens the door for wisecracks and unkind remarks from unsympathetic classmates. It puts all the students into a position where social problems are likely to develop.

Most learning-disabled students sit in class praying they won't be called on to read aloud or put something on the board. Wise teachers see to it that their prayers are answered.

Chapter XI

Adjustments in Testing

LEARNING-DISABLED STUDENTS constantly protest about unfair practices that make them fail tests. "I knew that stuff backwards and forwards; I just couldn't get it all on the paper," they complain. When faced with a failed test, it is common for LD pupils to insist that they *knew* the material, but some aspect of their disability made it impossible for them to demonstrate their knowledge. Either the questions were written in a way too difficult for them to read, or the test format caused them confusion, or they didn't have enough time to finish, or they couldn't record their answers in the form that was required, or there was something about the setting that was so distracting that they couldn't concentrate. When LD students do study, they often fail tests anyway.

For the pupil who can't read the words, or understand the directions, or record his answers accurately, an F means lack of success in dealing with the test itself. It says nothing whatever about the student's knowledge of the subject matter.

After two years of LD therapy, Jack entered the ninth grade full of determination and confidence. By the middle of the first semester, the youth was in danger of failing biology. Mrs. Richards, the boy's mother, went to the school for a conference.

The biology teacher, Miss Johnson, explained the situation to the student's mother. Jack had gotten an A+ for producing the best bug collection in the class. He had a perfect record with homework. He had passing scores on all his lab work, experiments, and classwork. But he had failed all four major tests. Altogether, his grades averaged out to a low D.

"With no big project to help him pull his grade up during the second half of the semester, I don't think Jack can make it," Miss Johnson concluded sadly.

Fortunately, Mrs. Richards understood her son and his learning disability. She asked to see the tests that were causing the problem.

All four proved to be very long, and the reading was extremely difficult. Surprisingly, Jack had managed to finish each of them.

With a reassuring smile, the teacher explained, "Because of his learning disability, I always give Jack extra time to finish his work—especially on tests."

Mrs. Richards spread the test papers on the table, then requested that the teacher help her analyze her son's mistakes. "He always has done poorly on tests," the mother commented. "But maybe there's something that makes these particularly difficult."

The teacher immediately replied, "The only thing that always costs him a lot of points is spelling." Miss Johnson picked up one of the papers to demonstrate her point. "The first section is fill-in-the-blank. Out of twenty questions, Jack missed twelve." She checked down his answers quickly. ". . . Seven were misspelled; five were totally wrong."

The student's mother tried to be diplomatic and hide her surprise, but still her eyebrows shot up just a bit. "If the answer is misspelled, you count it wrong?"

"Yes, of course." To the teacher the system seemed perfectly logical. She returned her attention to the test paper. "On the multiple choice, he usually does pretty well. Here he has twenty out of twenty-five. That's definitely okay."

Mrs. Richards nodded.

"On the true-false, he got fourteen out of twenty. That's not bad."

The mother agreed, then added, "Jack doesn't read with precise accuracy. He usually finds true-false questions difficult."

Miss Johnson went on, "Then on these last two sections, he did very poorly." The teacher pointed to a page covered with red circles and X's to mark the numerous errors. "On the three essay questions, it was possible to score fifteen points. Jack got five and a half. And on the labeling section, out of twenty points possible, Jack got six!"

"Jack is such a poor writer," the boy's mother said. "I'm surprised he did that well on the essays."

"Oh, he doesn't do that badly," Miss Johnson countered. "I can always tell that he knows what he's talking about." She indicated the first essay question as an example. "Here on this one, Jack got four points. His answer was *very* good. But since he made more than three errors in spelling, punctuation, capitalization, and so forth, he lost half his credit."

The teacher turned to the last page of the test. The paper was covered with a large picture of a frog. Long arrows pointed to twenty different parts of the animal. Miss Johnson scanned over the words Jack had written in the blanks at the ends of the arrows. "It was his poor spelling that made him get so many wrong on this part, too." She shook her head, then noted, "If he had spelled all the names correctly, he'd have gotten thirteen points for his labeling. As it is, he got six."

"I think Jack would have passed this test if he hadn't lost so many points because of his bad spelling," Mrs. Richards concluded.

The teacher agreed. "It's possible."

"Could you count it up and see?"

To satisfy the mother's curiosity, the biology teacher rescored the test without counting off for spelling. "If he hadn't made all those mistakes, he'd have gotten a seventy-three. That's not terrific, but it *is* passing."

"From a fifty-three to a seventy-three. That's quite a difference." Mrs. Richards sighed, then asked, "Why do you count off for spelling in a biology class?"

"It's department policy," came the simple reply.

Mrs. Richard made a sweeping gesture toward her son's failed test. "This F does not say anything about Jack's success in learning biology. All it says is that he can't spell!" She paused, then stated the crux of the issue. "Jack has a learning disability. It's not fair to fail him in biology because of his poor spelling."

Miss Johnson tried to be patient and sympathetic as she explained what she believed to be a hopeless situation. She talked about high standards, college preparatory programs, school policy, and the grading procedures used in the science department. Finally she suggested a possible solution. "Jack will have to make fewer spelling mistakes on his tests." She paused, looked up, then presented what she believed to be the only other alternative: "Or he'll have to study harder so he can make up the points by doing better on the rest of the test."

The mother's voice was no longer totally sweet and calm. "He can't improve his spelling." Then, crisply, she pointed out the simple arithmetic of the teacher's suggested solution. "If he loses twenty points per test for spelling, a perfect paper with every single answer correct would only get him an 80! If he missed just ten questions, instead of a high B for a ninety, he'd just barely pass with a seventy!"

By this point, both women were very frustrated. Miss Johnson was irritated that this mother wanted her to lower her standards. She didn't believe in teaching some watered-down course and passing it off as biology. Mrs. Richards was disgusted with a system that cheated her son out of what success he could achieve. She was tired of fighting the same old battle. She was tired of well-meaning teachers who simply did not understand what the system did to crush LD children.

After a minute, Mrs. Richards quietly asked, "Would it be possible for you to give Jack two grades on his biology tests—one for his answers, and one for his spelling?"

The teacher shook her head. "I'm sorry, but I couldn't do that."

Still the mother persisted. With careful, polite control she asked, "Would it be possible for the head of your department to give you permission to do that?"

Despite the cool tone of her voice, the teacher still maintained a cooperative attitude. "Yes," she said. "He would have the authority to make such a decision."

Gradually Miss Johnson and Mrs. Richards resigned themselves to the fact that they could not resolve the problem. The teacher provided Jack's mother with photocopies of the boy's four failed tests, along with the name and phone number of the department head.

The mother and the teacher managed to part on friendly terms. It was obvious that Jack's parents were *not* going to stand idly by and let their LD son fail biology because he couldn't learn to spell the names of the parts of a frog.

It's been happening for years. Learning-disabled children often flunk tests covering material they truly have mastered. Even when LD students fail because they did not try, their lack of effort is usually a direct result of a system that allows them no chance for success.

To be fair, tests must be designed to let the pupil show what he *has* learned in the subject being evaluated. Teachers must guard against test situations that merely provide another proof of the LD child's deficits in the basic skills.

A few simple guidelines can help teachers make test adjustments that are both practical and fair.

1. Because the LD child's material was adjusted or adapted, he may not have been exposed to all the information presented to the rest of the class. It is not fair to test him on points that were never presented to him in assignments or discussions.

An adjusted test is easily created by omitting or striking out inappropriate items on the LD student's copy of the test, then adjusting the scoring accordingly. All questions that are deleted should be clearly marked on the pupil's paper *before* the examination begins. Crossing them out is more effective than merely circling their numbers.

2. Because the learning-disabled student reads slowly, he is rarely able to finish a test in the normal time allowed. It is often most practical simply to shorten his test by crossing

out some of the questions. This method saves the youngster from the social pressure that makes him want to hurry and finish so that he can appear to be just like everybody else. It also spares him the embarrassment caused by adjustments that single him out and make him look different.

Some teachers allow the student himself to decide which parts shall be omitted. If the examination is made up of several sections, they get the pupil to select entire sections to be skipped. (For instance, on his biology test, Jack would have been wise to skip the essay questions and the labeling.) In some cases, it's more practical to have the pupil select a certain number of pages to be omitted. (For instance, on a six-page social studies test, an LD student might be told to do *any* three pages.)

There are several ways to shorten a test without adjusting it to accommodate a student's weaknesses. The child can be told to do a certain portion of the questions in each part. Or he can merely start at the beginning of the test and work straight through until he runs out of time. When using these approaches, the questions that were not attempted are not counted off. (For example, if an LD student answered the first sixty-eight questions on a one-hundred-item ex-amination, *his* grade would be based on how many he got correct out of the sixty-eight he tried. His test would be cut down in size by thirty-two questions.)

The most common method of adjusting a test to fit the slower work pace of LD students involves giving them extra time. Unfortunately, this approach is almost always ineffec-tive. The extra time allowed is usually just a token!

Teachers often say, "I let him have as much time as he needs." Usually that means, if the child will ask for more time, he may have it. Also, it normally means the student has permission to stay in his place and keep on working. No matter what goes on in the classroom—noise, children

moving about the room, changing classes, the teacher starting a different lesson—he'll be allowed to keep on working
on his test through it all. Unless the teacher can see to it
that an LD pupil is provided with adequate time *in an
appropriate environment*, she should use some other method
of adjusting a test to fit his slower pace.

3. Because most learning-disabled children are poor readers, the pressure of a test can make even the easiest material
too difficult for them. Special provisions need to be made
for a youngster who has trouble reading *any* of the words
on a test. If the child needs to ask, "What's that word?"
someone should be readily available to help. The "good
neighbor policy" can be effective during tests, as long as the
LD child does not require very much help.

An LD aide or volunteer is an especially appropriate person to provide an LD youngster with help during a test. It
is also common for the LD specialist to become involved in
assisting with examinations. When a learning-disabled pupil
is going to need assistance on a particular test, the special
education department and the LD teacher can usually be
relied on to help the teacher make suitable arrangements. It
is *not* practical for the classroom teacher to assume this role
herself. She cannot adequately supervise the rest of the class
while she is out of the room reading test questions for one
of her pupils. Helping the child within the classroom doesn't
work well, either. All the talking involved disturbs the other
children and makes the LD student feel embarrassed.

A cassette tape recorder makes the ideal reader for an LD
child during tests. A recorded version of the test can be
played through a headset to allow the pupil to work independently while remaining within the classroom.

In two years of LD therapy, Joel had overcome almost all of his
reading problem and was doing fine in a regular sixth-grade class.

The boy had gotten to the point that he needed special adjustments only when taking tests. Like many LD students, when faced with an examination, the youth panicked and forgot all the skills he'd learned. Under the pressure of a test, Joel could not read material that would be ridiculously easy for him at any other time.

This sixth-grader did not need someone to sit at his elbow and struggle through every part of a test with him. He was ready to work independently. But he did need something to give him confidence. It was necessary to give Joel just enough help to get him past his panic so that he could use his own adequate skills.

With the help of a tape recorder and a student teacher, all of Joel's tests were read onto a tape casette. The boy had to take his exams in the classroom in the standard way. But, to help him with the reading, the cassette player and a headset allowed him to hear each question read aloud once.

It wasn't much help. But for Joel it was enough. Once he was certain that he knew what a question said, he had no trouble figuring out the answer.

Without the tape recorder, Joel's test grades were in the fifties and sixties. With it, he made B's and C's.

4. Because LD students have trouble writing, certain types of tests should be radically adapted or avoided altogether. Essay questions usually put the LD child at his worst possible disadvantage. As much as possible they should be avoided entirely. If a test segment that requires a great deal of writing simply cannot be omitted, then a method of adaption is essential. This can be accomplished through one of two basic approaches: (1) Keep the requirements of the essay format, but change the form from written to oral. The student would still have to present his answer in a complete set of well-structured paragraphs. But he would dictate his essay to the teacher, an aide, a volunteer, or a tape recorder. (2) Require the student to write out his own answer, but change the format so it doesn't have to be in the form of

carefully structured interlocking paragraphs. In a list or rough outline, the pupil would present the substance of what would be contained in an essay.

Learning-disabled youngsters also have trouble writing out definitions, answers that must be in complete sentences, or quotations from long memorized passages. Wherever possible, these should be eliminated or adjusted to fit the student's weakness in writing.

What kinds of test questions are best suited to learning-disabled pupils? Any type that keeps the need for writing down to a minimum. True-false, multiple choice, fill-in-the-blank, matching—all of these rarely require more than one word per answer.

5. Because some LD students have trouble with math, teachers must be prepared to adjust tests in other areas that may involve math. Many learning-disabled children have difficulty with science courses. Charts, graphs, and statistics sometimes make it difficult for them to succeed in social studies.

Margaret was a high school senior. She had never had trouble with reading, writing, or spelling. Math was her weakness. By counting on her fingers, she had reasonable skill with addition and subtraction. Multiplication was difficult for her because she had never been able to memorize the multiplication tables. And the girl could not do division at all.

In her high school physics class, Margaret did all right with everything except the problems that had to be solved mathematically. She could memorize the formulas. She could even set up equations. But she could not manipulate the numbers well enough to solve the problems and come up with correct answers.

The girl flunked her first two physics tests. Every single question that required mathematical computation was marked wrong.

After a conference with Margaret, the physics teacher adjusted the requirements of the girl's tests. The student no longer had to concern herself with working out the arithmetic and coming up with correct answers. For Margaret, using the proper formula and setting up the problem correctly was considered ample proof that she had mastered the material. This LD student's teacher understood that a wrong answer meant Margaret was not good at working math problems. It did *not* mean she didn't understand physics.

For the LD student with a disability in math, arithmetic errors should not count off on work outside math class. For the LD student with a language disability, spelling errors should not count off on work outside spelling class.

6. Because LD youngsters have trouble concentrating, they need a test environment that is isolated and quiet. They often find it impossible to tune out distractions for more than a few minutes at a time. Just knowing others are in the room can prevent them from keeping their attention focused on their work. From first-graders to college seniors, learning-disabled students often need to be provided with a small private place where they can take tests.

The library is *not* the ideal spot. What's needed is a place where the student can be alone. And the smaller it is, the better.

One resourceful LD teacher converted her elementary school's book storage room into a special quiet place for LD students to use when taking tests. Floor to ceiling, all four walls shelved textbooks. Carpeted, air conditioned, and windowless, the tiny room was totally private and soundproof.

LD children were allowed to use the book room for taking tests. It was an ideal spot when used individually by those who did examinations orally with cassette tape recorders.

Many of the teachers felt uncomfortable inside that small, windowless little cubicle. None of the children showed any reluctance to use it. They seemed to find it safe and cozy.

*   *   *

A huge old high school building had a strange three-room suite of chemistry laboratories. In the most inaccessible and least used of these rooms, there were two "gas chambers" that looked like isolation booths used on TV quiz shows. Although they were created for use in experiments requiring special ventilation, they were also soundproof.

When an LD specialist was first assigned to this high school and asked for special areas where LD students could take tests, the science department chose these two chambers as the private places they would use when LD students took tests. The English department adopted a tiny workroom off the library as their isolation area for LD students. The math teachers used the office assigned to the head of their department. All over that antiquated building, little nooks and crannies were set up as test booths for learning-disabled pupils.

But the gas chambers in the science department were the ones the students liked best. Even when taking tests in other subjects, they tried to reserve a space in what they jokingly referred to as "The Inner Sanctum."

Learning-disabled children do not always outgrow their distractibility. At all ages, they need special adjustments to help them perform well despite their problems with concentration.

7. Because they have trouble understanding and following directions, LD students need to have test instructions carefully explained to them one section at a time. (This calls for use of the three-step process: tell him, show him, have him do one for himself.) Thus, the teacher gets the pupil started off on the first part. But then the question arises,

who will help with the directions of the other sections of the test if they're to be explained as the youngster gets to them?

If the child is taking his test outside the classroom, he will have to have someone to go to for help at the end of each segment of the test. More than likely, the teacher will assume this responsibility while supervising the others taking the exam. The student could also get help from the LD teacher, an aide, a volunteer, the librarian, or even the school secretary. The child simply needs someone to go over the directions with him at the beginning of each new segment of work.

When an LD pupil takes a test in the classroom, his "good neighbor" can explain directions as needed. When the "good neighbor policy" is allowed during tests, both children must understand clearly the types of problems they are permitted to discuss. Generally, the helper will be permitted to assist with three kinds of questions: "What are we supposed to do?" "What's that word?" "How do you spell———?" If the student has other types of difficulties, he'll have to consult the teacher.

8. Because learning-disabled youngsters become easily lost on a printed page, certain types of tests confuse them and put them at an unfair disadvantage.

In administering standardized tests, schools find it less expensive to provide children with answer sheets so that the test booklets can be used year after year. Standard form sheets full of circles or squares are easier to check. Often they're even machine scored. They are efficient for the teacher, but can cause an LD pupil great difficulty. Some learning-disabled children cannot keep their place among the little spaces numbered to match the questions. Skipping lines by mistake, putting some answers in the wrong column, marking two in the same place—there are a variety of ways in which LD students make a mess out of an ordinary answer sheet. Allowing LD children to record their answers directly in the test booklet saves everybody a lot of time and annoyance.

Occasionally teachers concoct an examination that has a truly unusual and complicated format. Matching tests with as many as forty or fifty items are sometimes used. Once in a while a student is required to flip back and forth between different pages or sections of items. Questions presented in confusing forms or formats make it impossible for the learning disabled to demonstrate their knowledge of a subject.

An ingenious test was created by a teacher who was tired of always doing the same old stuff with her seventh-grade English classes. She knew its complex structure would give Wayne difficulty. As the boy's LD teacher, I acted as his helper when he took the test.

On the first page, there was a short story. The directions at the top merely said, "Read the story below." Wayne did that silently with no difficulty.

Page two was a solid mass of fill-in-the-blank comprehension questions on the story. My student got tired of flipping back and forth to find answers and copy words. With patience and determination, he managed to do it on his own.

The real fun began on page three. Directions covered the top, blank lines filled the bottom, and the middle was divided into three columns. First we were told to go back over the story on page one and underline all the verbs. After that was done, each of the verbs was to be copied into one of the columns. The descriptive active words went into Column A. Those that were just regular active were to go into Column B. And the last column was for those that were passive or showed a state of being. It nearly drove Wayne crazy. He'd find a verb on the front page and decide what type it was. Then he'd reread the directions on page three to see which column was for that category. By the time he was ready to choose the column, he'd forgotten the word. In the process of going back to find it, he'd forgotten where to put the answer. In desperation, he asked me to help.

My job was to remember the word while he struggled to figure out what to do with it. Wayne read, ". . . the old man sputtered. . . ." Without glancing up, he instructed me, "Okay, you remember sputtered."

I jotted the word down.

Mumbling under his breath, my student made the decision that the word was active. "But is it descriptive?" he asked himself. "Descriptive active or regular active?" In order to refresh his memory on the difference between the two, he reread the examples. "If it says, 'He bounded across the porch,' that's descriptive. If it says, 'He walked . . . ' that's just plain active." Suddenly he paused, looked up at me, and questioned, "What was the word?"

"Sputtered."

"Sputtered— Yeah, sputtered." Then he returned to thinking out loud. "The old man sputtered or the old man said. . . . It's gotta be descriptive." Looking at me again, he asked, "Sputter?"

"Sputter*ed.*"

"How do you spell it?"

We got through it and Wayne did well. But the process was sheer agony.

For the other students in the class, this clever test was a pleasant break from the routine. They completed it successfully in one fifty-minute class period. For Wayne the test was fiendishly difficult. It hit at all his weaknesses. Even with a trained professional helping him, it took the LD student more than two hours to complete this routine test.

Some test formats require a child to use skills he does not have. If some other method of examination cannot be arranged, then the teacher must consider it her duty to provide the LD pupil with a professional helper. Guiding a learning-disabled student through a test that he finds complicated and confusing is *not* a job for an amateur.

Chapter XII

Adjustments in Grading

SALLY HAD ALWAYS had trouble with math. In grades one through five, she was in the bottom group of the lowest track. She could read and write and spell. She was sweet and cooperative. But no matter how hard her teachers tried, they couldn't seem to help her learn arithmetic.

Sally's family moved to a different state. The girl's new school used a math program that was totally individualized. The students were assigned work at their own level. All work was graded pass/ fail. Report card grades simply indicated how quickly the pupil was progressing through his individualized arithmetic lessons.

Since Sally was a hard worker, she faithfully completed all the material assigned her. It was nowhere near sixth-grade level; but at the end of the year, the math grade on her report card was an A.

That summer the family moved again. Sally's application was submitted for entrance into a private country day school. The prospective student and her parents went in for an admissions conference with the school's headmaster. When asked about their daughter's academic record, the parents produced her sixth-grade report card. A solid year of very high grades attested to the fact that Sally was an excellent student. Except for math, that was a true picture of the girl's performance in school.

The parents carefully explained their daughter's good grade in sixth-grade arithmetic. "All it means is that she finished the book." They made it clear that Sally was *not* good at math.

The headmaster nodded, assuring them the child would be placed in an appropriate class.

When her new private school began, Sally was assigned to the top seventh-grade math class. It was pre-algebra. She lasted about three days! Recognizing the error in their judgment, the school moved her down to a regular class. She did better. But after a few weeks she began falling behind. During the sixth week of school,

Sally was switched again. This time she was put into the low math group where she should have been placed in the beginning.

Because of that one deceptive A, the new kid in town had to deal with the embarrassment of looking stupid in front of three different groups of her new schoolmates. And, after only a month and a half of school, she was already behind the other students in the lowest math class.

The teacher who gave Sally that A in math had not done the girl a favor!

A single letter grade cannot give a fair indication of a learning-disabled child's progress in school. A student can be making phenomenal progress while working far below grade level. An A would indicate his great attitude, excellent work, and strong improvement. But it would imply superb work at or above grade level. Such a mark would not be fair to the youngster, his classmates, or his next teacher.

Failing a child when he is doing the very best he can is equally unfair. An LD child who is far below grade level shouldn't be given D's and F's when he's working hard and making good progress. Any success he achieves deserves a reasonable reward.

Arthur had an adjusted and adapted spelling list. His classmates did twenty words a week out of a sixth-grade book. Most of them spent about fifteen minutes a night on their spelling. Arthur had eight words a week from a third-grade book. He struggled to master two a night. To pass his weekly test, Arthur spent at least forty-five minutes on spelling every night.

The system was working. Arthur passed all his Friday tests with at least an 80%. The youngster was delighted by his accomplishment. For the first time in his life, he was highly motivated.

At the end of the first marking period, Arthur's report card had a D − for spelling. The boy was crushed. When his mother came in for a conference, the teacher sweetly explained, "He can't do sixth-grade spelling at all. I really *should* have given him an F. But I just couldn't flunk a child who is trying so hard."

The mother took the matter up with principal, supervisors, and several high-level administrators. The school system felt that the teacher was being exceedingly generous to give Arthur any kind of a passing grade.

There was nothing anyone could do. No matter how hard Arthur worked, the best grade he could possibly get would be a D —.

Or he could quit trying.

The boy gave up. But, in the traditional pattern of failure, he did not merely give up in spelling. It started there but gradually spread to include a very special hatred for his teacher, serious behavior problems, total lack of interest and effort, failure in all his subjects, and finally a two-week expulsion from school for stabbing another student with a fork.

Arthur was not a "bad" boy. But for him, the sixth grade was a very bad year.

Standard grading and reporting procedures simply do *not* fit the needs of teachers trying to give an honest evaluation of a learning-disabled student's progress. Three adapted methods are available. None of them is ideal.

1. The double grade

It is often possible to give two marks for different aspects of the same work. Rather than combining effort and progress along with level of achievement, the two can be kept separate. A fifth-grade LD youngster who is working hard and having good success with his adjusted assignments at third-grade level would perhaps get a B for effort and progress. The level of difficulty would be indicated separately from his grade. In the appropriate box on his report card, he would get a B/3.

LD children are not very fond of this method. It seems to remind them that they're not quite like everybody else. But at least it *is* fair. And it's honest.

An alternate method of using the double grade allows teachers to separate form from content. For the LD pupil who wrote his own papers, B−/D+, A/D−, C+/F accurately describes knowledge of the subject (top or left) and quality of presentation (bottom or right). The double grade can also fit the situation when an assignment has been drastically adapted. On a tape-recorded term paper, a logical mark is C−/0 or B+/LD. The 0 or LD clearly indicates that only the content can be fairly evaluated.

Another alternative for the double grade enables teachers to honestly state the level of achievement without judging effort or progress. A seventh-grader with third-grade reading skills might be marked 3/LD. Such a grade makes no comment on the student's progress yet explains the reason for his low achievement level.

2. The nongrade

Sometimes it is impossible to give any kind of evaluation of an LD student's performance in a particular subject area. Fifth-grade report cards often have a blank where teachers are to grade the quality of the cursive writing students use in doing their regular classwork. LD pupils at that age are often just beginning to learn cursive and aren't yet competent enough to use it at all in class. Rather than giving an F (which wouldn't be true), or a 0 (which wouldn't be fair), the teacher can either leave the place blank or enter LD.

Some schools will not allow teachers to use double grades. Without such a system, it is impossible to give learning-disabled children honest marks in subjects such as reading, spelling, math, high school English, or any others that have been heavily adjusted. When the double grade is impossible, the nongrade is the reasonable alternative. In the blank beside the course in question, instead of a letter or number, the teacher can put LD. The parents will understand, the child will understand, and next year's teacher will understand.

3. The written report

A fair explanation of a learning-disabled youngster's progress in a subject can usually be presented in one concise paragraph. It allows the teacher to be both fair and honest. Unfortunately, it takes a great deal of time to produce good written reports.

For those teachers willing to write out an explanation of a student's progress, a typewritten statement can be stapled to the regular report card. Each page should have a basic heading stating student's name, his grade placement, subject being evaluated, current date, and the teacher's name. One paragraph should be written to cover each of the basic subjects.

Each paragraph should clearly and specifically name the child, name the subject, then evaluate attitude, effort, material covered, homework record, test scores, concepts mastered, adjustments made, and special difficulties. The grade level at which the student is working can be included when known and applicable.

Sample A

Carl has been working very hard in his sixth-grade spelling class. With a weekly list of five words from the third-grade book, he has passed all but one test with a grade of 80% or better. He has failed to bring in his homework only twice. Carl finds it especially hard to locate the words in the glossary and break them into syllables. He has mastered saying the alphabet in order and is having good success in learning to alphabetize. Overall, I'm pleased with Carl's progress in spelling.

Sample B

Helen has been neglecting her work in our seventh-grade math class for the past six weeks. Out of thirty-two homework assignments, she failed to bring in eleven of them. She is often inattentive and uncooperative in class. Despite daily help one-to-one, Helen is still unable to do long division. Through the use of a new game, she has made some real progress in mastering multiplication. She can now multiply three-digit numbers by two-digit numbers. We have not yet begun to work on carrying. On tests, she passes the sections on addition and subtraction. Helen has improved in working with decimals and fractions. Although she is not in a regular math book, she is now working successfully on about a high fourth-grade level.

Whether or not teachers use the written report at the end of each marking period, it should be considered a *must* at the end of each semester.

Adjusted Scoring Systems

To simplify scoring and grading, teachers try to devise tests and assignments that work out to an even one hundred points.

Many assume that adjusted assignments throw the whole system off. That's not necessarily true. By using a variation of the normal system, teachers can get adapted work to yield normal percentage scores.

If Jack's biology teacher had omitted the essay questions from his test, she'd have removed a section worth 15 points. Thus, if the boy had turned in a perfect paper, he'd have gotten 85 points. This figure is the new *adjusted total* of points possible, and it becomes the bottom number of a fraction: /85. Adding up the points for correct answers gives the top number. If Jack got 63 answers right, his adjusted score is computed by putting the 63 over the 85 to make the fraction $^{63}/_{85}$. Dividing the top number by the bottom one (63 ÷ 85) gives an answer that tells what percent Jack got right on his adapted test. The resulting 74% (rounded off) could be entered in the grade book as is. It could also be converted to a letter grade.

No matter what the method used to alter the assignment, the basic principle of adjusted scoring always remains the same: How many were possible? How many did this child get right? Make a fraction with correct answers on top and number possible on the bottom. Divide out the fraction. The result is a percentage score.

Most children do a twenty-word spelling list every week. Since a perfect score is 100%, the twenty words count five points apiece ($5 \times 20 = 100$). If a child's list is cut to ten words, they count ten points each ($10 \times 10 = 100$). If the student has only five words to learn, they are worth twenty points each. One misspelled word on the test gives a grade of 80%. Missing only two words means a failing 60%. The fewer words on the list, the more points each one counts.

A custom-designed spelling program was used with a class of learning-disabled eighth-graders. Each week the class had a list made up of twenty words. Numbers one through five were always very easy. The next five were more difficult, but still part of the elementary basic sight vocabulary. Numbers ten to fifteen were more challenging. And the last five were on or above eighth-grade level. From this weekly set of twenty words, every student was assigned his own personal list.

Three boys with severe problems in spelling were assigned only the first five easy words. Those who were not so severely disabled were given the first ten. Those who had already mastered the basic sight words were assigned numbers one through fifteen. Two very bright students with no problems in the language area had the whole list every week. For them, numbers fifteen through twenty provided a challenge, and the first fifteen acted as review.

The class had thirteen students each working on his own version of the spelling list. Yet it was not at all difficult to administer and grade the weekly test. When the children numbered their papers, each wrote down only the numbers for the words he had studied. Everybody had the first five. Some had been assigned the first seven, or the first twelve. A few had truly personal lists composed of a combination from the different categories of difficulty. At the top of his test paper, each pupil also put a number between one and twenty to indicate how many words were assigned him for that week.

To grade the tests, the teacher used the fraction method to get a percentage score. After a few weeks she devised an even easier system using a conversion table (see below). Even with such a highly specialized and individualized spelling program, marking and scoring weekly spelling tests was not at all difficult.

The teacher in the above story had a copy of the following chart taped to her desk. For scoring assignments that have twenty items or less, it is an even faster system than the fraction method. It is important to remember that these figures are rounded off.

1 word = 100 points	11 words = 9 points each
2 words = 50 points each	12 words = 8 points each
3 words = 33 points each	13 words = 7½ points each
4 words = 25 points each	14 words = 7 points each
5 words = 20 points each	15 words = 6½ points each
6 words = 16 points each	16 words = 6 points each
7 words = 14 points each	17 words = 5¾ points each
8 words = 12 points each	18 words = 5½ points each
9 words = 11 points each	19 words = 5¼ points each
10 words = 10 points each	20 words = 5 points each

For example: in a list with seven words, the teacher counts fourteen points off for each mistake. A child who makes two errors gets a score of 72% (at 14 points each, the 2 errors equal 28 points off; 100 − 28 = 72).

When an assignment includes a total of more than twenty items, the above process gets far too complicated. Sometimes a more precisely accurate percentage score is desired.

For such situations, the fraction method is most practical. The child above got five right of a possible seven. The fraction ⁵⁄₇ divides out to be 71.42. The recorded score would be 71%.

Adjusted assignments make a revised grading system essential. Those discussed above are easy, fair, and objective.

Grades Can Be Good

Like everyone else, learning-disabled students need standards—something to measure themselves against as they strive toward real success. They need something that tells them how good is good enough. When the goal is attainable, aiming for the 100% of perfection is a challenge.

Some educators think a learning-disabled pupil should not be given grades. Many teachers believe that abandoning this routine practice makes the youngster *feel as if* he's succeeding. Eliminating grades does relieve the child of reminders of failure. But it also deprives him of the rewards for success.

Realistically, grades do not harm children. What hurts them is failure. Tricks that hide failure do not create success.

By adjusting the work of an LD pupil, teachers make it possible for him to succeed. Then grades put a twinkle in the child's eyes as they tell him of real success.

Chapter XIII

Adjustments in Homework

FUNDAMENTAL to all educational philosophy is the belief that formal instruction equips the individual to think independently. Thus schools are intended to do more than teach skills and transmit information. They are also responsible for systematically preparing the student to use his knowledge on his own. A person has not been successfully educated until he can apply his learning in the context of his own life.

The practice of assigning students schoolwork to do at home is a logical product of this philosophy. Through homework pupils develop skill in working independently.

Within actual classrooms, these lofty ideals tend to get lost. Many teachers no longer assign homework regularly. They have found the old traditional system of nightly preparation to be more trouble than it's worth.

Learning-disabled students can quickly kill a teacher's faith in any kind of homework program.

LD pupils usually don't do any homework at all. Everybody else works. They do absolutely nothing besides play, feel guilty, and cause trouble. Yet, even more than other students, LD youngsters need the benefits daily independent study can provide. They need opportunities to learn to be productive despite their tendency to be disorganized, unmotivated, and forgetful. They need that sense of accomplishment that comes from doing a satisfactory job on even the tiniest assignment. They need the feeling of self-confidence that comes from working successfully on their own.

The First Parent-Teacher Conference

Homework is schoolwork, assigned by a teacher, to be done at home, under the supervision of the parents. It directly involves both the home and the school. If an LD student is to succeed with his homework, there must be coordination and cooperation between the parents and the teacher. Mutual understanding must be developed from the very beginning.

During the first two weeks of school, the classroom teacher needs to have a formal conference with a learning-disabled pupil's parents. (The school's LD specialist should be included as well.) Through this meeting, the teacher takes the lead in establishing good communication between school and home. And she accomplishes three major objectives. First, she gains helpful information about the child and his previous school experiences. Second, she has an opportunity to explain general policies concerning the way she will run her class. Third, she and the parents can thoroughly discuss homework. Although it will be too soon for the teacher to give specific details on just how the youngster's homework will be altered, she should give the parents an idea of the general approach that will be used. The mother and father need to understand exactly how often their child will have home assignments. The teacher needs to understand just how much supervision and help the parents are willing and able to provide.

From the time their sons first entered school, the Dixsons were positive that both their boys had a specific language disability. Books and magazine articles confirmed their suspicions, but they couldn't get educators to do anything to help. As the father's work moved the family all over the country, the two boys were repeatedly tested in various clinics and schools.

When George was twelve and Bill was nine, they were finally diagnosed correctly and provided appropriate therapy.

Despite his severe learning disability, George had successfully passed grades one through five. He was in the midst of squeaking through grade six. As a third-grader, Bill was still a nonreader. Although always on the brink of total failure, the child had passed the first and second grades.

What success the boys had achieved was totally due to the efforts of their parents. For six solid years the Dixsons had devoted all their evenings to schoolwork. They hadn't merely helped their sons with homework. They had systematically retaught everything that had been done in school. Reading to them, recording their answers to questions, explaining, drilling, discussing, practicing, studying for tests—for all practical purposes, George and Bill were being educated at home. For all four of the Dixsons, "family life" meant schoolwork shared.

It took two years of LD therapy to get Bill and George to the point where they were capable of doing their own homework. Then it took another two years under the supervision of a psychiatrist to get the family to break away from their long-established pattern of spending their entire time together huddled over schoolbooks.

Even though it had been absolutely essential for them to become involved in their sons' studies, Mr. and Mrs. Dixson had found helping with homework to be habit-forming.

It is equally common to find parents of LD children who have either given up or never gotten involved with homework in the first place. There are also families who care very much and will provide encouragement and supervision, yet are not capable of supplying the type of assistance the child might occasionally need. Many LD children have LD parents. Before the teacher designs the system by which the child's nightly assignments will be altered, it is important to find out exactly what kind of assistance can be expected in the home.

Twelve-year-old Brad was the fourth of the Johnsons' six children. He and his three older brothers were all learning disabled. His two sisters were having no trouble with school, but they were in only the first and second grades.

Brad's parents had never been officially diagnosed, but it appeared that they, too, were learning disabled. Mrs. Johnson had to read recipes six or eight times in order to figure them out. She had dropped out of high school because of the trouble she had with reading comprehension. Mr. Johnson had dropped out of college because of his trouble with writing and spelling. The man once confessed to me, "When I'm on a business trip, I have to call my secretary to get her to spell words for me."

There were eight wonderful, warm, loving people living in the Johnson home. Every one of them was eager to offer Brad any kind of assistance he needed. But there wasn't a single one of them capable of helping him with his sixth-grade homework.

No matter how much or how little help is available for the child at home, teachers should adjust and adapt assignments so that learning-disabled students are able to do the majority of their homework on their own. In the first conference, parents should be encouraged to avoid any direct involvement in their youngster's nightly assignments. They should be guided to understand that their role is to provide an appropriate time and place to study, show interest, and offer encouragement or sympathy when needed. Other than that, they should stay out of the evening homework as much as possible.

Enabling the Child to Work Independently

In changing homework to fit the needs and limitations of an LD pupil, the teacher should concentrate on developing the child's reliability and independence. By making assignments in accord with the following guidelines, teachers can use homework to help a youngster develop independence, establish good study habits, and build self-confidence.

1. Carefully consider the attention span of the particular LD child. Under the very best of conditions, how long can he work at one stretch? In the controlled, quiet environment of the classroom, can he work for ten solid minutes on math? How many minutes of spelling can he do before his mind drifts off to something else? For young children it will probably be two to five minutes at best. For the older ones, ten minutes is usually about the maximum.

Find out how long he *can* concentrate, and start with that. The student may be given three or four different assignments in one night, but no single one should require a greater amount of working time than is contained in one of his short bursts of focused attention.

Keep in mind that for the learning-disabled child, doing homework includes getting organized. Five minutes worth of actual work takes ten minutes of finding papers, sharpening pencils, getting to the right page, figuring out directions, and so on. Changing from one subject to another means the student needs another ten minutes to get reorganized.

This first step sounds easy. Actually, it asks for a radical change in the way homework is selected and assigned. Teachers have always thought it's unfair if one student isn't required to do as much work as the others. This attitude is based on the idea that work must be measured by the number of pages read, problems done, or questions answered. The standard is set according to the size of the finished product rather than the amount of time involved in producing it. Thus, good students are rewarded for working quickly; and LD students are punished for working slowly. In a mere half an hour, the competent student can breeze through ten pages of social studies, write out the answers to the questions at the end of the chapter, have a snack, and go off to play with friends. In attempting the same assignment, the

LD student takes two agonizing hours to figure out half the words in the reading, write garbled answers to a few of the questions, have a tantrum, and go off to his room to sulk. Learning-disabled children have always known that a system that gives everyone assignments of equal size treats them unfairly. Teachers have to come to that same realization. Until teachers can shift away from the traditional method of measuring assignments, they're not in the position to make appropriate adjustments in the homework of LD students.

2. Be sure the student understands the directions and has two samples to copy (one that was done for him, one that he did himself). The LD student's unreliable memory means that today he knows how to carry in addition, tomorrow he may not. The fact that he did work like this in class every day this week does *not* mean he'll remember how to do it when he gets home tonight. A good set of directions and two samples give him a chance to figure out what to do when he forgets.

3. Be sure the student has the exact assignment written down correctly. Learning-disabled children have memories that leak. They *cannot* be trusted to remember their homework assignment. The most practical and effective way to work around this is to insist that they carry a small spiral notebook in their hip pocket at *all* times. Every home assignment must be recorded in this notebook. And someone must check to be sure that it was written down accurately (an ideal job for a "good neighbor").

Ricky was a darling fourth-grader with boundless energy and a thousand reasons why he didn't do his homework. Over a period of six weeks, I plugged most of the loopholes that were providing the youngster with excuses for not completing his nightly assignments.

Despite all my clever tactics, the child was producing homework only about once a week.

I got Ricky a small spiral notebook that he was to carry in his back pocket all the time. I explained to him that LD people need a "memory jogger." On the days when he did have it with him, I made him record his assignments in it. And those assignments usually got done. But as often as not, the little notebook got left at home in his other jeans. When that happened, the boy would dutifully write the various page numbers on a scrap of paper and stuff it into his pocket. Reminders done in that form usually got lost or forgotten.

At home, Ricky's mother was having the same problem. Night after night her son was unable to do any studying because he'd left his assignment book at school.

It looked as if Ricky were deliberately giving us the runaround.

In a long phone conversation, Ricky's mother and I came up with a wild solution.

Years of punishments had done nothing to get the boy to do his home assignments. We decided on a system of rewards. (My student's mother insisted on calling them "bribes.")

Ricky was trying to earn enough money to go to soccer camp. As much as possible, his parents were trying to give him lots of opportunities to earn extra money by doing things around the house. "Right now, that kid'll do anything for money," his mother explained.

We agreed to make a major issue out of the assignment notebook. Money would be the reward.

As Ricky walked out the door in the morning, if he had his spiral notepad in his pocket, his mother gave him a dime. When he got to school, he showed me the little spiral and got me to sign it. That signature was worth another dime. At the end of the school day, I checked to see that he had all his assignments accurately recorded. If he did, I signed again. That signature was also worth ten cents. He got the payoff for my two autographs by taking his assignment book home so that he could show them to his mother. Only fresh signatures produced money.

Ricky turned into a reliable little homework machine. He earned thirty cents a day every day for three weeks. At that point he'd reached his goal of financing his trip to camp. And the habit of carrying the memory jogger had been well established.

To maintain Ricky's new reliability with homework, I continued signing his notebook twice a day for the rest of the semester. For every week with ten signatures, his mother gave him an extra fifty cents allowance. Ricky earned lots of spending money for camp. And he learned to rely on a hip pocket notebook to make up for his unreliable memory.

4. When requiring practice or drill, assign only work that involves concepts the child has already mastered in class. If he's just learning a skill and is still having trouble with it, he should not work on it without supervision. If subtraction problems with borrowing always confuse him, he shouldn't be expected to tackle them alone. As much as possible, assign tasks with which he is nearly certain to succeed.

5. Give the child an escape route. Teachers will not always succeed in predicting accurately what an LD pupil is capable of doing on his own. It is especially hard to judge how long it will take him to do a particular task. When an assignment proves to be too difficult, the child needs a way to get out of the painful situation.

For children who can use a clock, a time limit is ideal. In the front of his notebook, the student should have a list of the maximum amounts of time to be allowed on each subject. If his routine study schedule includes fifteen minutes daily for spelling, the limit for that subject would be about twenty minutes. Any spelling assignment that took more than twenty minutes would be considered too difficult. After putting serious effort into the assignment for the full time allowed, the child would draw a line, write down the time spent, and *quit*.

For those who can't tell time (and that will be many of them, including a lot of the older ones), a phone call to the teacher offers escape in emergencies. The child may not know how long he's struggled with some task, but he does know when it's giving him trouble and he's had all he can stand. If the teacher is called at that point, the youngster can either get help with the assignment or get permission to give up. In the event that the teacher cannot be reached, the mother and father should have the authority to tell the child to stop work. In such situations, the parents would write a brief note of explanation to the teacher: "Jimmy spent a lot of time on his spelling and couldn't do it. I gave him permission to quit."

When homework becomes torture, students turn off. If an escape route lets them give up today, the chances are they'll come back and try again tomorrow.

6. Adjust the assignments in size, not quality. If, in five minutes' time, a child is capable of doing either ten easy math problems *or* five harder ones, sacrifice the quantity rather than the quality. Assign work that is challenging. Do not assign homework that is so easy that it's an insult to the child's intelligence.

7. Develop a pattern or routine. Learning-disabled youngsters thrive in structured situations. Doing the same old thing day after day does not bore them. In fact, it seems to make them feel secure.

In a self-contained LD class of fifth- and sixth-graders, our day always started with a highly structured session of LD therapy. We did half an hour of tracing, copying, and handwriting; twenty

minutes of phonetic practice and drill; forty minutes of word attack exercises and reading; and half an hour of dictation, proof-
reading, and correcting.

By midwinter, I found the routine to be deadly dull. I thought
of myself as some kind of lunatic who hung from the rafters
spouting phonics.

One gloomy Friday morning in late February, I indicated my
boredom to the twelve boys in my class. "Well, guys . . . " I groaned.
". . . you think you can stand it one more time?"

Bobby, one of my more outspoken students, tartly replied, "What
do you mean, 'stand it'? This is the best part of the day!"

The others immediately chimed in with their agreement. "Yeah,
we like this stuff."

"I'd rather do this than math."

"Ain't nothing about this that's so bad."

Even the older, more sophisticated twelve-year-olds indicated
that they found nothing at all objectionable about our morning
routine.

Until that moment, I'd never thought about it. But my boys
were right. Those two highly structured hours were the most productive part of our whole day.

It did feel good to have two hours every day when we knew
we would be successful.

In setting up a homework program for an LD student,
the more steady and predictable the routine, the better. Ten
minutes of math every night. (*Every* night means Monday,
Tuesday, Wednesday, and Thursday—not weekends.) Ten
minutes of spelling every night. Fifteen minutes of reading
every night. Ten minutes of science or social studies or health
every night. Help the student build up a system, develop a
rhythm.

In junior and senior high, teachers need to work together
to coordinate the homework assigned to learning-disabled
pupils. If a youth has five subjects—English, history, math,
science, and an elective—each teacher should agree to give

a certain amount of homework regularly. If each teacher held assignments down to a maximum of fifteen minutes per night, that would be an hour and fifteen minutes of work, plus organizing time. For older students, that's a reasonable amount of time for the daily homework routine. A combination totalling somewhat less would be suitable for younger children.

8. Eliminate copying entirely, and keep writing to an absolute minimum. In an unsupervised study situation, the LD student's weaknesses can make him so frustrated that he gives up in disgust. If it's necessary to assign some writing task, it's better to have him do it at school where someone is available to help him when he gets stuck, sympathize when he gets discouraged, and pick up the pieces when he blows up. Homework should increase learning, not frustration.

9. Always do something to recognize that the assignment was successfully completed. Homework does not always have to be collected or corrected. But at the time it is due, the teacher must at least scan it over, comment on its overall quality, and give the student credit in the grade book. Neglecting to give credit for home assignments gives the impression that they're not at all important. If their efforts aren't regularly recognized, LD children are very quick to turn off to homework.

Education courses teach that every piece of student work has to be corrected, scored, marked, and recorded in the grade book. If a pupil's paper isn't going to be looked over very carefully, it shouldn't be assigned.

There were lots of times when I didn't dare make an assignment. The students might have needed the work. But I couldn't handle any more papers to grade. It was especially difficult to teach expressive writing, where just one batch of essays produces a mountain of homework for the teacher. For years I was caught between what was best for my students and what was possible for me.

One fall I tried a revolutionary new approach with a class of LD seventh-graders. To develop their skill in expressive writing, they wrote a one-page essay every night. But—not all the papers they produced were corrected. In fact, most of them were never even read. As in music lessons, where the pupil spends an hour or so daily perfecting his technique, most of my students' nightly essays were considered "practice." At the beginning of class, they were collected, checked off in the grade book as completed, and thrown into the wastebasket. Once a week the essays were kept for careful evaluation, correcting, and grading.*

My LD students had some surprising reactions to this experiment. Only one part of the assignment gave the class trouble. Most of the students found it terribly difficult to think up suitable topics on such a regular basis. Some of them had to rely on the ideas that I provided daily. It made perfectly good sense to them that one would practice writing in much the same way one would practice the piano. The students never complained about having their work thrown away ungraded. As long as they got credit for having done the assignment, they were content. Also unexpected was their reaction to my choosing papers to keep. My teen-age pupils always responded enthusiastically when I announced, "The random selection machine says today's papers—these gems I now hold in my hand—will be graded." From the day our project began, the students never slacked off. Each night each pupil put maximum effort into producing an essay of good quality.

As a result of this daily writing program, the quality of the students' writing improved so dramatically that the pupils got a great deal of satisfaction out of the tremendous progress they were making.

10. Assign nothing that the child cannot complete successfully entirely on his own. If the social studies book is

---

*I am indebted for this idea to Daniel N. Fader and Elton B. McNail, *Hooked on Books: Program and Proof*, (New York: G. P. Putnam's Sons, 1968).

just barely within the youngster's level of readability, he might be using it successfully at school. But in the classroom he can use a "good neighbor" to help when he gets stuck on a word. Adjusted assignments that are realistic in the classroom are often too difficult for totally independent study.

When homework is done successfully, students get satisfaction from both the finished product and the process that created it. When assignments are designed to assure pupils' success, studying becomes a challenge with attainable, worthwhile rewards. In the hands of a wise teacher, nightly assignments can build the students' interest, confidence, and motivation.

Section Four

LET'S PRETEND that Al, the young wino I met on the river bank in Chapter I, could take us back to relive his experiences in school. In our imagination we can return to the first grade with him and let him show us what his days were like. In our mind's eye we can create a scene that will let Al guide us through one of his days in the fifth grade. Through the magic of fiction we can witness his classroom struggles as a learning-disabled teen-ager.

The journey back into the classroom with Al offers the reader an opportunity to witness three vital aspects of the learning-disabled child's failure to succeed in school: (1) Al clearly demonstrates almost all of the characteristics that are typical of the LD youngster. (2) Al's teachers demonstrate that standard classroom procedures are generally ineffective, if not downright destructive, for LD pupils. (3) Over the ten-year period of the three observations, Al's attitude toward himself and the world gradually deteriorates. As is the case with most of the learning disabled, Al's failure to learn causes him emotional damage.

Chapter XIV

For the LD Child, First Grade Isn't Much Fun

MOST OF THE CHILDREN were already in their seats when the bell rang to start the day. The teacher took her place behind her desk and waited for Al to finish hanging up his jacket on the coatrack at the back of the room. The boy stooped down, peeped into a grocery sack he'd brought with him, folded up the top of the bag, and carried it with him toward his seat.

The traditional greeting began the day. "Good morning, class."

"Good morning, Miss Dowell," thirty-four small voices chorused back.

Al was nearly up to his seat at the front of the room next to the teacher's desk, so roll call began. After the fifth name, Miss Dowell glanced up from her record book. She was not at all surprised to find that Al had gotten sidetracked on his way to his seat. The youngster was leaning over the cage of hamsters kept on the cupboard by the window.

"Al . . . " the teacher called gently.

The boy was so engrossed in tapping on the glass and talking to the furry creatures that he didn't seem to hear.

Miss Dowell called in a louder voice, "Al . . . "

Startled, the child looked over his shoulder. "Huh?" he grunted.

"Will you please take your seat. It's time for class to get started."

The youngster started toward his desk, returned for the

paper sack he'd left by the hamsters, stuck his face near the cage to whisper a parting word, and moved slowly toward his place.

Convinced that Al would actually reach the desired destination this time, Miss Dowell went back to taking the roll. She glanced up to see the boy nearing his chair. Encouraged by his progress, she resumed her morning routine.

But the child didn't stop at his seat. Al walked right by it, and on up to the teacher's desk.

"For lunch today, we have beef stew with . . . "

"I found this great big lizard down by the creek last night," a little voice piped right beside Miss Dowell's shoulder.

The teacher jumped with surprise, then turned to look straight at the child who had interrupted her. She wanted to pick him up by his scrawny little shoulders and carry him to his seat. But there was nothing there to grab.

Al was bending over to remove something from the brown bag. "I ain't never seen a lizard as big as this one. And he's a weird color, too—got all red around his head and back there where his tail is broke off. He must of lost that tail piece in a fight, but it'll grow back . . . " Rising with his prize displayed in a jar gently cradled in his hands, the child looked straight at his teacher. "Did you know lizards can grow new tails?" he asked.

He was stunned into silence by the glowering look in Miss Dowell's eyes.

"Al," she snarled in a dangerous low voice. "This is *not* the time for that. Put the lizard away and get into your seat."

The youngster started to say, "I just wanted . . . "

But the teacher cut him off. "Get into your seat, Al— NOW!"

The little boy's eyes watered up, and he swallowed hard. The whole room was deathly quiet as he very carefully put the jar back into the bag, folded the brown paper down securely over the top, and walked to his chair.

His teacher waited in silence, thinking how unfortunate it was that most of Al's days started off this way.

Once the announcements were finished, the morning's writing lesson began. As a warm-up exercise, each child printed the alphabet across the top of his paper. Miss Dowell moved around the class checking the papers. One by one the children got their star for the alphabet and began copying the day's special writing assignment that the teacher had neatly lettered on the board. Al was always the last to finish the alphabet. In fact, the teacher usually had to stand at his side and help him if there was to be any hope that he'd complete it at all. It was part of the daily routine.

Miss Dowell took her customary position next to the struggling youngster. "Al, you're doing well today. You're already up to the *o*, and you haven't got any letters in the wrong place."

The child was trying so hard to concentrate that he didn't even look up. His brows were furrowed, and his lips were set in a thin, straight, determined line. He clutched the thick first-grader's pencil in a vicelike grip.

"You want me to help you?" the teacher asked softly.

The tousled head nodded.

"Are you stuck?"

"Yeah. I can't figure out what comes next."

"Well, before we start, how about holding the pencil the way I showed you."

The boy's dirty fingers strained to find the "correct" position.

Taking the child's right hand, the teacher gently moved his thumb so that it no longer curled up over the top of the lower knuckles. "The way you hold it, it's a wonder you can write at all," she chuckled. She knew Al hated to hold the pencil properly. He'd often told her it didn't feel right. To-day he didn't complain.

A glance around the room assured Miss Dowell that the rest of the class was hard at work, so she pointed to the *o* on Al's paper and whispered, "Now, let's have a look. . . . You need to figure out what comes after *o*. Let's try the little song. That usually helps." Singing the a-b-c's in a low voice next to her student's ear, she got him started again.

Al's eyes lit up. "*P,*" he said in a voice just a little too loud.

There were a few chuckles and snickers from the other students. Miss Dowell stood up tall, surveyed the room sternly, and warned, "Class—you have work to do. And it doesn't require *any* noise." The quiet resumed.

Returning her attention to Al, the teacher found three letters had been added to his alphabet: *p*, *q*, and *u*. "Oh, Al, you're not stuck anymore. That's good."

The boy grinned.

"But one of those letters doesn't belong there. Let's do the little song again and you can figure out which one."

They tried the song twice. It didn't help.

Children were starting to move about the room as they finished their writing and looked for other activities. Miss Dowell glanced at the clock. It would be time to start read-ing soon.

Anxious that Al at least finish his alphabet, she told him, "The *u* doesn't go there. It's *p*, *q*, *r*, *s*. . . ." She helped Al struggle on through to *v*, while trying to keep an eye on the increasingly restless class.

By this time Al was feeling a great deal of pressure to finish. Quickly he slapped down the *w x y z*, then looked up with relief.

Miss Dowell scanned his messy paper, then took out her

red pencil. As she began marking the errors, she explained, "You make the corrections on these letters, and we'll let the rest of the assignment wait until recess."

The child sighed and slumped down in his chair. He hated it when he missed recess because he hadn't finished his work.

"Al—you're not listening."

The little boy looked up at his teacher. She'd been telling him something, but he hadn't heard. His mind had drifted off to thoughts of recess. And Miss Dowell knew it.

"Al, I'm trying to help you," she said in an impatient voice. "If you would just pay attention."

The boy returned his gaze to the handwriting paper in front of him. It now had bright red circles around four of the letters.

"You need to make these corrections, Al. Your *d*—it's backwards. See?" the red pencil pointed. "Your circle is on the wrong side. It looks like a *b*. Look down here next to the *a*. . . . This is your *b*. . . . Which side is the circle on?"

The youngster thought a minute, then ventured in a questioning tone, "The left?"

"Write a *b* for me here at the bottom," Miss Dowell instructed.

Al drew the straight vertical line, paused, glanced at the letter next to *a* in his alphabet above, then put the circle in its proper place.

"Now, which side did you put the circle on in order to make that lovely *b*?" the teacher asked.

"The right?"

"Yes, the right." The teacher looked at her pupil. "Show me your right hand."

The child looked at his hands, then held out the correct one.

"Yes," Miss Dowell nodded with approval. "Your right hand is the one you write with, isn't it?"

Al nodded in agreement.

The teacher continued, "To make a *d*, you put the ball on which side of the stick?"

Al glanced at his hands, then replied, "The right."

"No, that would be a *b*." In frustration, the teacher checked her watch. "Look, Al, I'll write out the first four letters of the alphabet for you and you copy them exactly, okay?"

As soon as the four letters were there before him, the child nodded, reached for his pencil, and tried to do as requested. But Miss Dowell's hand was still on his paper.

"Not yet, Al," she said crossly. "Wait until after I tell you about *all* the corrections."

He withdrew his hand.

The teacher hurriedly continued, "The *m* needs another lump. The way it is you have an *n*. The *j* is backwards. It needs to face the other way. And down here at the end, the *w* is upside down." Miss Dowell stood up, adding, "Now, you work real fast, and make those letters right. It's time for reading."

As the teacher moved away, Al followed her with his eyes. Students clustered around her to turn in their papers. He wondered if they ever noticed how pretty Miss Dowell was when she smiled . . . and especially how pretty she was when she wore her hair all bunched up in the back like today.

The sound of footsteps at his side didn't register fast enough to spare Al the surprise thump on his head with an accompanying snicker. "Hey, dummy. Ain't you done yet?"

Al took a quick swing at Bobby, the boy who had stopped by to taunt him.

"What's so hard that's taking you so long?" the tormenter asked, then grabbed the paper from Al's desk to have a look. "All you got here is the alphabet—and it ain't even right!"

As the color rose in Al's face, another boy joined in the fun. "You mean he took all that long just to write that little dab?" Tom asked with a vicious laugh. "Golly, I didn't know *anybody* was that stupid!"

Jumping from his seat, Al grabbed for his paper.

"What's going on over there?" Miss Dowell challenged.

The handwriting paper was quickly placed back on Al's desk. The three boys faced each other in silence.

The teacher surveyed the scene. "Bobby and Tom, get back to your seats and get ready for reading. You've got no business over there." Miss Dowell motioned for the two to move along. "Al, have you finished your handwriting?"

"No," he mumbled.

"Young man," the teacher said in that special warning voice, "you've got one minute to finish your corrections and get your paper turned in."

Since he'd forgotten what Miss Dowell had told him to do with the letters circled in red, he copied them down below—more neatly, but facing in the same directions—and handed in his paper.

"The Eagles, the Robins, and the Cardinals get out your pencils and your reading workbooks," the teacher instructed from the front of the room. "And the Bluebirds bring your books and come up into the reading circle." Al was a Bluebird.

As Al bent over to get his book out of his desk, his attention was caught by the grocery bag on the floor next to his chair. He pulled back the paper and peeped inside just to be sure the lizard was all right. Thinking maybe the animal wasn't getting enough air, he removed the lid of the jar and fanned his hand across the top several times. The lizard scurried to make an escape, but Al clapped the top back on and twisted it down tight. He was glad to know his little friend was fine.

"Al," Miss Dowell's voice called. "You're supposed to be getting out your reading book, not playing with your lizard."

The jar was eased back into the bag.

"We're all up here waiting for you, Al." The teacher lapsed into a meaningful pause, hoping to hurry him along.

Reading class started. Al shuffled up to join the Bluebirds. They were the low group. *Everybody* knew they were the slow group. The rest of the class had already finished three or four reading books this year. They were up into nice thick books with interesting stories and hard words. The Bludbirds were still trying to get through the baby books with the big print and the big pictures.

The half hour spent in the reading circle with the Bluebirds was one of the most trying periods of Miss Dowell's day. The children in the group found reading very difficult. They constantly lost their place and even stumbled over the easy words. Most of them had an unusually short attention span. This meant the teacher always had to contend with a lot of wiggling and looking out the window. In all these things, Al was just like all the other little Bluebirds. He found it very difficult to sit still and pay attention. And his oral reading sounded absolutely awful.

Many of the youngsters in the group had trouble understanding the simple stories. When asked the comprehension questions, they couldn't remember the details and often weren't able to explain the main ideas either. However, Al had no such difficulties with comprehension. Once the boy figured out what a passage said, he always understood what it meant.

The reading circle was Al's least favorite part of the school day. He dreaded sitting there knowing his turn was coming. It was hard to pay attention when he knew that in just a few minutes he was going to have to go through the agony of trying to read out loud. As always, all too quickly, his turn came.

"Al," Miss Dowell asked, "do you know where we are?"

He shook his head.

"Carol, will you show Al the place?"

The boy tried to cooperate as the little girl next to him fumbled to turn several pages of his book and point out where he should start.

Al pressed his finger hard against the page to keep the place and began:

Al: "Mother was . . . "

Teacher: Not "was," Al. "*Saw.*"

Al: "Mother saw . . . Bill . . . on top of the . . . house. He . . . "

Teacher: Not "*he*," Al. The word starts with *s h* as in shhhhhh.

Al: "She saw . . . "

Teacher: "*Was.*"

Al: "She was not. . . . " (The child paused, then looked up at the teacher.)

Teacher: You know that word. Joe, tell us what that word is.

Joe: "*Happy.*"

Teacher: Right—"*happy.*"

Al: " . . . happy to see . . . him up . . . here. . . . "

Teacher: Not "*here*," Al. "*There.*"

Al: " . . . there. 'Come down, . . . Bill,' Mother called."

Teacher: "*Called Mother.*"

Al: " . . . called Mother. 'Come down off . . . ' "

Teacher: "*From.*"

Al: " 'Come down from there this minute' . . . "

Teacher: No, Al. It doesn't say "this minute." Take another look. What are those last two words?

The reading circle finally ended. Miss Dowell gave her low group three worksheets, carefully explained the directions for all three, sent the Bluebirds back to their seats, and called for the Robins to come up to the front.

Al made a circuit of the room on his way back to his desk. He stopped for a drink at the fountain, paused in front of the Indian mural to admire the part he was working on, sharpened his pencil to a nice fine point, noticed the pencil sharpener was nearly full of shavings and started to empty it.

Miss Dowell called from her seat in the reading circle with the Robins, "Al, that doesn't need to be done now."

He carefully put the pencil sharpener back together and wandered toward his desk. Since Miss Dowell's watchful eyes followed him every step of the way, he went there slowly but directly.

A few other members of the Bluebirds were still just getting started. Most of the students, however, were already hunched over their desks, busily working. During the remaining hour of reading, Al stayed quietly in his seat. Ten minutes were devoted to getting out his crayons and ruler. Five minutes went to playing with a large rubber band he discovered in his desk. For ten minutes he attempted to do the worksheets. On the first one, he'd forgotten the directions, so he quickly and easily finished it but did it all wrong. The second page was of a familiar type, but he kept getting stuck on the hard words. He knew better than to interrupt Miss Dowell while she was reading with another group. He figured out the words as best he could. Getting more and more frustrated, he began guessing at answers. By the end of the sheet, he was circling words he didn't know to answer questions he hadn't even tried to read. Before starting on the third page of his work, Al colored the pictures on all three sheets, took a peek at the lizard to be sure he was doing all right, drew several pictures of the lizard and the creek that was his home, watched a fly buzzing against the glass at the very top of the window, drew a picture of the lizard enjoying the fly for a meal, experimented with coloring the large rubber band, used the now striped rubber band to draw circles and ovals, tried doing some block printing by stamping the crayon-colored rubber band against his paper and pressing down hard, and before he knew it, reading class was over and it was time for recess.

Unfortunately, Al had to miss part of recess so he could finish his handwriting. (The reading worksheets he had failed to finish would probably deprive him of *all* of his recess tomorrow.)

The children gathered up their sweaters and jackets. The captains for the week got the kickball out of the closet. Chattering and laughing, the class lined up at the door, waited for the teacher's signal, and filed out to the playground.

Al was standing at the window trying to catch the fly when Miss Dowell came over to him with the handwriting paper. "I don't like you to miss your play period," she began. "You need a break like everybody else."

The little boy left the window and returned to his seat. "I wanted to catch that fly and feed him to my lizard," he explained.

"That would be a good idea. I'll bet your old Granddaddy Lizard would like that. Maybe after we have our lunch we could take a minute to catch him some lunch, too."

Al's eyes sparkled enthusiastically. "We could put the fly in the jar while it's still alive and watch to see how the lizard catches it. I'll bet he's got a long sticky tongue like a frog and he'll shoot that tongue out . . . "

"Hold it. Hold it." Miss Dowell stopped the excited child. "Let's get the handwriting done now. We'll see about the lizard's lunch later."

Dutifully, Al picked up his pencil.

"Since I think it's important for you to get at least part of your recess, I'm going to have you write just the first sentence of the story on the board." Miss Dowell patted the child's head to encourage him. "You concentrate on doing a good job with just that one sentence. When you're done and I've corrected it, you and I are both going to get to go outside."

It took ten minutes and a lot of erasing, but Al put his heart and soul into that one sentence. His paper wasn't exactly neat, but for him it looked good. With a proud smile, he took his work up to his teacher for approval.

Miss Dowell looked at the words her student had copied from the board. Instead of reaching for her box of stars, she picked up her red pencil. "Al, I can understand that you have trouble writing your letters when you have nothing to go by. But I do not understand why you make so many mistakes when all you have to do is copy something off the board." The teacher's disappointment was easily seen in the way she frowned and shook her head. "First of all, you left out a whole word. Look at the third word on the board. It says 'kite.' Look at your third word. . . ."

Al gulped. Sure enough. He didn't know for sure what his third word said, but he knew it wasn't "kite" like it was supposed to be.

The teacher put a red X where the missing word should have been. Then she pointed to the fifth word and asked, "What's this word supposed to say?"

The boy studied what he had written down. "It," he replied.

"How do you spell *it*?" Miss Dowell asked. Then she added, "You should be able to spell *it* without even looking at the board."

Nevertheless, Al checked to see the correct spelling on the blackboard. "Oh," he said, "I got the letters mixed up."

"Yes, you did. It's supposed to be *i t, not t i*." The red pencil put a big circle around the word that had been written backwards. "There are two other tiny mistakes." Miss Dowell paused to let the child attempt to figure out what they were. When he didn't respond, she said, "This *i* needs a dot." The red pencil supplied the small mark required. "And this *t* is missing something."

Al reached over to his paper and crossed the *t* himself.

Finally, recess had arrived.

Al burst from the door and dashed across the playground to join his classmates. To get into the kickball game, which was already in progress, Al merely took a position in the outfield. Enthusiastically, he danced around hoping to get some action.

When the captain noticed Al, he shouted, "You're not on *my* team. Go on in with the other side."

The opposing team's captain hollered back, "I didn't pick Al. He ain't on *my* team."

Al meandered up to the pitcher's mound to ask the captain, "Can I pitch?"

"You ain't even on my team, stupid," came the snarled reply.

The third baseman shouted, "Had to stay inside because he can't even write his alphabet. Get out of the way, baby, you're holding up the game."

Al started walking toward home plate.

Betsy, the girl who was captain of the team then at bat, confronted him with her hands on her hips. "I told you, you ain't on my team, Al. Go drop all the fly balls for those guys."

Miss Dowell arrived just in time to settle the issue. She

forced Betsy to accept Al on her team, and then stood back behind the backstop to observe. Al was at the end of the line. With luck, he'd get one chance to kick before recess ended.

Fate gave the team's new addition a turn at bat. With two outs and two men on, Al stepped up to the plate.

"Oh, boy," groaned the captain, "Here comes our last out."

Nervously, Al waited. As the ball rolled toward him, he ran up on it and gave it a walloping kick with his left foot. The ball sailed out of bounds by third base. On the second pitch, he tried again. This time he missed the ball entirely. Blushing crimson, he returned to his position behind the plate as his teammates jeered, "Can't you do anything right?!"

The next pitch dribbled and wobbled toward him. Somehow Al's left foot managed to catch the ball way underneath and squarely in the middle. It was a high infield fly. Four different children moved to get into a good position for the catch. Each one called, "I got it. I got it." It looked like an easy out.

Al raced toward first base. To his delight the ball plopped to the ground amid the four scrambling infielders. He was safe.

The next child at bat made the third out and recess was over.

Al bounded inside to get a drink and start in on the long hour of math that separated him from lunch. Arithmetic presented all the difficulties of reading and writing classes put together. The child had trouble getting organized, paying attention, and following directions. He read numbers backwards and wrote them facing the wrong way. Although he understood what math was all about, he couldn't deal with it effectively when it had to be put on paper. As usual, the class was over before Al's messy, error-filled paper was finished.

Lunch was a cinch as long as Al was careful to avoid Bobby and Tom and some of their friends. Then came the afternoon. That was the good part of the day.

Story hour was a great time for Al. While the teacher read aloud to the class, the children were free to move about the room doing anything they liked—as long as they were quiet. Al was good at that. He could wander all over doing whatever he liked and still never miss a word of the story.

After the story, it was time for show and tell. Next to getting safely to first base, Al expected this to be the best part of the day. Miss Dowell let the children come up and sit on the floor in a circle. When it was Al's turn, the jar with Mr. Granddaddy Lizard was passed carefully from hand to hand. The lizard's proud owner told all about how he'd caught the wonderful creature. A lot of the children asked questions.

"Will he bite?" one of the girls wanted to know.

"No, he ain't got no teeth," Al replied.

"Well, then, how does he eat?"

"He just grabs a bug whole and swallows it down." Al demonstrated with his hands. "To see them little bitty bugs, I think a lizard must have pretty good eyes," he added.

The last hour of the day was social studies. The class was studying about Indians. Miss Dowell had read them stories and taken them to a local musuem. Today she showed a film strip and then let the children work on the mural that covered the whole length of the wall at the back of the room. Al loved it. He knew a lot about Indians. And he'd been eagerly waiting to work on his part of the huge picture.

Before the children cleaned up and put their paints away, the teacher had each one stand by what he'd done that day and explain it to the class. Some had painted a teepee, or a horse, or a warrior. Most had worked on sky, grass, trees, and other background. Al had done a bush. He proudly showed the bright green leafy mass to his classmates. "I even put in some of the branches and twigs," he explained. "And a bird's nest," he added, pointing to a grayish circle off to one side.

"What are those two brown things sticking out of the top?" Miss Dowell asked.

"Them's feathers." Al grinned playfully. "There's a Indian hiding behind my bush. He don't know it, but his feathers are sticking out so *I* know he's there."

The teacher beamed. "What a clever idea."

Anita flounced her curls with a huff. "I think it looks silly."

"Two ugly brown blobs sticking out of a bush," another girl added, then pointed at Al's work. "That's dumb. Those don't look like feathers!"

Miss Dowell stepped quickly to Al's side. "That's enough of that," she snapped at the two girls. "Nobody criticized *your* work like that."

"But we didn't ruin the mural," Anita protested.

"Yeah, he's ruined our mural," chorused several of the children.

"Al hasn't ruined anything." The teacher concluded in a very firm warning voice, "And there won't be another word about it."

Half of the class worked on cleaning brushes, picking up the newspapers spread on the floor, and other jobs concerning the messy painting project. The rest of the children were involved with routine end-of-the-day chores. It was Al's week to wash the blackboards.

He was a cooperative but unreliable worker. It took him a long time to get the sponge and water because he spent a few minutes playing with the faucet. Then he stopped to admire the mural on his way by. And, of course, once he did get started, he worked very slowly. Despite repeated warnings that he needed to hurry up, the bell rang before Al had finished. "You can go on, Al," the teacher offered.

"I'm almost done," the child explained, without speeding up his slow pace.

Miss Dowell went to the door to see the other children off. They said their good-byes, broke into pairs and small groups, and left.

Al finished shortly. All of his classmates had already gone. But he always walked home alone anyway. At least this day he had his lizard to keep him company—and it had been an especially good day, too.

As a six-year-old, Al was eager to learn. His boundless energy and inquisitive nature made him interested in everything around him. He was so quick to forgive that he remained optimistic and trusting of his peers despite repeated rejection and ridicule. Although constantly criticized for his behavior, Al was innocently oblivious of the ways in which his actions irritated others.

Chapter XV

Fifth Grade and Still Failing

"AL, YOU'RE TEN MINUTES LATE." Mrs. Carswell looked up over her bifocals as the student casually approached her desk.

"I had to stop at the office," the boy replied, fishing around in the hip pocket of his jeans. "I got an excuse."

"Speaking of excuses. Do you have the note you promised me? Remember? You were absent Monday and Tuesday. You were supposed to get your mother to write an excuse."

"My mom didn't get off work until late last night," Al answered, rummaging through the other back pocket.

Mrs. Carswell set her spelling book aside. "Al, you and I need to have a talk," she said, motioning for the boy to follow her out to the hall.

As she led the youngster toward the door, Mrs. Carswell announced to the class, "The spelling test will begin at ten minutes to nine. Please get your papers ready." Al followed his teacher out of the room. She closed the door behind them.

Mrs. Carswell set a hand on her pupil's shoulder and tried to look into his face. "Al, it's the middle of April and you have F's in almost every subject. If things don't improve, you're going to have to repeat the fifth grade." She sought the boy's eyes, but he was staring at the floor. The youth had been held back once. He was already a misfit—bigger and older and wiser than his classmates. "Al, I don't *want* you to fail." The teacher's tone was almost pleading.

Al shifted his weight, then stuffed his hands in his back pockets so they no longer dangled limply from his slumping shoulders. He made no remark.

Mrs.Carswell opened her record book and held it down where her student could see it. He stared at the page with unfocused eyes.

"You have missed. . . ." the teacher paused, counting under her breath. "You've missed eighteen days of school this semester. Of course, two whole weeks of that were the ear infection you had in February. But you've gotten so far behind in your work."

Al said nothing.

The teacher flipped the pages in her book. "In language arts, we've had four book reports." She pointed to the four zeros that represented Al's grades. "You were absent for the first one and never got around to making it up. For the second one, you picked a book that was too hard and didn't finish it. On the third one, I helped you select a book; you got halfway through and decided you didn't like it. . . ."

"I lost the book," the boy muttered.

"Yes. Then you lost the book. The fourth report was due Monday. But you were absent Monday."

Assuming a no-nonsense attitude, the teacher sternly asked, "Have you read a book for this report?"

"I ain't done with it yet," the youth muttered.

"What book are you reading?"

"It's one I got at home."

"You know I'm supposed to approve the books that are used for the reports."

"This is a good book. It's all about a pioneer family living out on the prairie." Al give a brief summary of the plot. As he warmed up to his subject, he began describing an especially exciting scene. "There's one part where the Indians are about to attack the cabin. The father knows he can't stand them off by himself. So he leaves his wife and the children locked inside the house, and he slips off out the back and sneaks up into the woods behind the Indians—they're all up there sitting around a campfire waiting for the moon to come up before they attack. . . ."

As she was swept along by her student's enthusiasm, the teacher's eyes lit up with recognition. "Oh, I know that story. That's a very famous western." Pausing, Mrs. Carswell pondered, then added, "Al, that's an adult western. It'll take you forever to wade through that great big thick book."

"But it's a good story."

"I think you're making a mistake to try to read such a difficult book, Al. That's way too hard for you."

"I'm doing okay," he reassured her.

Mrs. Carswell was delighted that Al had finally found a book that truly interested him. Smiling, she offered encouragement. "Well, if you can read it—more power to you. . . . Did you know they made a movie out of it?"

"Yeah."

"In fact, it was on TV not long ago."

"Yeah, I seen it. That's how I got interested in the book."

"Al," Mrs. Carswell sighed. "You already know the story. If you saw the whole thing on television, there's no point in reading the book."

"But it's an interesting story. I like the part where the chief's two sons have the contest to see who gets to keep the pony."

"Have you gotten to that part in the book?"

"No, not yet."

It was almost time to start the spelling test. The teacher decided to settle two issues immediately and drop the others until later. "On Monday, you are to bring two things to school with you. One, I want to *see* this book you say you're reading." For emphasis she tapped the first line of the note she was writing to the youngster's mother. "Monday, you bring the book." She paused for Al to nod that he understood, then moved on to her second point. "With the two days you were out this week, you now have five days of unexcused absences. I've written the dates down here." Again she tapped the note for emphasis. "You give this message to your mother. And when you walk in that door Monday morning, you'd better have that book in one hand and a note to excuse your absences in the other—OR ELSE!"

Al stared at the bright red letters of the message to his mother. Slowly he took the paper, folded it, and stuffed it into his pocket.

The noises made by thirty-two restless students drifted out into the corridor. It was nearly nine o'clock. Mrs. Carswell could not ignore her class any longer.

Opening the door, she announced in a loud, threatening voice, "The spelling test will begin in thirty seconds." She paused, returning her attention to the boy still standing beside her in the hall. "Al—for Monday," she insisted gently. "The absence excuses and the book. Okay?"

Al's only response was a small nod. Head lowered, eyes on the floor, he slipped quietly by her and moved toward his seat in the back row.

The teacher knew there was only a slim chance that she would ever get to see either the book or the note. In fact, it was possible that the issue might never come up again. Al had a habit of being absent on Mondays.

As Al got to his seat, Charles, the boy in the desk next to his, teased, "Hey, Al, you in trouble with the teacher again, boy?!"

Al grinned, then climbed into his seat by throwing a leg up over the back as though mounting a horse. "I'm *always* in trouble," Al chuckled. He lightly punched the heavyset boy seated diagonally in front of him. "Right, Larry?"

"That sure is right, Al." Larry nodded as he pivoted around in his chair to look directly at his pal. Grinning and bobbing his head up and down in wide-eyed agreement, he earnestly stated, "You're in trouble just about more than anybody else in the class."

A whoop of laughter burst from the youth in the desk directly behind Larry. "You said that right," Todd chortled. The boy's wide smile emphasized the roundness of his freck-led cheeks so that he looked like an impish cherub. He gave Al a cuff on the shoulder. "Always in trouble—you just never do behave."

Al shrugged his shoulders. "What do you expect from us guys here in the back?" Charles, Todd, and Al snickered under their breath. Larry snuffled and snorted with loud guffaws.

"The boys in the back—ain't no way we can keep out of trouble." Charles snapped his fingers and rolled his black body to an imaginary beat. "The boys in the back—we back here because we *bad*." He rolled the last word out on his breath. To cover up their laughter, Al, Todd, and Charles bent over and pretended to be getting out some books.

At that moment, the teacher called, "Al, would you come up here for a minute?"

Todd's eyebrows shot up in feigned alarm. "Uh-oh. You're in trouble again."

Al slowly got out of his chair.

Charles prodded him in the behind. "Now you gonna get it, boy. Get on up there and take your licks."

Al bent over as though to pick up something he'd dropped. While out of the teacher's line of vision, he quickly untied Todd's sneaker, shoved a wad of paper up under Charles's shirt, and smiled in triumph. With Mrs. Carswell watching, there was no way his friends could get even.

From the front of the room came a repeat of the teacher's request. "Alvin, I need to see you NOW."

Setting his face into a serious look, Al turned and headed toward Mrs. Carswell's desk.

Impatiently, the teacher waited.

One of the students near the front complained in a loud voice, "Awww, come on, Al. We want to get started."

It was 9:07. Thirty-two children had just spent more than fifteen minutes waiting to start their spelling test. That one disgusted voice expressed the way the entire class felt toward Al.

Rather than scold about wise remarks, the teacher carefully enunciated the first spelling word and gave a sentence to go with it. The room fell silent immediately. She pronounced the second word, and then the third. By then Al was standing awkwardly at her side. As she continued with the spelling list, the conversation with Al was squeezed into the pauses between words. "You got here so late this morning I'd already sent down the lunch count and attendance," Mrs. Carswell explained. She said a spelling word for the class, told Al the two selections on the lunch menu; gave the class another word, wrote down Al's decision; pronounced a spelling word, filled out an adjusted attendance slip. When Mrs. Carswell removed a hall pass from her drawer, Al reached out his hand for the messages he assumed he would be taking to the office.

The teacher scanned the room, then fastened her gaze on a bubbly little blue-eyed girl in the front row. "Sally," the teacher requested sweetly, "would you come up here for a minute, dear?"

While Sally carefully set her pencil aside and turned her

letter-perfect paper face down on her desk, Mrs. Carswell explained tartly to Al, "Every time I send you out of the room on an errand, you're gone for at least half an hour. You've wasted enough time this morning already." With a firm nod, she sent Al to his seat and Sally to the office.

At 9:15, on spelling word 11, Al's school day finally began.

Throughout the rest of the spelling test, Al struggled to get out of the mess he was in. "Hey Charles," he whispered. "Call out them first eleven words for me." His friend tried, but it didn't work out very well. Even with his paper right in front of him, Charles didn't know for sure what most of the words were supposed to say.

Al tried the same approach on Barb, the girl sitting in front of him. Mumbling behind her hand, she tried to help him out. That didn't work either. The teacher overheard them and issued a loud order. "I don't want to hear any more whispering back there. Al, you leave Barb alone."

At the end of the test, Mrs. Carswell instructed the students to pass their papers forward.

Al left his seat and started toward the front. He had to find out what to do about those eleven words he'd missed.

The boy had gotten only a few feet from his desk when the teacher stopped him. "Alvin, there is no need for you to be up walking around. *Pass* your paper in like everybody else."

"But I need to ask you a question," Al protested, paused, then proceeded toward his teacher.

"Go back to your seat, Al," Mrs. Carswell ordered. "If you have a question, raise your hand and ask it from there. That is the accepted procedure."

Cheeks flushed, fists clenched, Al returned to his chair. An uncomfortable, thick silence fell over the room. Even

Todd and Charles found no humor in the situation and made no comment.

Angrily, Al folded his spelling test and shoved it into his desk.

From the front of the room, the teacher commanded, "Get that paper out of your desk, Alvin, and pass it up to the front."

"It ain't finished," the infuriated youth snorted.

Mrs. Carswell stalked over to Al's desk and glared down at him. "You're the one who's just about finished, young man."

The boy's cheek muscles twitched over his clenched jaw and stiffly set lips. A thin film of tears washed over the anger and hate in his eyes.

Gingerly, the teacher fought to keep control. She had seen Al explode before. At all costs, she wanted to avoid a really ugly scene. Forcing calm into her voice, she quietly requested, "May I *see* your paper?"

Halfheartedly, Al rummaged among his books. When he found the spelling test, he unfolded it, pressed it out flat, printed his name at the top, then shoved it at his teacher.

"I see that numbers one through eleven are missing," Mrs. Carswell observed without emotion. "Is that what you wanted to talk to me about?"

"Yeah," the boy replied sharply. "I wanted you to call them out so I could finish."

"But I don't want to take the time to do that right now, Al," the teacher explained in cool, smooth tones. "Because of you, the class was fifteen minutes late getting started. I don't think it would be fair to make thirty-two others wait for you *again*." She wanted to add, "Besides, you haven't passed a single spelling test this year. Those words won't make any difference." But from the way the youngster had slouched down into his seat, she saw that it wasn't necessary. "I'll dictate the rest of the list for you at our 10:30 break." Briskly she placed Al's paper on the top of the stack, snapped a paper clip on to hold it in place, and strode back to the front of the room. "Get out your materials for reading," she instructed the class. "I'll work with Group II first today."

Al, Charles, Larry, Barb, and four others comprised Group IV, the low group. They were in a big thick third-grade reading book—everybody knew it was a third-grade book from a pattern of dots printed on the back cover. For most of Group IV, even this easy book was too difficult.

Mrs. Carswell moved methodically from one reading group to another, handing out worksheets, making assignments, and explaining directions. Once all the children knew what they were supposed to be doing, she sat down to work with Group II.

As usual, Al had trouble getting down to business. His pencil point was worn down to a thick fat stub. He didn't want to risk a trip to the pencil sharpener, so he spent several minutes gnawing at the wood with his front teeth.

Disturbed by the sounds coming from his neighbor, Charles punched him in the ribs with an elbow. "Hey, boy, knock it off with all that noise. You sound like a rat."

Al curled his lips back to bare his front teeth and made smacking sounds with his tongue. "Naahhh, I ain't a rat. You don't know nothing. I'm gnawing on wood—see." He smacked again on the pencil for effect. "I'm a beaver."

From his seat on Al's left, Todd interjected, "You sound more like Bugs Bunny."

Pretending the pencil was a carrot, Al shifted his voice up to a high squeak, "Annhh, what's up, doc?"

At this, Barb turned around in her seat to make a loud shushing noise.

Without even looking around, Mrs. Carswell called, "Al. Charles. Todd. Get to work."

In imitation of Porky Pig, Charles stammered, "That's all, folks!"

The three boys giggled for a minute, then turned to their work.

During the half hour that Group IV worked independently , the teacher had to speak to Al four times: once for making noise (he was whittling on his pencil with a pocketknife); once for getting out of his seat (he had gone to the wastebasket to throw away the wood shavings); again for making noise (he was punching holes in a piece of paper with the pocketknife); once for getting huffy (angry about the confiscation of his knife, he slammed his books shut and refused to go back to work).

Promptly at 10:00, the students in Group II returned to their seats, and Mrs. Carswell called Group IV up to the big table. They were scheduled to work with the teacher for fifteen minutes.

"Be sure you have all four worksheets, your book, your pencil, and a checking pencil," the teacher warned the students who were gathering at the table around her.

Barb, Charles, and Larry returned to their desks to get something. Al flopped into a seat.

"You have only two pages there, Al," Mrs. Carswell observed.

"I ain't done with the others," the boy replied, slouching further down in his chair.

"Please go get the other two sheets," the teacher requested politely. "We're going to check all four of them. I want you at least to be able to follow along."

The youth made no move toward obeying. Instead, he shrugged casually and said, "I got nothing to correct."

The teacher replied in a voice that she forced to sound sweetly calm, "I understand that. But I would like you to have your papers here with you so you can participate in the discussion."

As though the argument were too silly for serious consideration, Al sauntered over to his desk to get the two mimeographed sheets he'd never even touched.

Of the allotted fifteen minutes, five were gone before Mrs. Carswell managed to get Group IV started.

As they went around the circle reading the first page of comprehension questions, Al gave correct answers both times it was his turn. When the group got to the ninth question, it stumped everybody.

Mrs. Carswell reread number nine: "Why did the horse run back into the fire after Bob had led it out to safety?"

The children stared at their papers in silence. Nobody wanted to be the one called on. Carl got chosen first. "I got that he ran back in to try to get his friends out." Carl looked up and shook his head. "But you said that was wrong."

"Larry, what do you think?"

Words rolling slowly from his lips, Larry replied, "That was a real smart horse. I think he went back in to put out the fire. He could have stomped it out. . . ."

"Oh, the fire was too big for that," Mrs. Carswell explained gently. "The picture shows flames coming up clear through the roof."

The teacher searched the faces of her seven poor readers, then said, "Surely some of you know about horses and animals."

Most of the children shook their heads. Carl, Larry, and Al just sat there.

"Al, what do you think?"

"He panicked," Al muttered.

"Who panicked?" Mrs. Carswell asked.

"The horse," Al said flatly.

With lively new interest, the teacher requested, "Could you explain what you mean?"

Al spoke as though he were bored by having to tell the group something everybody already knew. "Frightened animals don't always act logical. They get so scared they act crazy."

This piece of information supplied the spark needed to make the other children understand.

Racing against the clock, Mrs. Carswell got Group IV through the rest of the first sheet and began entering their scores in her grade book. Out of fifteen questions, most of the students got ten or eleven right. When she called Al's name, he said "Fourteen."

"Fourteen?" The teacher's eyebrows shot up in surprise. "You missed only one, Al?" Her amazement quickly turned to suspicion. "You'd better count that up again."

The boy nodded, recounted the checks he'd put on his paper, and repeated, "Yup—I got fourteen."

"Let *me* have a look." The teacher took Al's paper and ran her eyes over it quickly. The youngster had filled all the blanks with single words and short phrases instead of the sentences the directions required. "You don't get fourteen, young man. You get a zero. You didn't even follow the directions." She set the paper down with a disgusted snap.

"Them answers is all right," Al protested heatedly, then added, "Well, all but one. . . ." He paused to await the verdict.

"Everybody else followed the directions and wrote sentences. It wouldn't be fair to them if I let you get away with one-word answers."

"That ain't fair," Al argued. "I got more right than anybody."

Returning her attention to the grade book, Mrs. Carswell asked, "How many did you get right, Barb?"

Al looked across the table at Charles. "I got more right than anybody else! Don't that count for nothing?"

Silently, Charles shrugged his shoulders.

The teacher wanted to stop Al's whining complaints with a starchy comment like "They spent *their* time working. You spent *yours* playing with your knife. You deserve exactly what you got." But she refrained.

After Mrs. Carswell had recorded all the scores for the first page, she gave Group IV their new assignment. To Al, she added, "If you make those answers into sentences, I'll be happy to take the zero out of the grade book and put a fourteen in its place." Without responding, Al turned away and walked to his desk.

Al had the small spring-powered motor from a wind-up toy in his pocket. Careful that its whirring noise didn't attract the teacher's attention, he spent the remaining twenty minutes of reading class playing with it.

Morning break finally arrived. "Rows one and two may go to the lavatory and get a drink," Mrs. Carswell announced. "Al, bring your pencil and come up here."

Al took a seat beside the teacher's desk. She called out the words for him as she graded the rest of the spelling papers and supervised the activities of the class's free time. When Al's messy paper was complete, she took it from him and said, "While you're right here to watch, I'll go ahead and mark your test."

Al sank back into the chair as she proceeded.

The red pencil flashed down the column of words. Check, X, X, X, check, X, X. . . . The boy couldn't do the arithmetic involved in figuring up his score, but he could see that he'd failed again.

Instead of letting the youngster take his break, Mrs. Carswell leaned toward Al, explaining, "I want to take just a minute to point out a few things about your test." Using her red pencil as a pointer, she began. "In the first place, the weekly spelling test is supposed to be done in cursive. You'll notice that you printed." Then she pointed to the heading across the top of the page. "You are supposed to have your full name—first *and* last— here on the right. You have just your first name."

Al watched Charles dance toward the door to go for a drink. Silently, he turned back to his teacher as she began a careful analysis of the types of spelling errors he'd made.

"I see you left out a number again," she observed crisply, then added, "You might not be able to spell, Al. But surely you can number a paper from one to twenty."

The boy made no comment.

"Two of these words would be right if you hadn't switched the letters around to the wrong places. . . ." The teacher fixed the youth with a harsh, accusing gaze. "Careless errors, Al. Most of your mistakes are just carelessness."

Todd sauntered into the room. From behind the teacher's back, he caught Al's eye, made a face, pointed at Mrs. Carswell, tossed off an obscene gesture, grinned, and ambled to the back of the room.

Mrs. Carswell was vigorously circling Al's careless mistakes. "This *f* is backwards. . . . You left out a whole syllable. . . . You wrote *b* instead of *d* twice in one word. . . ." The teacher's voice trailed off. Suddenly she counted up the check marks by fives, slapped a 35% at the top, and told Al, "Go on and take your break." Quickly, she gathered up her sweater and purse and hurried toward the teachers' lounge.

Al strode to the door without drawing any interest from

the other children. He was bigger and tougher than most of them. Trouble seemed to follow him around. As much as possible, his classmates stayed clear of him.

But Charles had been waiting for his pal. Grabbing Al from behind in a surprise attack, the tall black youth playfully wrestled him to the ground. As they struggled to pin each other, Charles asked, "Hey, man, what'd you do with that little wind-up motor? Me and Larry want to look at it."

Larry moved closer to the two flailing bodies and bobbed his head up and down. "Yeah, Al. Can I look at the little motor? I promise not to hurt it."

"Tell this hunk of junk to get off me so I can get it out of my pocket," Al grunted from under the weight of Charles.

Reaching into the squirming pile of arms and legs, Larry grabbed Charles's collar. "Get off of him. He's got it in his pocket."

A small tearing noise came from the tautly stretching fabric. "Hey, man, let go. You're ripping my new shirt," Charles barked up at Larry while trying to maintain his hold on his opponent.

The collar remained in the grip of the strong, outstretched hand.

"Let go. Let go," Charles insisted, straining to pull his shirt free.

Several children had come over to watch what they thought was a real fight. The teacher was still out of the room.

The tearing sound was heard again.

One of the onlookers charged over to Larry and shouted up into his face, "Ain't you even smart enough to let go? Your hand can't be as dumb as you are!" Then he grabbed Larry by the wrist.

Charles and Al scrambled up from the floor. Todd raced toward the scene from the back of the room.

"You take that back," Al demanded.

"But he was ripping Charles's shirt," the youth protested.

"I don't care what he was doing. Don't you *never* call Ole Larry names like that!" Al shouted with rage.

Charles put an arm around Al's shoulder to draw him away. "Save your breath, man. They don't know nothin'." With a jerk of his head, he motioned Larry to follow. "Come on. Let's us four go get a drink. The air ain't so good in here." Charles herded Al and Todd out into the hall.

Al flustered and blustered under his breath. When he and his three buddies got to the fountain, he'd cooled down enough to sigh heavily and conclude, "We could beat the stew out of every one of them, Charles. . . . But ain't no way they'd ever understand."

When Mrs. Carswell returned from the teachers' lounge, the classroom was unusually peaceful. Children were talking, reading, playing games. Even Al, Charles, and Larry were quietly amusing themselves with some toy.

Humming lightly to herself, the teacher moved about the room handing back math papers. To call the class back to order, she announced, "You'll find yesterday's tests on your desks. Group I and Group II, stay in your seats and make your corrections. Group III, bring your tests and your pencils and come up to the table. I'm going to help you with your papers."

Groups I and II were both doing fifth-grade arithmetic. Group III used the fourth-grade book and did a lot of worksheets. Al, Larry, Charles, Mary Lou, and Pam were the only students in the low group.

The five joined their teacher at the table.

As soon as they all got settled, Mrs. Carswell began. "Let's start with the addition problems at the top of the first page. Did anybody get all of the first row right?"

Pam's hand shot up.

"Okay, Pam, you go to the board." She handed the girl

some chalk, then continued, "Charles, did you miss the first problem?"

"Nah, I didn't miss nothing until the last one in the row," he replied.

Larry waved his hand. "I missed that one."

"Okay, Larry—tell Pam what to put on the board."

Slowly the boy called out the numbers and told her what to do. Together they arrived at an answer of 93.

"Anybody who doesn't have 93 for the answer needs to figure out what went wrong," Mrs. Carswell said.

"I know what I did wrong," Larry spoke right up. "I said three plus six equals eight. It should have been nine."

"Very good, Larry." The teacher scanned the papers for others who'd made errors on that problem. "Al, what did you do wrong?" she asked.

"I didn't do nothing wrong," the boy snapped.

"But it's got an X on it," Mrs. Carswell noted.

"I figured out the right answer," Al growled. "You put a X on it because I messed up when I wrote it down."

"What does your answer say?"

Al studied his paper in silence, then said, "I got ninety-three."

"No, Al. That's what the answer is *supposed* to be."

"Oh, then I got thirty-nine."

"Right," Mrs. Carswell nodded.

Mumbling to himself about "stupid dumb mistakes," Al changed the reversed numbers.

When they got to the harder addition that involved carrying, almost every problem on Al's paper was marked wrong.

"Charles, you go to the board," the teacher directed. "Al, you call out the first one to him."

Al began, "Twenty-six goes on the top."

Charles wrote 26.

"Put eighty-six underneath it."

Charles wrote 86.

Al snorted in disgust, "That ain't eighty-six, Charles. Come on, be serious."

"Yeah, it is, man." The youngster at the board appealed to the teacher for confirmation. "Ain't that eighty-six, Mrs. Carswell?"

She nodded. "It sure is."

With that, Al's building frustration snapped. Grabbing his pencil, he smashed it down on his paper, slashing and scribbling with rage. "I hate math. I hate math," he snarled.

"Yeah, man, I know that," Charles responded. "But what you want me to do with these here numbers?"

"You really want to know what you can do with them numbers, nigger?!" Al challenged.

Mrs. Carswell gasped.

"Nahhh," Charles drawled back at his friend with a knowing chuckle and a wide grin. "I mean other than that."

Al jumped out of his seat, snatched up his paper, and stuck it under Charles's nose. Stabbing at it frantically, he said, "Copy this . . . this blasted number here. . . ."

"Oh, that—that's sixty-eight," Charles said casually.

"I don't care what it is! Just copy it down."

Charles did as he was told. Looking up at Al, he asked, "Now what?"

"Now you just stay there and keep your big mouth shut. I'm going to tell you how to work it." Al yanked his chair out and flopped back down into it.

Mrs. Carswell relaxed with a sigh of relief. Al had flared up and cooled off so quickly there was no need for her to interfere.

Al took a deep breath and cleared his throat. "Okay," he said in a calm, low voice. "Six plus eight is . . ." he counted on his fingers, ". . . fourteen."

Charles stood quietly, chalk poised.

"Put down the one and carry the four."

The numbers went on the board as ordered.

"Four plus six is . . ." again Al paused to count out the answer on his fingers, ". . . ten, plus two is . . . twelve. Put down the twelve."

Larry leaned across the table and pointed to the problem on the board. "You did your carrying wrong, Al. You shouldn't have wrote down the one; that ought to have been the four."

Al couldn't follow what Larry was trying to say. Pam and Mary Lou chimed in. Charles wrote. Mrs. Carswell explained. Al tried. Finally Larry went to the board. Al followed the boy's slow explanation very carefully. And the light dawned. "I see what you mean, Larry. I see what you mean. The number is 14—I should have put the four down in the answer and carried the one!" Larry was so delighted, he patted Al on the shoulder.

Al slapped Larry affectionately on the back. "Thanks, man."

In congratulating Al on his success, Mrs. Carswell said, "Now that you know how to carry, you won't have any difficulty making your corrections."

Al looked down at the twenty problems he'd missed. The idea of reworking every one of them took the edge off his excitement.

To speed things up, the teacher sent all five pupils to the blackboard. That way they could do a whole row at once. Al had a terrible time getting his problems copied correctly onto the board. But he had no further trouble working them.

Back at the table, the five started in on the subtraction problems they'd missed on the test. Al's paper was covered with row after row of X's. On every single set of numbers, he'd added instead of subtracting. Thoroughly disgusted,

Al shoved his paper aside. "Ain't no way I can get all them done." Shaking his head, he silently sulked in defeat.

The other four took turns at the board as they reworked the subtraction problems. Al moped over his paper until Mrs. Carswell drew him aside and worked with him privately.

Everything was fine until Al and the teacher got to subtraction problems that required borrowing. By reading the numbers in the wrong order, the boy made a mistake every time. On $46 - 18$, he said, "Eight take away six is two, four take away one is three."

The teacher carefully pointed out his error.

The next example was $73 - 45$. Again, Al found a way to subtract the smaller number, even though it was at the top, from the larger one. "Three from five is two," he said.

Mrs. Carswell drew pictures with bags of apples. She gave him beans from a jar. Al understood her illustrations. Yet, on paper, he continued to work in the wrong direction.

Group III accomplished a lot in their thirty-minute session with the teacher. As they were dismissed, they were rewarded. "You go back to your desks, finish your corrections, and then have a good time with this dot-to-dot puzzle." Most of them were delighted.

Al dragged himself back to his seat, tossed down his test and his puzzle, and sank slowly into his chair.

"What's the matter with you, boy?" Charles asked playfully.

"Oh, man, I got a headache," Al moaned. Folding his arms for a cushion, he put his head down on his desk.

It was lunchtime before the teacher noticed Al. As the other children prepared to leave for the cafeteria, she walked quickly to the back row, asking Al, "Why do you have your head down?"

When the snoozing boy didn't respond, Todd gave him a gentle nudge.

Raising his drowsy head, Al looked up to see his teacher's angry face staring down at him.

"If there's anybody in this room who can't afford to sleep through math class, Al—it's you!"

"I had a headache," Al mumbled.

"Headache—humph!" The teacher blustered. "You get ready for lunch, young man. We'll talk about this later."

Flanked by Charles and Todd, Al found the noon meal pleasant and almost trouble-free.

The twenty minutes between lunch and physical education was story time. Mrs. Carswell read to the children as they remained in their seats drawing or quietly playing. The book for this week was a true story about the construction of the Golden Gate Bridge. Al found it fascinating. He got a box of lego and a ball of string out of the cupboard. Once he'd spread all the pieces on his desk before him, he carefully removed the little wind-up motor from his pocket. He was going to build a steam shovel that really worked.

Al's hands deftly fitted pieces together as he listened to every word Mrs. Carswell read. Running a string through the hole in a plastic ruler, he experimented with the boom until he hit on a design that would work.

Several times Charles requested, "Hey, man, let me help."

Twice Todd asked, "What are you making?"

The only response from Al was a brief "Shhhhh."

The last thing to go into place was the small wind-up engine. Al used rubber bands to strap the motor to a platform at the back of his contraption. He even bent a paper clip so the derrick could hook onto the things it lifted. On the first trial run, Al flipped the switch, the gears turned, and the string got all tangled up. After a few adjustments, he tested it again. This time the weight of the object being lifted threw the whole thing out of balance. It toppled over and fell apart. With calm patience, Al snapped the pieces back together. Then he added an extra set of pieces as counterweights at the back. Two more tests, and the machine was ready. A pack of chewing gum, a tiny model car, and a roll of caps, a hunk of modeling clay, a golf ball—the machine hoisted each one with equal ease. Al, Todd, and Charles spent the rest of the story hour gleefully watching the crane lift a huge assortment of objects they dug from the depths of their desks.

During the forty-five-minute softball game in phys. ed., Al didn't get to play much. He was chosen last and put at the end of the batting order. When he dropped an easy fly ball, one of the boys on his team shouted, "Butterfingers. Can't you even catch a ball right?!" Al lit into the youngster with fists and foul language. The other boy had to sit out for the rest of the inning. Al was sidelined for the rest of the game.

The last part of the day was devoted to working on projects for health class. Armed with pencils, paper, and dire warnings about good behavior, the class followed their teacher down the hall to the library. Once there, they were split into two groups. The librarian supervised the research activities of twenty students. Mrs. Carswell worked with a group of twelve.

Charles, Larry, Al, and Todd scrambled into adjoining seats at the large round library table. Chuckling and rolling his eyes, Charles whispered, "We got all the bad guys from the back row right here."

Todd nodded. "Mrs. Carswell is keeping us all to herself. I guess she doesn't trust us!"

The teacher gave her small group a long explanation on how to use the card catalogue. Then, two by two, she sent them to look up their topic in the drawers full of cards.

When it was Al's turn, his partner was Mary Lou. Her topic was bones. His was teeth.

"Al, you go over and stand on the right side of the cabinet," Mrs. Carswell directed.

On his best behavior, Al took his pencil and paper and walked directly to the left-hand side of the large set of drawers.

The teacher corrected him. "That's not the right side, Al."

The boy looked surprised. "It's not?" he muttered under his breath, then quickly moved to the other side.

"Yes," the teacher nodded her approval. "Now, Mary Lou, you go over to the left side."

With both children in the proper places, Mrs. Carswell continued. "Mary Lou, where are you going to look to find *bones*?"

"Under B," the girl replied.

"Then find the B drawer and pull it out." Looking at Al, the teacher asked, "Where are you going to find *teeth*?"

"Under T," he replied.

"Good. Find the T drawer and pull it out."

Mary Lou already had her B drawer open and ready. Slowly Al surveyed all the drawers in front of him. When he couldn't locate the T right away, he ran his finger under the letters as he read each label. He started at the J.

"Al," Mrs. Carswell called to him from the table. "You're looking at the middle of the alphabet there."

The boy tried to speed up and read the labels faster.

"No, Al," the teacher called. "Don't waste your time there. *T* is near the end of the alphabet. Move over to the drawers farther to your right."

Hesitating for a second, Al moved the desired direction and began searching in earnest.

Mrs. Carswell left her chair and went up to help him. "Do you know where *t* comes in the alphabet?" she asked softly.

"Yeah. Near the end."

"Do you know what letters come before it or after it?"

Al looked at her blankly.

"Say the alphabet for me, Al. We'll figure out where the *t* is."

Quickly, he rattled off his version of the alphabet. It was perfect up to *o*. But from there it went, "*p q u r s t p u v. . . .*"

Apparently his speed compensated for his lack of accuracy. The teacher did not complain about his errors. "What came just before the *t*?" she asked.

Under his breath, Al repeated the entire alphabet to himself. "*S*, then *t*," he replied.

"Good." Mrs. Carswell smiled. "And what comes before *s*?"

Again Al raced through the whole set of twenty-six before answering, "*r*."

The teacher patted him on the shoulder. "Very good—*r*, *s*, *t*. Now you're ready to find T in the card catalogue. It comes after the R and the S."

It took a lot of help, but Al finally succeeded in finding three books on teeth. Back in the classroom, he used the research period to pore over them intently.

Al looked through all three of his library books. He studied the pictures and charts, copied some of the illustrations. He began drawing teeth—a human incisor from the book complete with labels on all the parts, a whole set of human teeth, gorilla teeth, dog teeth, horse teeth, shark's teeth, bat teeth, vampire teeth, Dracula's fangs, blood dripping off Dracula's fangs, the dead victim of Dracula, a werewolf howling over the corpse, Frankenstein. . . . And before he knew it, the day was over.

As the children departed for home, Mrs. Carswell gave Al an unusually cheery good-bye. She felt very much encouraged by the interest he'd shown in the health project. It even seemed remotely possible that this time the boy might actually complete an assignment.

Al felt good about things, too. Between the success with the crane and the fun with the teeth, a typical day had turned out to be just a little bit special—and he hadn't been sent to the office once!

In six years of school, Al lost a lot of ground. His quick mind and good reasoning ability were no longer readily apparent. The free-flowing interest in everything around him had all but disappeared. Very little remained of the enthusiasm that had formerly made the youngster eager to talk and share and express his ideas. Any motivation that might have been there was gone. Self-confidence was gone. Socially, he'd become an outcast.

Chapter XVI

Fifteen and in the Eighth Grade

AL PAUSED IN THE DOORWAY of the math lab and serenely contemplated the scene before him. The beak of his baseball cap arched up over his eyebrows to frame his watery, pink, translucent eyes. Affixed to the battered cap was an embroidered emblem advertising rolling papers. Next to the sweat-stained patch a small tin button displayed a bright green marijuana leaf.

All the other students were at their seats working intently. No two were engaged in the same activity. Al's eyes took in the purple and white of worksheets, the undulating curve of open books, the shining reflections from plastic coatings on brightly colored work kits, and the exquisite geometry of the various cubicles, cubbyholes, and cupboards. Visually, the math lab was a feast, and Al savored it thoroughly.

Miss Wintle looked up from her desk as though aghast that any student would dare to enter her classroom a full forty minutes late. Although she saw Al so infrequently that she couldn't remember his name, she was certain that he was on her roll book as a member of this first-period class.

Al couldn't remember Miss Wintle's name, either. But that didn't worry him at all. In an emergency he would call the wide-eyed first-year teacher "Ma'am." The grin that she used to radiate her idealistic optimism made him intensely uncomfortable. Math classes and math teachers always made Al uneasy.

Without fanfare, Al and Miss Wintle went through the routine ceremony of greetings, tardy slips, and checks in the roll book. Noting that this student attended class on an average of once every two weeks, she thought to herself, "It's a good thing this program is individualized." The teacher escorted her pupil to the files and helped him get out his work folder.

"Ah, yes," Miss Wintle said, removing a page of problems from the manila cover with Al's name on it. "You were half finished with this subtraction sheet."

"I'll have to get a pencil," Al muttered.

"No problem." Miss Wintle calmly pointed to a supply table in the front corner of the room. "Get one out of the pink coffee can." Then, stopping Al before he could start in the indicated direction, she patted her ears and stammered, "Oh, oh, better yet, take this one." With a light chuckle, she pulled a long, new, freshly sharpened, bright green pencil out from behind her ear, where it had been hidden by her long hair.

"It even has a good eraser," she observed, and handed it to her student.

The new arrival took a seat at one of the empty tables in the back. Miss Wintle pulled a chair up beside him. The heavyset young woman seemed all bouncy with enthusiasm.

Al stared at the worksheet that had been placed in front of him and awaited instructions.

"Since you almost finished the first two rows before, I think you could just put today's date here at the beginning of the third row and pick up where you left off."

Al took up the pencil, put his hand in the proper position, began to write something, then looked up and asked, "What's the date?"

"November fourth," the teacher replied.

With flashy speed, Al dashed off 10—4—78.

"November's not the tenth month," Miss Wintle corrected.

Her pupil looked startled by his error.

Quickly the teacher explained, "November is the *eleventh* month. That date should read, *11*—4."

Al made a heavy extra-dark one over the zero.

Miss Wintle paused as though debating about something. Then she pointed to the four-digit subtraction problems he had previously completed. "What kind of problems are these?" she asked.

When Al didn't respond immediately, she tapped the minus sign to give him a clue. "What does this sign tell you to do?"

"Oh, take away," Al nodded. "Yeah, those are take-away problems."

"Right," Miss Wintle agreed. "I'm going to sit here and watch to be sure you haven't forgotten how to do them. I want you to take the first problem in row three and work it out loud."

Al looked at the figures in question. " Let's see." His eyes narrowed as he tried to think. "Three take away three is zero." He wrote down the number. "Four take away two. . . .." His fingers tapped out the figures on the desk. ". . . is two. Seven take away one is. . . .."

The teacher interrupted, "That's not seven take away one."

Pausing in confusion, Al stared at the problem, then corrected his mistake by saying, "Seven from one is. . . ." Again his fingers worked against the desk. He gave his answer, "six," and wrote the number down.

Miss Wintle stopped him once more. "No, that won't work. You've got to do it in the other direction." With her finger she pointed to the figures that illustrated what she was saying. "You have to start with the top number and take away the bottom number."

"Oh, yeah." Al nodded his head slowly. "I forgot."

"You have to say, 'One take away seven,'" the teacher coached.

Her pupil repeated, "Right, right. One take away seven is . . . " This time his fingers flew through the computation. "One take away seven is six."

"No, Al, that's still not quite it." Miss Wintle shook her head and pointed to the numbers. "You're *saying* it right, but you're still working it upside down."

"I am?" Al asked in total amazement.

The bell rang before Miss Wintle had drawn enough apples and pears to get her pupil to understand borrowing. As the students put their folders away, she offered Al a parting word of encouragement. "We'll work on that borrowing one more time, and I think you'll have it."

He didn't reply. Instead, he handed her the pencil she'd loaned him, said "Thanks," and ambled out of the room.

When Al sauntered into his second-period history class, no one seemed to notice his presence at all. The other teenagers were chattering and jostling. The teacher was writing on the blackboard. Without considering whether or not there were assigned seats, Al took a desk in the back row and slouched down into a comfortable lounging position.

No one talked to him. He never said a word. Within his shell of isolated silence, he looked relaxed and content.

The bell rang. A few late arrivals hurried to their seats. The teacher, Mrs. Edmonds, took attendance and class began.

From a position front and center, Mrs. Edmonds cleared her throat and waited for quiet. "You should have before you your own partially labeled world map. Monday we did the continent of North America. Tuesday we worked on

Central and South America. Wednesday it was Europe."
Instead of looking at the class over her half glasses, she took
the little spectacles off and used them as a pointer. "You'll
find all the instructions you need right here on the board.
This continent is to be labeled . . . " she touched the word
Asia. "These major cities are to be located." Her finger swept
across a very long list. "Population figures are to be ascer-
tained and appropriately noted." She looked sternly at her
students, admonishing, "After working on this project for
three whole days, we can trust that you know how to do
that. . . ." At the teacher's pause, no one protested, so she
went on. "You will, of course, locate and label these major
geographical features." Her finger tapped insistently against
the slate to indicate a long column of names for rivers, seas,
and mountain ranges.

To the left of the teacher and just over her head a large
globe of the world was suspended from the ceiling. In the
sharply angled glare of the morning sunlight, the orb's tiny
contoured mountains made a pattern of highlights and
shadows across the surface of the garishly colored relief
map. Al found the suspended ball intriguing. Staring at it
and squinting his eyes, he could feel himself an astronaut
coming back from outer space and trying to land on that
little speck of a planet. He had progressed deep into the
scenario of his fantasy when an authoritative female voice
said, "Alvin."

Al looked up to see the teacher moving quickly toward
his desk with a quizzical look knitting her brow. "Alvin—
that *is* your name, isn't it?"

Al nodded, "Yeah."

Mrs. Edmonds flapped the back of her hand against Al's
shoulder. "Sit up straight in your chair. Take off that hat."

Al quickly complied.

Fluttery motions accompained the teacher's crisp, clipped words as she handed her pupil an atlas and a blank map of the world. "Since you missed the first three days of this assignment, it's pointless for you to try to catch up. Just start with the new work I put on the board this morning."

Al was stuffing his cap into the hip pocket of his tattered jeans as his head slowly bobbed up and down in agreement.

Mrs. Edmonds started to walk away, then turned back to Al and added, "I'd suggest that you begin with the geographical features. After I get the rest of the class started, I'll come back and explain the proper procedure for putting in the cities and other political markings." Without waiting for a comment from her pupil, the teacher turned on her heel and walked away.

Al carefully spread out the large blank world map he'd been given. He was intrigued by the strong black lines meandering around on it to form intricate designs. He noticed the oddly shaped enclosed areas, and the random patterns outlined within them by a network of lighter black lines. Al stared at the outlines through narrowed eyes. Just as children see shapes in the clouds, Al watched illusions emerge from the patterns of his map. It excited him that each one gradually took on the characteristics of the entity suggested by the general form. To Al, the configuration of the Baltic Sea became a rampaging elephant with its head thrown back. It seemed alive as he watched it charging across the area of the map representing Northern Europe.

Al's interest in the fantasy shapes waned. His attention returned to the globe. While he was recreating the astronaut-searching-for-home experience, the contrast of oranges and browns seemed to pulsate against the intense blues that dominated the color scheme of the orb. With a jolt Al realized, "That orange is s'posed to be land!" This startling new perception made him see the globe in a whole new way, then led him to wonder if he could tell the difference between the earth and the sea on the flat black-and-white map in front of him.

Al picked a spot, then stared at the globe in an attempt to find it. It took several tries. Finally, at the southern tip of Africa he could see the relationship between his map and the globe. And he could see the difference between the land and the water. The continent stood out so clearly for him that he ran his finger around the black line that separated it from the surrounding oceans. Sometimes an optical illusion would play tricks on his eyes. The outline of the Mediterranean Sea would stand out as the dominant land mass on his colorless map. And Africa would be seen as a large body of water. This would make Al lose his perception of the generally accepted relationship between earth and sea. Every time such a visual reversal occurred, Al put his finger back on the southern tip of Africa and started over. He was in the midst of this process when Mrs. Edmonds returned to his side to give him the instruction she had offered earlier.

The teacher seemed to be startled by the fact that Al's map was still blank. She drew herself up tall, set her jaws and shoulders, and asked, "Young man, why are you not working?"

Al shrugged. "I ain't got no pencil."

To correct her pupil's faulty grammar, Mrs. Edmonds repeated his statement with precise emphasis on the part she substituted for the word "ain't." "You say you *don't* have colored pencils." She paused, then continued, "Colored pencils are on the supply list for this course."

Al said nothing.

Disgust put an extra sharp edge on Mrs. Edmonds' clipped diction. "Do you have *any* pencil?"

Al shook his head. "No."

"Humph." The teacher glared at him over her glasses,

shot a quick look at the clock, then snapped, "I suggest that you go to your locker and get one."

There *was* no pencil in Al's locker. He knew that before he left the history room. But he also knew that if one wandered the halls of a large school, a stray pencil could almost always be found on the floor somewhere.

A display of trophies in the hall caught the young man's attention. He paused to stare through the glass case and see if any had the current year's date.

Farther down the hall, he wandered into the bathroom to have a cigarette. While there he noticed that the paper towel dispenser was broken. It took him only a few minutes to remove the cover and determine the cause of the problem. Using his pocketknife, he took the mechanism apart and fixed it.

Unfortunately, the bell rang before he got the cover back on. With young males streaming in to use the facilities, Al was forced to abandon his project and move on to his third-period class.

Al strolled into the auditorium through a door near the stage. Fifty-five chattering teen-agers were taking their places in the front section in preparation for health class. As the students clustered together into groups with their friends, the huge amphitheater echoed with the sounds of cushioned seats thudding down into place.

Al never even glanced at the crowd to check for familiar faces. He strode up the aisle, climbing the steps of the rising tiers two at a time. With the casual certainty of one taking his favorite spot, the solitary youth eased down into a seat in the center of the last row. Stretching his feet out on the chair in front of him, he leaned comfortably back until his head rested on the wall of the projection booth behind him. His blank, unfocused eyes stared calmly from beneath the visor of the baseball cap.

Noises from the booth behind him indicated that the teacher was setting up a movie. Al closed his eyes and listened carefully to the hollow snapping sounds of celluloid being handled. He could hear sprockets moving, a tiny spring pulling into position, the rasp and whir of an empty reel. In his mind's eye he pictured the activity of hands, film, and machine. In his imagination he could see every step of the threading process in 3-D wide-screen technicolor.

Mr. Armsley, the school's baseball coach, bounded out of the projection booth and down the steps toward the front of his class. His strong, enthusiastic voice perfectly complemented his vigorous, sure movements. "Okay, troops. Let's get it together here." With his straight white teeth, close-cropped hair, starched plaid shirt and conservative tie, Coach Armsley was so vibrantly wholesome that he looked as if he'd just stepped out of an ad for physical fitness.

"Got a film on diet," he announced. "It's a long one, so we'll see it today and have a discussion and a quiz on it tomorrow." All bustle and efficiency, he grabbed his roll book off the top of his desk and looked out at the sea of attentive faces. "Adams . . . "

"Here," a male voice called in alert response.

"Andrews . . . "

"Present."

"Arrington . . . "

Al listened until the roll call got to his name and gave a sharp, snappy, "Yo."

As soon as the lights were dimmed, Al leaned farther back in his seat, pulled the brim of his cap over his eyes, and settled down for a nap. As far as he was concerned, green leafy vegetables were boring.

Al awoke when the lights came back on. He flexed his shoulders and stretched his neck to get the kinks out. Craving a cigarette, he eagerly awaited the sound of the bell.

When it finally rang, he flowed down the aisle, eased past the swarm of departing classmates, skirted around the extreme edge of the throng in the halls, and headed for the back door.

As soon as he was outside, Al dug his lighter out of his pocket. A cigarette was in his lips before he got halfway across the lawn. At the curb he paused, checked for traffic, flicked his lighter, stepped off into the street, and applied the flame to his cigarette. All tension drained out of him with the first exhaled cloud of smoke. Al stopped on the road's center line, took a second pull on his cigarette, inhaled deeply, and sighed with content. From his vantage point, he scanned the faces of the young males who had already attained the safety of the territory just across the street. All had long hair and wore blue jeans. Most had beards or mustaches. Many wore hats. The ones in leather, chains, and assorted motorcycle paraphernalia looked muscular and violent. Those in denim, bandana handkerchiefs, and T-shirts emblazoned with slogans appeared to be gentle and idealistic.

Al crossed the street and joined the crowd on the curb.

A tall, thin young man with a hugely drooping mustache clapped Al on the shoulder. "Hey, man, good to see ya," Joel greeted him warmly. The two joined closed hands to form one bonded fist in the ritualistic handshake of hippies.

"You still makin' music?" Al asked.

"Yeah. Yeah." The full length of Joel's slender body undulated as an extension of the movement caused by his nodding head. He stared into Al's face with open affection. A broad grin stretched across his mouth as he repeated, "Yeah, I'm still makin' music."

The two fell silent. Al lit a second cigarette from the butt of the first. His mind drifted off momentarily.

"Gotta light?"

Al didn't bother to come out of his reverie. Automatically, he fished out his lighter and offered it.

The smell of burning marijuana caught his attention. With casual, slow-moving eyes, Al turned back to focus his gaze on Joel.

The tall, lean youth allowed a large cloud of smoke to burst from his lungs, then took a series of noisy little puffs, inhaled powerfully, and, while holding his breath, offered the joint to Al.

With an easy movement like that of an athlete, Al took the joint and pivoted around on one foot so that his back was to the school. Sucking in one steady draw, Al filled his lungs to capacity.

The crowd started to thin. Joel cocked his head to one side and looked at his companion with hooded, dreamy eyes. "Want one more toke?" he crooned.

Al stayed for one more round.

The bell rang as he, and a host of others, crossed the street on the way back to school. Al had a couple of candy bars stashed in his locker. At that moment, he wanted one so badly that his tongue tingled. It didn't occur to him that he was already late for his fourth-period biology class. It didn't strike him as odd that he walked right by the biology room on the way to his locker. With a confident swagger, humming a rock tune under his breath and beating out the rhythm on an imaginary guitar, he strode through the empty halls intent on his mission.

As he walked into his fourth-period class, Al was licking chocolate off his fingers and lips. The room was totally silent. All the students were huddled over their desks writing answers in the blank spaces of a mimeographed sheet.

The teacher, Mrs. Tuttle, rose from her desk and mo-

tioned for Al to join her in the hall. Her glorious smile and
short Afro made the tiny black woman look almost playful
as she led her student to a spot just outside the door. "The
rest of the class is taking a unit test," she whispered. "Since
you've missed so many classes, you couldn't possibly make
a passing grade on this test." Pursing her lips, she cocked
her head and looked up at Al knowingly. "I think we'd
better put you back in the workroom with a film strip so
you can catch up on the work that you've missed."

Al looked surprised, or perhaps confused.

"Does that seem fair to you?" the teacher asked, then
explained without waiting for a response. "You can get ready
to take a make-up test sometime next week."

Al nodded his head slowly.

"Get some paper and colored pencils off the corner of my
desk and meet me in the little back room."

Again Al nodded.

Mrs. Tuttle thrust her head forward to look her pupil
straight in the eyes. "Is this okay with you?" she asked.

"Yeah, sure." Al actually grinned.

Mrs. Tuttle and her tardy student tiptoed through the
quiet classroom. Very few students even looked up. Al gathered up his materials while the teacher took a small, shiny,
red box out of her file cabinet. Like conspirators, they softly
padded into the workroom and closed the door.

As though unveiling a treasure, the biology teacher slid
open the red box and revealed its contents to Al. "With
these four filmstrips, we're going to introduce you to the
anatomy of a frog," she explained.

Al stared at the small film canisters and cassette tapes
nestled in their neat rows of perfectly fitting compartments.
With respect that was nearly reverence, he stretched out his
hands and accepted the offered gift.

"Do you know how to work these individual filmstrip machines?" Mrs. Tuttle queried.

Al was so enthralled with the magic of the red box that he didn't respond.

"Here," the teacher called gently. "Come over here and let me show you how to work the projector."

The youth took the chair indicated, then watched closely as the various mechanical procedures were demonstrated. He was eager to don the headset and begin his private showing.

The teacher gave Al his final instructions. "Don't forget," she added, "you won't have time to see all four today, so take as long as you want to look at them in any order that suits you."

Al nodded.

Mrs. Tuttle smiled and left the room.

The filmstrips featured the giant American bullfrog. The frogs were the biggest Al had ever seen. He was fascinated. He viewed tape number 1 and was on his second time through number 3 when the teacher had to roust him out of her back room and force him to go to lunch.

Mrs. Tuttle scooped up her purse and escorted her student to the door.

"You ever seen any of them big frogs?" he asked.

"We've got some of the tadpoles," she replied.

Al's eyes widened. "Where?"

"In that first aquarium by my desk."

"Can I see 'em?"

The teacher was glad she'd just finished locking the door. Al was so enthusiastic about the tadpoles that he seemed eager to forego his meal in order to see them right then and there. "We have to go to lunch now," she answered. "But next time you're in class, go over and take a look."

Al strolled along beside his biology teacher. His slow, languid gait easily kept up with her quick, tiny steps. "You gonn.. let 'em get all growed up?" he asked.

"No, we don't have the proper equipment for that."

"That sure would be interestin'."

Mrs. Tuttle's fast-moving high heels clickety-clacked down the wide marble stairs, then paused for just a second at the entrance to the faculty dining room. She laid a hand lightly on Al's shoulder. In farewell, she reminded him, "The aquarium right next to my desk. They really are wonderful. Come by tomorrow and see."

The school cafeteria held no appeal for Al. No one he knew would be found in there. He wasn't interested in nutritious institutional food anyway. He headed across the street, where vending machines offered the soft drinks and snack foods that he liked. He could eat outside with the gang at the curb.

Al started off with a packet of peanut butter crackers and a bottle of cola. He was thinking of heading back to the machine for something sweet when he remembered that he'd heard talk of amphetamines. Try as he might, he couldn't quite recall who had mentioned the uppers, so he wove his way through the crowd making inquiries.

Several youths told him to see J. C.

The small-time dealer grinned as Al approached. J. C.'s frizzy hair stuck out around the edges of the greasy red bandana he used as a headband. Except for his size, there was no reason to suspect that he'd been the star of the school football team for three straight years.

Al and J. C. had known each other since grade school. They clasped hands in warm greeting. After exchanging a few pleasantries, Al asked, "You really got some good speed?"

"White cross," the former athlete responded. Lowering

his eyelids and sighing blissfully, the dealer added, "Pharmaceutical quality for the connoisseur."

"Real white cross, huh?" Al pressed for further confirmation.

J. C. reassured him. "Same stuff they use in the hospital."

The prospective customer pondered a moment, then nodded. "How much?"

"Fifty cents a hit."

"All I got on me is a buck," Al protested.

"This is good stuff, man. Two hits of this and you'll be right until past midnight."

A crumpled dollar bill emerged from the customer's hip pocket, and the transaction was completed.

Al washed both pills down with the remaining swallows of his soft drink. Since speed didn't mix well with school, he headed for the highway. Al didn't have any particular destination in mind. He just felt like hitching a ride.

At the age of fifteen, on the eve of abandoning his attempt at formal education, Al displayed few of the true causes of his academic difficulties. His casually apathetic attitude masked the intense shame he felt about his repeated lack of success in school. Since he produced almost no work, he rarely demonstrated his terribly inadequate basic skills. He seemed to be a loner by choice. Nearly every aspect of Al's scholastic failure had been obscured by absences, drugs, and lack of motivation.

Yet, behind it all, there still remained a spark of curiosity and delight in the world around him.

Section Five

THE TERM "learning disability" focuses attention on the special deficits of those who are LD. It implies that they have their weaknesses, and that, if they're lucky, in a few areas they are average. By emphasizing only the negative, it suggests that the learning disabled have no special attributes or talents.

This view is a gross misconception.

Is it possible that Leonardo da Vinci, Thomas Edison, Auguste Rodin, and Albert Einstein have nothing more than their learning disabilities in common? Surely it's not merely coincidence that they are also four of our civilization's greatest creative geniuses.

Many experts have known it for years. Now, as a result of recent research, it can be proved scientifically: There is a strong positive side to being learning disabled.

Chapter XVII

The Final Analysis

FOR MORE THAN SIXTY YEARS, scientists struggled to come up with a logical explanation of what causes a learning disability. Medical doctors, psychologists, and other highly specialized researchers exhaustively studied brains, chemicals in the blood, genetic variables, body chemistry, teaching methods, nervous systems, and any other factors that might conceivably be connected with the problem. Many came up with theories. None of them offered conclusive, or even very convincing, proof to back up their ideas.

A whole new field of research opened up in the late 1950s. After ten years of careful investigation, a group in California released the results of their "split brain studies" in 1968. Their findings revolutionized our concept of the human brain.

The original discoveries were based on studies done with a small group of epileptics who had had the connecting link between the two halves of their brain severed in an attempt to control their seizures. Doctors had always known that the human brain is shaped like the meat of a walnut, with one thick piece of connecting tissue joining the two halves. The relationship between the two hemispheres had never been adequately explained. The left side was pretty well understood. The workings of the right side remained a mystery. With the cooperation of the split-brain patients, scientists were able to experiment on living humans to determine exactly how the two separate brain hemispheres function.

Through ingenious and fascinating tests, it was discovered that while the two halves of the brain are almost mirror images of each other, they work in entirely different ways.

They take in different types of information, and they do their processing by radically different methods.

The left brain is designed to deal with abstract information. It is highly organized and analytical. Its processing is called "reasoning." The left hemisphere is the seat of the "computer" which rules the realm of logic.

The right brain is designed to deal with concrete reality. It is highly intuitive and creative. Its processing is called "feeling." The right hemisphere is the seat of the "spirit" which rules in the realm of inspiration.

To summarize the characteristics of the two hemispheres of the human brain very briefly:

the left brain

- is "verbal." It takes in and processes messages coded in language. It thinks by talking to itself as it manipulates words and numbers.
- has a keen and constant awareness of time. Much of its evaluating and organizing is done in reference to an inner clock.
- has no sense of space.

- breaks information into small, manageable pieces.

the right brain

- is "nonverbal." It deals directly with reality. Its thinking is done without the use of words or numbers.
- has no consciousness of time.

- has a highly developed awareness of space. A great portion of its thinking is done in terms of manipulating concrete or imaginary objects in space.
- takes in data as whole units.

- organizes material by putting its component parts into a specific order. Sequence is a vitally important element in most of its processing. It works with step-by-step logic.
- focuses attention very narrowly on small pieces and component parts.
- specializes in analyzing. It notes differences between parts so they can be evaluated or categorized.
- prepares factual information for storage in memory.

- reasons its way to a conclusion without feelings or emotions. It figures things out by being factual and systematic.

- organizes information by seeking relationships and recognizing similarities between wholes: It works in analogical leaps.

- expands the focus of attention to deal with large whole units.
- specializes in synthesizing. By making analogics, it seeks to build, alter, create.

- produces sudden insights which are stepping stones to still bigger revelations.
- feels its way to conclusions by hunches or trial and error. It knows intuitively by being sensitive, imaginative, and whimsical.

Sometimes the two hemispheres work together as a team. To play tennis, the right brain controls the quick precise body movements while the left brain plans the strategy. In writing a short story, the right hemisphere supplies imaginative ideas while its counterpart takes charge of spelling, grammar, and punctuation. In such endeavors, both sides of the brain are involved in different aspects of the same project.

For other tasks, the two hemispheres take turns. Balancing a checkbook is best done with cool, calm reason. Creativity or emotion would complicate an otherwise simple manipulation of factual information. Dancing is best done in the free-flowing manner of right-brain processing. A rational, analytical frame of mind would kill the beauty and spontaneity of the movements.

Ideally, an individual shifts back and forth between the two modes of thinking as needed.

For most people, this is not always the case. When the smooth natural division of labor does not take place, the two hemispheres work in opposition to each other. One side can insist on doing a task for which the other half is better suited.

In "developed" countries, society accepts and admires the logical man of reason. Systems of formal education foster skill in intellectual pursuits. Through training and the process of acculturation, children are deliberately shifted to near total reliance on the left brain. Thus, it is common for intelligent, highly educated adults to say, "I'm not very creative," "I'm not very good with my hands," or, "I can't even draw a straight line." Such individuals (and there are many of them) have almost no access to the tremendous capabilities of their right brain. Their creative mind cannot produce its insights and inspirations because their reasoning mind acts as a dominating bully which refuses to relinquish control. For adults thus trapped in their left brain, it is a long, hard struggle to reestablish contact with the right. Meditation, jogging, gardening, yoga, craft courses, drugs, dance lessons, biofeedback, backpacking, self-improvement courses—Western man is working to get back in touch with the right side of his brain and restore balance to his life.

People with an "artistic temperament" consistently tend to favor the right-brain mode of thinking. Writers prefer to devote their energy to ideas and insights. They rely on editors to take care of the tedious details of grammar and punctuation. Musicians love to perform and create. They pay managers to organize schedules and take responsibility for business details. These artistic types *can* do left-brain thinking. But they shift into sequential reasoning only when it's absolutely necessary.

As soon as results of the split brain studies were released, experts realized that the learning-disabled individual is a right-brain person. On first hearing about the new research, LD adults almost always recognize the connection. One former student asked me, "Do you think my left brain has died?" Another claimed, "I feel like I'm trapped in my right brain."

Split brain theory has hurled researchers into a vast new area of investigation. The top ranking specialists pretty much agree that the LD individual is indeed strong in right-brain function and weak in left-hemisphere activities. "Why is this true?" has become the question new intensive studies are trying to answer.

New discoveries about learning disabilities have accumulated rapidly. After extensive investigation, a Canadian researcher has pointed out that LD individuals are built as though they had two right brains. A handful of educators have discovered that LD youngsters learn best when the methods of instruction teach to the right side of the brain. Books (including this one) on how to do this are popping up all over the country. British doctors are experimenting with a drug that stimulates the left side of the brain. When this chemical is administered to dyslexics, the resulting increase in left-brain activity improves their skill in reading.

From every area of science, from all over the world, a new theory is building: Learning-disabled youngsters are different because they do not operate out of the left side of their brain. They are right-brain children. They have very special skills and talents not available to most of us. When placed in schools designed for the left-brain majority, they not only cannot succeed, but their unique gifts are systematically destroyed. When placed in an appropriate setting, they learn and thrive.

The term "learning disability" focuses on left-brain deficits without pointing out right-brain attributes that are there as well.

These youngsters can be seen from an entirely different perspective. Let me introduce you to "right-brain children." They are one of nature's wonders.

They Are Reality Oriented

Right-brain people are firmly rooted in concrete reality. The real world—the one that can be touched, tasted, smelled, heard, moved, watched—that's the world that makes sense to them. That's what draws their interest, holds their attention, leads to understanding, produces responses, and lodges firmly in their memory. Reality-oriented children live by their senses. It's in concrete reality that they are comfortable and competent.

Reading and writing involve deep levels of abstraction. The little printed symbols represent letters that stand for sounds and go together to produce a graphic picture of a spoken word which is an oral group of sounds blended into one unit which is used to express symbolically an idea or name of an object or action that did exist, will exist, might exist, should exist, could have existed, or does now exist in concrete reality. Language is abstract. Written language is infinitely more so. Right-brain youngsters are not oriented toward the abstract. Their minds thrive on the tangible, the physical, the real.

How does this show up in the classroom? At every possible opportunity the right-brain child shifts from the abstract to the real. Instead of filling in the blanks on a reading worksheet, he draws pictures on it, punches holes in it, or folds it into an airplane. He may try to do the assignment in the usual way, but when dealing with abstractions, he has trouble concentrating. He's easily distracted, or just can't "get into it." Once he shifts his attention to the concrete reality of a fly buzzing against the window, he has no further problem with distractions. He is absorbed completely. When his mind and his body are both involved, he has an incredible intensity of concentration. The reality-oriented youngster succeeds in concentrating, performing, and learning when the task allows him to immerse himself in it physically as well as mentally.

The right-brain child is built like an old-fashioned string of Christmas tree lights. One missing bulb and the entire string refuses to light. Either the individual is totally involved in an activity—eyes, ears, head, hands, heart, muscles, feelings, senses—or he's not involved at all. His senses must work in unison with his mind. It's as though he thinks with his whole body. This setup enables the youngster to learn beautifully. It also prevents him from learning in the ways preferred by schools.

Tying the abstract to physical reality gives right-brain students a chance to feed in the sensory information they need to activate attention, understanding, and memory. The highly abstract *can* be taught to them successfully provided it's done by methods that are firmly rooted in reality. One of the oldest and most highly respected methods of LD therapy is the Orton-Gillingham approach. Its effectiveness is largely based on the fact that it is multisensory. Almost all of the pupil's senses are employed in the teaching of reading, writing, spelling, and math. It is reality-oriented, well suited to the right-brain pupils it's designed to reach.

With very few exceptions, our modern educational systems are based on using and developing the verbal and abstract. In such schools, the natural tendencies and talents of right-brain children go unexplored, neglected, denied, and abused.

They Are Spatially Gifted

Years ago, a famous American researcher studied a large group of dyslexics. This scientist believed that all those with a disability in reading, writing, and spelling must have one particular "symptom" in common. After very careful investigation, she did find one characteristic shared by all her subjects. But, much to everyone's surprise, it was *not* a deficit. It was an attribute. Every one of them had, to a significantly measurable degree, a talent for dealing with objects in space. They were all spatially gifted. The three-dimensional world made more sense to them than it does to most people. Their minds were ideally suited to perceiving, understanding, manipulating, visualizing, and remembering real concrete objects that exist in space. They had the special talents needed to be builders, inventors, designers, mechanics, sculptors, architects.

Split brain research has clearly demonstrated that spatial ability is a function of the right hemisphere of the brain. Since learning-disabled children are right-brain youngsters, it is totally logical that they should have a talent for dealing with three-dimensional objects.

The spatially gifted can comprehend a whole, and the relationships of all its parts, regardless of its orientation. In concrete reality, size, shape, configuration, and location are relative. For example: a carburetor is at the end of the gas line and distributues fuel to the pistons. If seen from directly above, it is round. From the side it looks rectangular. From an angle above and off to the side it appears to be oval. Viewed from beneath, it's all but completely hidden by the engine block. No matter how its shape and location appear to vary, the actual carburetor remains the same.

To deal effectively with objects in space, orientation must always be taken into consideration. That's a major aspect of spatial ability. But, when this same processing technique is applied to the abstract world of letters and numbers, the effect is disastrous.

If the orientation is not considered to be fixed, how are a *u* and an *n* different? The only way to distinguish one from the other is a matter of right side up or upside down. If variable orientation in space is not considered significant, how are a *p*, a *g*, a *d*, and a *b* different? They're all the same! They are the exact same configuration viewed from different sides and angles. You can't fool the spatially gifted right-brain child. He knows a stick and a ball when he sees one. Turn it any way you want, it's still a line and circle.

Teachers point out that the *d* faces one way, the *b* the other. The right-brain youngster thinks of that as something that appears to happen sometimes, but not as a permanent significant condition. Sometimes a carburetor looks long and thin, sometimes it looks round. To the spatially gifted child, orientation always is conditional just as it is in concrete reality.

They Have No Concept of Time

Split brain studies have proved that functions concerning time and space are divided between the two hemispheres in a way that is almost totally mutually exclusive. The right brain does the spatial processing and deals with spatial tasks. The left brain is responsible for keeping track of time, doing the sequencing, and dealing with temporal matters. Thus, it is perfectly logical that, coupled with being spatially gifted, right-brain children have an awesome weakness in their concept of time. They live as though time didn't exist. They don't think in terms of time, don't measure their lives or events by standards related to time. Of all the learning-disabled people I have encountered, I have never met one who dealt with time in a totally "normal" way.

One LD adult of my acquaintance is an exceptionally good example of this strange contrast in abilities. At the age of twenty-two, he was a tremendously talented and highly successful landscape architect. The fact that he is spatially gifted made him ideally suited for his profession. But his total lack of a concept of time made it very difficult for him to supervise crews of workmen. Unless the men kept track of the time for themselves, their young boss forgot about breaks and meals entirely. In this situation, as in many others, the unusual characteristics of a right-brain person acted as both a blessing and a curse.

Sequencing is a technique that orders objects or events in time. Right-brain youngsters have no sense of timing; consequently, they have no sense of sequence either. They order reality in terms of relationships and space. In assembling a model airplane, spatially talented children rarely use or follow the printed directions. The sequence they use is not based on the step-by-step instructions of the manufacturer. They put the seat, controls, instruments, and pilot into the cockpit before they glue on the canopy. They determine this order in accord with the logic of working with objects in space: the interior parts must be completed first because you can't get to the inside after it's buried under the outside.

That's a very effective way of functioning when it comes to concrete reality. In the real world of experiences, it's called "good common sense." Usually, right-brain people have a lot of that.

This kind of nonsequential spatial reasoning does not work in the realm of the abstract. To impose order on the abstract, it is necessary to sequence in time. Children are taught, "To print a *b, first* make the stick, *then* add the ball." Instructions that must be followed step by step in a specific order are tremendously useful to most youngsters. To right-brain children, such a sequence is of no importance whatsoever. It's something that they don't notice on their own, that doesn't make much sense to them even when it's pointed out, that doesn't stick in their memory at all.

These three factors—added facility in dealing with space, lack of a concept of time (including an inability to sequence), and a strong reality orientation—work in conjunction to make it all but inevitable that the child will have great difficulty learning to read and write and spell. It seems a horrible irony that the right-brain child's greatest strengths combine to cause his greatest weaknesses.

They Are Unusually Observant

Right-brain children are tremendously observant of what's going on around them. It's as though their attention were focused through a wide-angle lens. No sight, sound, or sensation is too small to escape their notice. Constantly monitoring their environment, their mind is everywhere at once. This expanded focus of attention is a great asset when walking across a busy intersection or riding a bike through the park. In the real world, where both danger and beauty can spring up anywhere, keen powers of observation promote safety and provide an avenue for added pleasure.

One highly respected expert suggests that many of history's great warriors were learning disabled. He believes that the right-brain trait of being superobservant enabled Alexander the Great, General George Patton, and many others to lead men successfully in battle.

Yet, in typical classrooms, right-brain students are constantly criticized for "not paying attention." Their expanded focus of attention is considered undesirable. Teachers say these children are "distractible." They think youngsters who notice everything have a short attention span. Schools require a narrow focus of attention. They want children to zero in on their work and tune out everything else. Right-brain children can't comply; and in their failure to do so, they are accused of being uncooperative, disrespectful, and unmotivated.

Being highly observant is a tremendous advantage in the real world. In school, it's a handicap.

They Prefer Intuition over Logic

Schools train children to use logic. Great emphasis is placed on developing skill in the use of structured thought-processing patterns. Sound reasoning is the only acceptable method of arriving at any conclusion. Teachers are very careful to be sure a pupil's correct answer is not just a lucky guess. Get the facts, remember the facts, add up the facts—it's the rigid system used in formal education.

The highly organized reasoning process does not appeal to right-brain people. Their preferred thinking style is based on sudden leaps of insight. Just as they are extra observant in concrete reality, they are highly attuned to the very subtle signals that trigger intuition. Their endlessly active minds thrive on the hunches and brainstorms of direct inspiration.

Edison was working on this principle when he invented the incandescent light. The idea came to him as a fully developed realization produced by intuition. Others told him it was a totally crazy notion. Yet, after nearly two thousand unsuccessful attempts, he produced a bulb that would actually light. First came the inspiration; then experimentation and a process of elimination to make it work; and last, once it had been actually created, logic could be applied to explain *why* it worked. In thinking by intuition, step-by-step logic comes last. Its function is to explain why something happens in reality. The truth of what was discovered through intuition and experimentation is proved through reasoning.

For aborigines and Indians who live close to the land, for artists and writers and sculptors and inventors, this is a very effective way of thinking. First comes the whole concept; then, in the process of producing it, the details are taken into consideration.

This type of thinking is *not* very effective in school. In the classroom, the intuitive approach is called "wild guessing." Teachers dislike it intensely. Right-brain students rely on it heavily. When performing in an elementary school reading circle, these children give a classic portrayal of the attempt to apply intuition to a situation that requires logic. A systematic method of word attack is not their style at all. Rather than try to figure out a word, they call off what they expect to be there. Based on the pictures, the reading of the other students, plus the cues and corrections provided by the teacher, they piece together their own version of the story.

Thus, the oral reading of right-brain youngsters is usually full of substitutions. Pronouns, articles, and prepositions are especially vulnerable to transformation in their improvisational approach to reading. Yet, almost always, the word inserted makes good sense within the context of the sentence or story. In trying to read, "Come down from there right now," students who read by intuition might try any of the following (substituted word in italics): "*Get* down from there right now," or "Come down *off* there right now," or "Come down from there *this minute*." It would be highly unlikely that any LD child would substitute *frog* for *from*, so that the sentence read, "Come down *frog* there right now." That would be a good guess based on phonics. But it would be such an inappropriate word for that context and position that it would not be considered as a realistic possibility.

As right-brain children get older, their reading usually does improve. By the time they get to fifth or sixth grade, they've usually learned to look at the first letter of a word—then guess. Some get to the point that they'll actually look at the first letter and the last one as well—before they make their guess. The technique is more precise. It produces errors like: *carefully* read as *comfortably*, and *Tuesday* called *Thursday*. For those few who learn to pay attention to whole syllables before applying intuition, mistakes are made on more difficult words: *consternation* becomes *conservation*, *formally* is read as *formerly*, and *Austria* is pronounced *Australia*.

At every level the tendency toward improvisation remains strong. And always, it's the little words that are the most likely candidates for substitutions. Typically, right-brain students improve their skill at controlled guessing. The intuition that serves them so well in reading people, nature, and reality hinders them when reading books.

They Are Creative

The left side of the brain, with its controlled, predictable processing methods, is perfectly designed for the task of analyzing. The left hemisphere has a natural tendency to break wholes into component parts. As an aspect of verbal thinking, it automatically identifies and labels pieces. It is also the mind's center where judging is done. Thus, the left brain is well equipped to do the comparing and evaluating that are integral elements in the process of analysis. Once the information has been gathered and the judgments made, the reasoning left brain places the pieces into categories. Through some method of numerical, alphabetical, or chronological sequencing, these groups are then arranged and organized. If used immediately, the facts are added up in some systematic fashion so that a decision is easily reached. If filed away for later reference, the exquisitely organized material can be neatly stored in memory for easy retrieval at any future time.

From beginning to end, analysis is a process unique to the logical left brain. Step by step, element by element, it is the direct opposite of the special thinking methods unique to the right hemishpere.

The right side of the brain, with its sudden insights and surprising revelations, is ideally suited to the task of synthesizing. The right hemisphere has a natural tendency to want to put things together and build. In its type of processing, details and pieces are important only in terms of their relationship to the whole. As a part of nonverbal reasoning, it automatically manipulates visualized images of real or imagined objects. It tends to rely on mental pictures as it searches for connectedness, similarities. Synthesizing is aimed at an envisioned end result that has nothing to do with logical solutions and is in no way bound by traditions.

The right brain's findings are not of the type that can be categorized and organized. It's just as well, because the synthesizing mind has no method of organizing anything systematically. It operates outside the concept of time, sequence, and set order. It is guided by the leadings of curiosity. Synthesizing is a mental adventure that can be pursued with no sense of hurry. As long as options can be found, they will be explored.

Skill in analyzing tends to go along with a good memory. The two occur together because they're closely related. People who live by logic usually have a good memory for factual information. But, since they are left-brain people, they are

not particularly creative. Facility in intuition and an apti-
tude for synthesizing have just the opposite effect. They
usually occur in conjunction with a high degree of creativity
and a poor memory.

Albert Einstein, the mathematical genius, could never remember his own phone number. When he wanted to call
home, he had to refer to a file card on which he had the
information recorded. The right-brained mind is great for
some things. But memory isn't one of them.

Everyone is familiar with the vague kind of recollection
produced by dreams. The setting, theme, and emotional
reaction may be recalled. "I had this dream that I was in a
gambling casino and I won all this money. Boy, was I happy."
The details just slip away. Eventually, the whole thing fades.
Right-brain children seem to remember in much the same
fashion. They often say things like "Miss Jones tried to teach
me that last year, but I don't remember," or "I did a bunch
of problems with carrying last week. But now I've forgot."
Memory seems to rely heavily on the solid organizational
systems of logic and analysis.

The process of analysis prepares material so that it can be
systematically stored for easy accessibility in the future. Apparently, the brain's card catalogues cannot file away new
information unless the big concepts are broken down into
manageable pieces that are labeled, categorized, and organized. Logic both draws on and feeds into memory.

The mind's ability to synthesize makes it possible for man
to create. All of the right brain's special processing methods
work together to enable the individual to develop the NEW.
By using intuition, focusing on the whole, and processing
by means of synthesis, the right-brain person repeatedly
comes up with the innovative. Not bound by the way things
have always been, he yearns for the different, the improved,

the bigger, better, stronger, prettier, more wonderful. Never convinced that there is only one way to get something done, he quests for methods that are faster, easier, cheaper.

It has been scientifically established that right-brain children are more creative than average youngsters. In concrete reality, they have a special flair for developing the original. In problem-solving situations that come up in daily living, they have a knack for devising ingenious solutions. Teachers see this quality and rarely appreciate it. They prefer predictable, reliable students. In the classroom it's believed to be essential that pupils work in the prescribed, logical, fixed way. Innovations are not desirable.

The right-brain child has a great mind as long as he applies it to the type of mental processing for which it is suited. He was not designed for the left-brain world of the abstract where we read and write and spell and remember facts. His realm is the world of the concrete where he can explore, learn from experience, synthesize, and create.

They Are Very Sensitive

Right-brain people are observant, intuitive, and creative. They have an artistic temperament. They are unusually perceptive and extremely sensitive. In the inner world as well as the outer, they are strongly affected by what they feel. They tend to base their actions on emotions rather than reason.

For learning-disabled children, their natural right-brain makeup combines with their personal experiences to make them very, very sensitive. Over the years they lose their tolerance for teasing. No matter how carefully hidden or sugar-coated, any form of rejection hurts them deeply. Behind all the bluff and boisterousness they project, they are usually very tender-hearted, caring people. Their sensitive nature tends to make them especially compassionate toward all the world's underdogs. Their extra sensitivity applies to themselves and everything and everyone around them.

The right-brain child has an uncanny ability to read people. His unusual power of observation allows him to pick up on body language, tone of voice, and other unspoken signals. His high degree of intuition often leads to an amazing depth of insight. The two characteristics work together to make the right-brain youngster especially attuned to "the vibes." He seems to sense the real feelings of others.

This same sensitivity enables right-brain children to see through to the depths of situations. They can't read the words on the page, but they can read between the lines and in the margins to get the messages conveyed without language. They may have great difficulty with the mechanical process of reading, but they usually get what's implied, suggested, hinted, buried underneath, or even camouflaged. They are often brilliant in understanding metaphorical statement and symbolism.

The right-brain child has a strong sense of the absurd. His unusual spontaneous type of wit allows him to produce little quips and one-liners based on the reality of the moment. The jokes are clever, subtle, and quick. They almost always reveal a deep level of perception of human nature, specific individuals, or the particular situation. Some adults are quick to notice and appreciate this style of humor. Many are not. When a student drops a hilariously funny remark to explain his forty-seventh consecutive morning of tardiness, his teacher may not feel amused.

The right-brain child's sense of humor is rarely understood by his peers. To them, his unusual jokes merely prove that he's weird.

Their sensitive nature makes these creative youngsters very vulnerable to the compassionless attitude which pressures them to attempt conformity. Right-brain children are not damaged by being different. They are damaged by people and a system that cannot accommodate their differences.

At its best, the left brain can be efficient. A person possessing such a mind awes others with his intelligence.

At its best, the right brain can be exciting. A person possessing such a mind awes others with his inspirations.

Most start with strength in the left. A few begin with natural talents on the right. All aim for a perfectly balanced combination of thinking and feeling. Those few who develop such a mind awe others with wisdom.

Useful Addresses

The Orton Society
724 York Road
Baltimore, Maryland 21204

ACLD, Inc.
Association for Children with Learning Disabilities
4156 Library Road
Pittsburgh, Pennsylvania 15234

ACLD's in Canada
Kildare House
323 Chapel, Suite 101, 102
Ottawa, Ontario K1N 7Z2

Foundation for Children with Learning Disabilities
99 Park Avenue, 6th Floor
New York, NY 10016

Select Bibliography

This bibliography does not contain all the works available in the fields of learning disabilities and brain function. Some of the many others are listed in the following section, "Additional Reading." Please note that the term *advanced* as it is used here and in the next section does not necessarily denote reading that is difficult or technical. It simply means that the reader needs to acquire a basic understanding of the subject before the *advanced* materials and their place in the total range of these complex subjects can be fully appreciated.

Introductory Works

Learning Disabilities

Bond, Guy, and Miles A. Tinker. *Reading Difficulties: Their Diagnosis and Correction.* 5th ed. New York: Prentice-Hall, 1984.

Fader, Daniel, M.D., and Elton B. McNeil. *Hooked on Books Program and Proof.* New York: Putnam, 1968.

Osman, Betty B. *Learning Disabilities: A Family Affair.* New York: Random House, 1979.

Simpson, Eileen. *Reversals: A Personal Account of Victory over Dyslexia.* Boston: Houghton Mifflin Co., 1979.

Stevens, Suzanne H. *The Learning-Disabled Child: Ways that Parents Can Help.* Winston-Salem, N.C.: John F. Blair, 1980.

Brain Function

Blakeslee, Thomas. *Right Brain.* New York: Doubleday, 1980.

DeBono, Edward. *Lateral Thinking: Creativity Step by Step.* New York: Harper & Row, 1970.

DeMille, Richard. *Put Your Mother on the Ceiling.* New York: Penguin, 1967.

Edwards, Betty. *Drawing on the Right Side of the Brain: A Course in Enhancing Creativity and Artistic Confidence.* Los Angeles: Jeremy P. Tarcher, 1979.

Fugitt, Eva D. *He Hit Me Back First! Creative Visualization Activities for Parenting & Teaching*. Rolling Hills Estates, Cal.: Jalmar Press, 1983.

Hendricks, G., and R. Wills. *The Centering Book*. Englewood Cliffs, N.J.: Prentice-Hall, 1975.

———. *The Second Centering Book*. Englewood Cliffs, N.J.: Prentice-Hall, 1977.

Houston, Jean. *The Possible Human*. Los Angeles: Jeremy P. Tarcher, 1982.

Masters, Robert, and Jean Houston. *Mind Games*. New York: Viking, 1972.

Ornstein, Robert E. *On the Experience of Time*. New York: Penguin, 1969.

———. *The Psychology of Consciousness*. New York: Penguin, 1975.

Pearce, Joseph Chilton. *The Crack in the Cosmic Egg*. New York: Simon & Schuster, 1973.

———. *Exploring the Crack in the Cosmic Egg*. Washington Square Press. New York: Simon & Schuster, 1975.

———. *Magical Child*. New Age Books. New York: Bantam, 1977.

Pelletier, Kenneth. *Mind as Healer, Mind as Slayer*. New York: Delacorte, 1977.

Prather, Hugh. *Notes to Myself*. Moab, Utah: Real People Press, 1979.

Vitale, Barbara M. *Unicorns Are Real: A Right-Brained Approach to Learning*. Rolling Hills Estates, Cal.: Jalmar Press, 1982.

Advanced Works

Learning Disabilities

Bannatyne, Alexander. *Language, Reading, and Learning Disabilities*. Springfield, Ill.: Charles C. Thomas, 1971.

Crow, Gary. *Children at Risk: A Handbook of the Signs and Symptoms of Early Childhood Difficulties*. New York: Schocken Books, 1978.

Cruickshank, William M., et al. *A Teaching Method for Brain-Injured and Hyperactive Children*. Westport, Conn.: Greenwood Press, 1981.

de Hirsch, Katrina, J. J. Jansky, and W. S. Langford. *Predicting Reading Failure*. New York: Harper & Row, 1966.

Gearheart, William R. *Teaching the Learning Disabled*. St. Louis: C. V. Mosby Co., 1976.

———. *Learning Disabilities: Educational Strategies*. St. Louis: C. V. Mosby Co., 1977.

Goldberg, Hermand K., and Gilbert B. Schiffman. *Dyslexia: Problems of Reading Disabilities*. New York: Grune & Stratton, 1972.

Johnson, Doris J., and Helmer Myklebust. *Learning Disabilities: Educational Principles and Practices*. New York: Grune & Stratton, 1967.

Kratoville, Betty Lou, ed. *Youth in Trouble*. Novato, Cal.: Academic Therapy Publications, 1975.

Orton, Samuel T., M.D. *Reading, Writing, and Speech Problems in Children*. New York: W. W. Norton & Co., 1937.

Thompson, Lloyd J. *Reading Disability, Developmental Dyslexia*. Springfield, Ill.: Charles C. Thomas, 1966.

Witelson, Sandra. "Sex and the Single Hemisphere: Specialization of the Right Hemisphere for Spatial Processing." *Science* 193 (1976): 425–26.

———. "Developmental Dyslexia: Two Right Hemispheres and None Left." *Science* 195 (1977): 309–11.

Brain Function

Axline, Virginia. *Dibs in Search of Self*. New York: Ballantine Books, 1964.

Calvin, W. H., and George A. Ojemann. *Inside the Brain*. New York: Mentor, 1980.

Cousins, Norman. *Anatomy of an Illness*. New York: W. W. Norton & Co., 1979.

Frankl, Viktor. *From Death Camp to Existentialism*. Boston: Beacon Press, 1959.

Gallwey, W. Timothy. *The Inner Game of Tennis*. New York: Random House, 1974.

Hayakawa, S. I. *Language in Thought and Action*. New York: Harcourt, Brace & Jovanovich, 1964.

Huxley, Aldous. *The Doors of Perception*. Perennial Library. New York: Harper & Row, 1954.

Jaynes, Julian. *The Origin of Consciousness in the Breakdown of the Bicameral Mind*. Boston: Houghton Mifflin Co., 1976.

Jung, Carl. *Man and His Symbols*. New York: Doubleday, 1964.

Koch, Kenneth. *Wishes, Lies and Dreams*. New York: Random House, 1970.

Levy, J. "Differential Perceptual Capacities in Major and Minor Hemispheres." *Proceedings of the National Academy of Science* 61 (1968): 1151.

Maslow, Abraham. *Toward a Psychology of Being*. New York: Van Nostrand Reinhold, 1968.

May, Rollo. *Love and Will*. New York: Dell, 1974.

Samuels, M., and Samuels, N. *Seeing with the Mind's Eye*. New York: Random House, 1975.

Sperry, Roger W. "Split-Brain Approach to Learning Problems." In *The Neurosciences: A Study Program*, edited by G. C. Quarton, T. Melnechuk, and F. C. Schmitt. New York: Rockefeller University Press, 1967.

———. "Hemisphere Disconnection and Unity in Conscious Awareness." *American Psychologist* 23 (1968): 723–33.

———. "Lateral Specialization of Cerebral Function in the Surgically Separated Hemispheres." In *The Psychophysiology of Thinking*, edited by F. J. McGuigan and R. A. Schoonover. New York: Academic Press, 1973.

———. "Left Brain, Right Brain." *Saturday Review* (August 9, 1975): 30–33.

———. "Messages from the Laboratory." *Academic Therapy* 11, no. 2 (1976): 149–55.

Additional Reading

(Please see the Select Bibliography for a listing of other works and an explanation of the term *advanced*.)

Introductory Works

Learning Disabilities

Brutten, Milton, Sylvia Richardson, M.D., and Charles Mangel. *Something's Wrong with My Child*. New York: Harcourt Brace Jovanovich, 1973.

Burns, Marilyn. *The I Hate Mathematics! Book*. Boston: Little, Brown & Co., 1975.

Clarke, Louise. *Can't Read, Can't Write, Can't Talk Too Good Either.* New York: Walker & Company, 1973.

Crosby, R. M. N., and Robert Liston. *The Waysiders: A New Approach to Reading and the Dyslexic Child*. New York: Delacorte, 1968.

Gordon, Thomas. *P.E.T.: Parent Effectiveness Training*. New York: New American Library, 1970.

Hampshire, Susan. *Susan's Story: An Autobiographical Account of My Struggle with Words*. London: Sidgwick & Jackson, 1981.

Jones, Beverly, and Jane Hart. *Where's Hannah? A Handbook for Parents and Teachers of Children with Learning Disorders*. New York: Hart Publishing Co., 1968.

Levy, Harold B., M.D. *Square Pegs, Round Holes: The Learning-Disabled Child in the Classroom and at Home*. Boston: Little, Brown & Co., 1973.

Osman, Betty B., and Henriette Blinder. *No One to Play With: The Social Side of Learning Disabilities*. New York: Random House, 1982.

Underleider, Dorothy Fink., M.A. *Reading, Writing and Rage*. Rolling Hills Estates, California: Jalmar Press, 1985 .

Brain Function

Bruner, Jerome S. *On Knowing: Essays for the Left Hand*. New York: Atheneum, 1965.

Buzan, T. *Use Both Sides of Your Brain*. New York: E. P. Dutton, 1976.

Ferguson, Marilyn. *The Brain Revolution*. New York: Taplinger Publishing Co., 1973.

Keller, Helen. *The Story of My Life*. New York: Doubleday, 1954.

Advanced Works

Learning Disabilities

Bush, W., and M. Giles. *Aids to Psycholinguistic Teachings*. 2d ed. Columbus, Ohio: Charles Merrill Publishing Co., 1977.

Chall, Jeanne, and A. Mirsh, eds. *Education and the Brain*. Chicago: University of Chicago Press, 1978.

Cratty, Bryant J. *Active Learning: Games to Enhance Academic Abilities*. Englewood Cliffs, N.J.: Prentice-Hall, 1971.

Cruickshank, William M., James L. Paul, and John B. Junkala. *Misfits in the Public Schools*. Syracuse: Syracuse University Press, 1969.

Gaddes, William H. *Learning Disabilities and Brain Function*. New York: Springer-Verlag, 1980.

Jampolsky, Gerald G., and Maryellen J. Haight. "A Special Technique for Children with Reading Problems." *Academic Therapy* 10, no. 3 (Spring 1975): 333–37.

———. "Use of Hypnosis and Sensory Motor Stimulation to Aid Children with Learning Problems." *Journal of Learning Disabilities* 3 (November 1970): 29–34.

Kinsbourne, M. "Cerebral Control and Mental Evolution." In *Hemispheric Disconnection and Cerebral Function*, edited by M. Kinsbourne and A. Smith. Springfield, Ill.: Charles C. Thomas, 1974.

———. "Lateral Interactions in the Brain." In *Hemispheric Disconnection and Cerebral Function*, edited by M. Kinsbourne and A. Smith. Springfield, Ill.: Charles C. Thomas, 1974.

Lerner, Janet W. *Children with Learning Disabilities: Theories, Diagnosis, and Teaching Strategies*. 2d ed. Boston: Houghton Mifflin Co., 1976.

Mann, Lester, Libby Goodman, and J. Lee Wiederholt. *Teaching the Learning Disabled Adolescent*. Boston: Houghton Mifflin Co., 1978.

Siegel, Ernest. *The Exceptional Child Grows Up*. New York: E. P. Dutton, 1974.

Brain Function

Bandler, Richard, and John Grinder. *Frogs into Princes*. Moab, Utah: Real People Press, 1979.

Bruner, Jerome S. *Beyond the Information Given*. New York: W. W. Norton & Co., 1973.

Feldenkrais, Moshe. *Awareness Through Movement*. New York: Harper & Row, 1972.

Gazzaniga, Michael, et al. *The Integrated Mind*. New York: Plenum, 1978.

Gazzaniga, Michael. "The Split Brain in Man." In *Perception: Mechanisms and Models*, edited by R. Held and W. Richards. San Francisco: Freeman, 1972.

Hadamard, J. *An Essay on the Psychology of Invention in the Mathematical Field*. Princeton: Princeton University Press, 1945.

Leonard, George B. *Education and Ecstasy*. New York: Dell, 1968.

Pribram, Karl H. *Languages of the Brain*. Englewood Cliffs, N.J.: Prentice-Hall, 1971.

Prigogine, Ilya. *From Being to Becoming*. New York: W. H. Freeman, 1980.

Restak, R. M. *The Brain: The Last Frontier*. New York: Doubleday, 1979.

Simonton, O. Carl, Stephanie Matthews, and James Creighton. *Getting Well Again*. Los Angeles: Jeremy P. Tarcher, 1978.

Wittrock, M. C., and others. *The Human Brain*. Englewood Cliffs, N.J.: Prentice-Hall, 1977.

Zaidel, E., and R. W. Sperry. "Memory Impairment after Commissurotomy in Man." *Brain* 97 (1974): 263–72.

Index

Italics indicate case histories.

Absences, as excuse for failure, 48 (*Al*, 241, 243, 266, 270, 276, 279; *Harry*, 52–54)
Adolescents, special needs of, 79
Alphabetizing, difficulties with, 22 (*Al*, 226, 262–63)
Alternate materials, 160–64 (*Pete*, 161–62); materials for the blind, 164; parallel reading, 162–63 (*Rob*, 161); paraphrases and condensations, 163–64
Ambidexterity: *Al*, 9, 18
Attention span, 294 (*Al*, 227, 230, 236); and homework, 212; and teaching techniques, 125–26, 176 (*Fred*, 176; *Rick*, 125–26). *See also* Distractibility
Audio equipment, use of: in controlling distractions, 146–47 (*Ed*, 146–47); and grading, 202; materials for the blind, 164; for oral work, 167; in reading texts, 155–56; in tests, 191 (*Joel*, 191–92)

Basic skills, failure in, 28–33 (*Al*, 5, 279); and test failure, 185 (*Jack*, 185–89)
Behavior problems: patterns of, 94–96 (*Jimmy*, 94–95); preventing, 94–96. *See also* Child management techniques

Characteristics of the learning disabled. *See* Learning disabled, characteristics of
Child management techniques: avoiding lectures, 108–10 (*Elaine*, 109–10; *Miss Blackham*, 108–9); avoiding senseless questions, 104–8 (*David*, 105–7); making realistic demands, 100–104 (*football game*, 102–3); making rules broad, 113–16 (*Chuck*, 115–16); power of the name,

96–100 (*Carl*, 99; *Richard*, 96–97); threats and rewards, 110–13, 117–23 (*Jack*, 120; *Miss Green*, 120–21; *Miss Jennings*, 121; *Soda Shoppe* 111–12)
Computers, 170
Concentration. *See* Attention span; Distractibility
Concrete reality, 172, 288–90 (*Al*, 277–78)
Condensations, 163–64
Conferences, guidelines for, 63–69; formal, 62–63; major production, 63; nonconference or quickie, 59–60; small formal, 62; telephone nonconference, 61–62. *See also* Parents: conferences with
Copying: difficulties with, 31 (*Al*, 234, 258; *Ralph*, 55–57; *Stewart*, 74–78); eliminating in assignments, 151, 165, 213, 218
Creativity, 24–25, 297–99 (*Al*, 233, 238, 260–61)

Decoding, difficulties with, 31–32. *See also* Reading
Demonstrations: as substitutes for written work, 168; as teaching technique, 172
Directional confusion, 17–19 (*Al*, 8, 262); and handwriting, 182, 291 (*Al*, 227–28); and math, 32–33, 182 (*Al*, 236, 256–59, 268); and the printed page, 66, 67, 196–97 (*Joe*, 66–67; *Wayne*, 197–98)
Discipline, 101; consistency in, 129–31; and enforcing of rules, 123–24; and the LD child, 93; in public places, 124; student's understanding of, 131–34; teacher's role in, 134
Distractibility, controlling: with audio equipment, 146–47 (*Ed*, 146–47); with special rooms, 194–95; with